HEALTH
WANTED
INQUIRE WITHIN

A 5-Step Guide
to Lead Your Self and Your Team
from **Burnout** to **Brilliance**

CARA LENZ

First published in 2025 by Onyx Publishing, an imprint of Notebook Group Limited, Arden House, Deepdale Business Park, Bakewell, Derbyshire, DE45 1GT.

www.onyxpublishing.com
ISBN: 9781913206925

A CIP catalogue record for this book is available from the British Library.
Library of Congress Control Number: 2025911316

Typeset by Onyx Publishing of Notebook Group Limited.

ONYX PUBLISHING

For my mom, whose wisdom I carry in my heart every day.
For my dad, whose love, support, and optimism I cherish still.

For Dan, Liza, and Ryan, my first ever friends and
lifelong companions on this wild ride we call life.

Life is amazing. And then it's awful. And then it's amazing again. And in between the amazing and awful it's ordinary and mundane and routine. Breathe in the amazing, hold on through the awful, and relax and exhale during the ordinary. That's just living heartbreaking, soul-healing, amazing, awful, ordinary life. And it's breathtakingly beautiful.

— *L. R. KNOST*

This is possibly my favorite quote of all time. It highlights the roller coaster we often feel like we're riding throughout this journey called life—with it's incredible highs and devastating lows, sometimes in very quick succession. My hope is that this book will help everyone it touches to be even more present for the amazing, find strength and resilience through the awful, and deepen appreciation for the ordinary.

To your journey.

Cara

praise for

health wanted inquire within

Many authors attempt to move the reader into action- this one does. Cara Lenz has crafted a leadership development must-read primer that easily commands your attention and underscores the criticality of wellbeing as a key leadership trait.
—COREY B. SMITH
Fortune 50 Executive, Inclusion & Engagement

One of the earliest foundational lessons I learned as a young leader at Target was the importance of not only caring for your team, but caring about them. At Apple, I realized how paramount leading teams through the winds of change required a leader to put the wellness and enrichment of their individual team members before profits. In her book "Health Wanted Inquire Within," Cara Lenz examines the very real and often exasperating topic of self-care and wellness in the workplace. With a highly personalized and charismatic style, Lenz lays out the case as to why it not only makes good business sense for leaders and corporations to invest in their people's wellness, but also encourages focusing on self, first. If you are a leader who truly cares about your team and your own personal wellbeing, read this book and leverage the 'reflect to retain' exercises to jump start your skill building efforts. Trust the process. I promise this will prove an enjoyable and empowering journey.
—DUKE ZUREK
Former Global Sales, Learning, and Stores Director at Apple Retail

Structure is important in times of change. Cara has created a structure, for people leaders and individuals to take back their power and live an intentional life.
—MISSY DURANT
Former CHRO, Medica

Health Wanted Inquire Within *is a transformative guide that every leader needs in today's challenging work environment. Cara Lenz not only sheds light on the alarming health crisis in the workplace but also provides a clear, actionable roadmap for leaders to take charge of their wellbeing and inspire the same in their teams. With her five-step framework, Cara empowers readers to move beyond burnout and create workplaces that foster resilience, engagement, and brilliance. Her blend of personal experience, scientific insights, and practical tools makes this book an essential read for anyone committed to thriving, not just surviving, in their personal and professional life. Cara's heartfelt message and strategic guidance are a beacon of hope for leaders ready to prioritize wellbeing as both a personal and organizational value.*

—NATALIE BAIRD-KING

Supreme Court Certified Family Law Mediator and author of the book *Forgiving Unforgivable*

After spending over 30 years in a leadership role with Fortune 100 companies, I never heard anyone talk about the well-being of anyone within the organization. Finally, this book provides a clear roadmap for balancing an organization's demands while supporting the well-being of the team, not just giving it lip service.

—ARMANDO ALVAREZ

Partner M.C.A. Consulting L.L.C and Former VP of Best Buy and Geek Squad Services

Cara Lenz has created an insightful, actionable guide for leaders who are ready to make wellbeing a cornerstone of their leadership approach. Her five-step process isn't just a tool for personal growth—it's a pathway to building cultures that foster trust, engagement, and productivity across the entire organization.

—APRIL WHITSON

Global VP of HR (ABB Inc), Speaker, and Author of *The Stay Challenge*

This book was a game-changer for me. As someone who has spent years juggling career demands, mom responsibilities, and personal wellbeing, I often felt like I was running on empty. Cara's approach helped me see that wellbeing isn't just something you hope for—it's a skill you build. The exercises challenge the reader to rethink patterns, strengthen resilience, and take ownership of their mental and emotional health. I feel more grounded, more intentional, and more capable of leading both myself and others with clarity and confidence. This isn't just another self-help book—it's a roadmap to sustainable wellbeing.

—HEATHER POWERS

Former Director at Booz Allen Hamilton, executive coach, speaker and author of *The Power Lane*

contents

PART V. THE DEFINE PHASE

PART VI. THE DEVOTE PHASE

PART VII. THE DEDICATE PHASE

PART VIII. DELIVER

introduction

———

L ET'S START THIS JOURNEY WITH A trip back to childhood; to those sunny afternoons on the playground during recess or gym class, when you and your friends would engage in a fierce game of kickball.

For the natural athletes, the ritual of choosing teams was likely exciting. For the not-so-natural athletes, it was probably closer to terrifying. The captain had one job: choosing the players who'd give the team a competitive advantage. Selections were based on speed, agility, accuracy, and likability. As a player, that moment triggered a fundamental human instinct: the desire to belong, to be valued, to be chosen, and to contribute.

Now imagine we picked teams in the workplace the same way—but the only thing you had insight about was their mental and emotional wellbeing. Some people are Mental Wellness All-Stars. The others? Mental Wellness Rookies.

The Mental Wellness All-Stars:
- Regulate emotions well.
- Effectively receive and integrate performance feedback.
- Manage conflicting opinions and thoughts effectively.
- Stay focused and get things done.
- Manage their work and home commitments effectively.
- Have a positive attitude that raises the energy of the team.
- Show compassion and authenticity.

Meanwhile, the Mental Wellness Rookies:

- React poorly under stress and pressure.
- Avoid tough conversations.
- Become defensive or reactive, either acting out or shutting down.
- Procrastinate and/or underdeliver.
- Have difficulty managing their home and work commitments.
- Lack awareness of their impact on others.
- Complain often or lack initiative.
- Hold grudges and believe that everyone is out to get them.

Imagine you're face-to-face with this line of people. Who would you want to interact with your customers? Who would you trust with your business's success?

Most of us would take our pick from the Mental Wellness All-Stars. This is because deep down, we *already know* that employees who show the characteristics of Mental Wellness All-Stars are likely to be more productive, resilient, engaged, and successful. They're happier. They're more likely to stick around when the going gets tough (if the culture supports them). You've likely seen firsthand how these employees make for invaluable team members, leaders, and contributors.

Unfortunately, in today's fast-changing world, there are forces working against leaders and their employees' wellbeing.

- Workplace stress and burnout continue to increase.
- Mental health (in adults and children) continues to decline.
- Helpful resources are more difficult than ever to access.
- Healthcare costs are out of control.

Organizations and their employees keep spending more and more money on "health," yet everyone keeps getting sicker.

I was once one of those individuals. On paper I had it all: a job with one of the most sought-after employers in the world, excellent pay and benefits, fun coworkers, and work I loved. But the weekly travel, the insane hours, and a newly promoted (and somewhat Machiavellian) boss took their toll. I tried to stay "healthy," but I had a deep-seated feeling that my work was killing me, figuratively and literally.

So, I quit my job and moved to an island. Literally.

I was lucky enough to have that choice. However, not everyone can just quit their job and run away—nor should they have to.

No one *should have to quit their job so they can find their health.*

After some time spent reflecting (usually on the beach with a cocktail in hand, or underwater on a dive), I came to the realization that *I* was part of the problem. A big part of it, actually. Although my job was stressful and my boss was demeaning, I didn't deal with those stressful situations well. I didn't have the skill set I needed to effectively handle the stress that came with my job. I was essentially a Mental Wellness Rookie. That's no excuse for my organization and leader, but I bore some responsibility here, too.

So I dove deep into the research available on this topic. I was curious, and I had a desperate need to figure out why I was struggling with workplace stress so much (and what I could do about it). I needed to go back to work at some point (I'm not a trust fund baby), and I wanted to do so without it killing me. What I learned during my research was that there was a lot I could do personally, and that my organization could do, to solve this problem. This book is the result of that period of study.

In the pages that follow, we will identify the "why" and "how" behind what you already know at an intuitive level: that mentally strong employees are key to any organization's success. We will explore what it means to be mentally well in the workplace, and why it matters. Specifically, we will delve into the qualities and behaviors that distinguish those who have learned mental wellness and those who have not. These qualities are not mysterious or elusive, and you already recognize them when you see them. We will look at how these behaviors and characteristics are linked to your workplace's bottom line, and I will provide you with practical strategies and a clear process to help you create a culture of wellbeing within your existing team, whether you are a formal leader or not. In short, I will show you how you can shift from being a Mental Wellness Rookie to a Mental Wellness All-Star (and how you can teach this process to your team, if you're a leader).

An important note before getting started: this process is not for everyone. If you are not concerned about your own wellbeing or that of your team or organization, this process isn't for you. If you realize the importance, but are looking for a "quick fix" for wellbeing, this book is also not for you. Just as weight loss pills don't provide long-term physical health, long-term mental wellbeing cannot be achieved through a quick fix. It's an investment. Any program offering a quick, one-size-fits-all remedy for mental wellbeing should be approached with caution. It just doesn't work that way (even though we all wish it did).

If you are:

- A leader who wants to create a truly effective and productive team…
- An individual who wants to experience joy and show up for their family and work in a better, more effective way…
- An executive or HR leader who wants to create a culture where employees can do their very best work and also thrive *outside* of work, or…
- A visionary on the forefront of bringing true wellbeing to your life and your organization...

…then this book is for you. Because mental wellness is a skill set. A skill set that can be developed. We all have a right and responsibility to access that knowledge and implement it in our lives and workplaces. We may not be on the playground anymore, but our desire to belong, to be valued, to be seen, and to contribute remains as strong as ever. And we all still want to win!

How to Read This Book

This book is designed as a practical guide; as a workshop meant to span over three to six months. It's aimed at instilling wellbeing as a sustainable skill set in you and your workforce.

There are two ways to approach it:

1. Read it straight through to get an overview of the five-step process, then return to each chapter to dive into the exercises.
2. Immerse yourself and take it step-by-step. Start with Chapter 1 and stay there. Do the exercises. Practice the skills. Don't move on until the material starts to stick.

Whichever approach you choose, I recommend spending about two to four weeks on each of the five steps. This pace will allow you to build and solidify your new habits gradually, giving you the time to learn, practice, and adapt. Importantly, you'll need a space to explore and reflect—so grab a journal to accompany you. This isn't just reading, it's a practice. Your journal will hold your answers, your insights, and your growth.

The goal is incremental growth. Getting 1% better, day after day, adds up to big change. Think of it like learning a new language: at first you fumble with the basics, but with daily practice, fluency grows. Eventually it becomes second nature and you're able to speak with someone in that language. Similarly, while the strategies in this book *will* offer immediate benefits, the transformative results will emerge over time as you consistently incorporate these practices into everyday life.

Wellbeing is a journey. As with any journey worth taking, steady and consistent steps lead to the most rewarding destinations.

One quick note as we get started: you'll see that I often intentionally separate "yourself" into two words to emphasize Self. It's a gentle reminder to focus on supporting the person at the center of your experiences—you. Many of us have lost touch with Self. Thinking of Self as an entity to care for can help shift that perspective.

At the end of each chapter, there are a few questions subtitled "Reflect to Retain." Please do not move onto the next chapter without completing (even quickly) these questions at the end of each chapter.

One final note for those reading this book for their own personal development journey outside of work: Focus your journaling and individual exercises to situations in your personal life, whether with family, friends, or those in your community.

Okay, I think that's everything you need to know before we get started. Make the decision to commit now and get ready for radical change!

Reflect to Retain

Are there currently any Mental Wellness All-Stars in my workplace or personal life? How about Mental Wellness Rookies? Who are they? What characteristics do each of these people have that put them in that category?

How would I categorize myself right now? What behaviors specifically put me in that group?

What is one characteristic I would like to improve upon (even if you already see yourself as a Mental Wellness All-Star)?

Spend some time on these questions before moving on. Once you have written (yes, physically written) detailed answers, feel free to progress to Chapter 1. I'm excited to see you there!

PART I

THE PROBLEM

chapter 1

---

the beginning

I WAS 28 WHEN I GOT the diagnosis. BRCA1 positive. Almost no one I told knew what that meant. Heck, the first three doctors I went to didn't really know, either. The third I had been referred to actually asked me, point blank, why I was there: "What do you want me to do for you?" I told him to act like I was his niece or daughter—someone he actually cared about—and give me some advice. I wasn't particularly nice about it. I was scared and confused, and I felt all alone.

BRCA is the genetic defect associated with breast and ovarian cancer, among other things. As it happens, my mom was part of the study that discovered the BRCA gene. Back in the 1980s, her doctor told her (and her five sisters) that the medical community knew there was a genetic component to breast cancer; they just hadn't found it yet. My grandmother and several other women in my mom's family had died from breast cancer, so they recommended that my mom and her sisters have a preventive mastectomy.

This was a radical suggestion at the time. People just weren't doing that then. Still, my mom and three of her sisters went through with the surgery and were followed as part of a study.

A System That Failed Us

In 2001, my mom was diagnosed with ovarian cancer. It was devastating. She was 57, and it was late stage III, which wasn't good. They call ovarian cancer "the silent killer" because there are no real signs of it. One doctor told me once they didn't even really know what it looked like on an ultrasound until stage III, and at that point they were saying the survival rate past five years was less than 20%. My mom started chemo and followed the doctors' advice, which was mostly focused on her port, chemo, pharmaceuticals, and checkups. She was told almost nothing about nutrition, exercise, rest, mindset, or supplements.

Every year after her mastectomy, my mom received a questionnaire from researchers asking various questions, mostly about what other health issues had come up. A few months after her diagnosis, she received her annual survey in the mail. She filled out the form, including the fact she had been diagnosed with ovarian cancer. They promptly replied that they had determined during their study that the genetic component that causes breast cancer also causes ovarian cancer… and asked whether she would be willing to be part of *another* study.

This was the first time I remember being truly angry at the medical community. My father was a hospital CEO, and I grew up respecting doctors, nurses, and everyone who worked in a hospital, so this felt like a huge betrayal. They had *known* she had this gene! They had *known* that it also caused ovarian cancer! But they hadn't reached out to her? They hadn't warned her? I knew and understood that there were rules around privacy and disclosure in research, but my mom had *helped* them with their study. So why couldn't they send a letter and say, "Hey, we cannot give you any details, but we have recently found that the genetic component of breast cancer is also related to ovarian cancer. You might want to go talk to your doctor"? That letter may have saved her life. Yet that's not how the establishment worked at the time.

My mom's diagnosis prompted me to get the BRCA test. After being passed off to those three doctors, I eventually found my way to a teaching medical facility and a team of oncologists who I saw at least every six months for the next 20 years. After a few visits, I asked one of them why this genetic defect meant I would get cancer. What was the gene physically doing to my body? He explained that everyone is born with two "things" that protect you from cancer: one of them breaks down in your thirties or forties; the other protects you until your seventies. This is why most people get cancer later in life. I was born with only one.

I wanted to know how that "thing" broke down and how I could slow its deterioration. This, to me, seemed like a normal thing to ask, yet almost no one was asking questions like that at that time. The doctor actually chuckled a little when I asked it. He told me they were not really sure; it was just a process that happened. Maybe environmental things? He essentially didn't have a helpful answer to my question. So, I let it go.

My mom died in 2004.

I was beyond devastated. My mom was amazing. She was wise and kind and giving and smart. She was clever and funny. She was an elementary school teacher who was strong in her faith and active in her church. She was the most patient and calm person I have ever met. I know it's common to canonize loved ones who have passed, but my mom truly was one of a kind.

Watching someone die is awful. Watching your mom suffer for weeks and die is beyond words. That experience catapulted my health journey. I cried for about a year after she passed, and once I crawled out of my paralyzing sadness, I started to think about what that doctor had said— that something was slowly breaking down the part of me that protected me from cancer. The medical community didn't have much to offer me by way of guidance here—the recommendation was essentially to have two intense surgeries (a double mastectomy ASAP and an oophorectomy by age 35), cross my fingers, and hope for the best—but I didn't want to do this. Something in my gut was telling me to look for answers elsewhere.

During my research, I found a website that recommended I look at four things when evaluating alternative approaches to preventive healthcare:

1. What alternative medicine values in itself.
2. What alternative medicine critiques about conventional medicine.
3. What conventional medicine values in itself.
4. What conventional medicine critiques about alternative medicine.

Basically, the message was, educate yourself. This is what I did.

Although I started this journey frustrated that no one seemed to have an answer for me, I learned a deeply impactful lesson along the way: that we have to take our health into our own hands. No one will care about your health as much as you do. Your doctor may care to an extent, but at the end of the day, you are just a number on a spreadsheet. However for you, your wellbeing is essential. Without it, you have nothing. *Nothing.*

The journey to educate myself was not linear. I fumbled around for a while, visiting random alternative practitioners. I remember one time telling my story to someone working at a nutrition center, and she responded, "Just quit eating sugar." I told her I was addicted to sugar, and I'll never forget what she said next: "You may as well say you're addicted to death, because sugar is death." That scared me enough to not go back there. I now know that she was right, but her approach wasn't helpful.

Corporate Success, Personal Cost

Fast forward 15 years—I had a great job with an amazing company. I was helping leaders and making a difference in the working lives of hundreds of employees. The catch was, it was killing me. I was on a plane almost every week, I worked 50- to 60-hour work weeks (and still wasn't getting everything done), and I was available to my employees during nights and weekends. I could feel the stress pulsing through me daily. I knew that this was not good, especially with my genetics. I gave so much every day, but it wasn't enough, because I was spread too thin. I continued to get feedback like, "We want to see more of Cara," which is great, except I was already exhausted and running every which way all the time.

I knew intuitively that the stress of the job and the habits that I had adopted as part of this fast-paced, get-it-done work culture were killing me. I had gone through the excruciating emotional and physical pain that came with a preventive mastectomy to protect my health, yet I was letting an inordinate amount of work stress into my life. It didn't make any sense.

While I was mulling these things over, our team was assigned a new leader. Theresa came from the business side—she didn't have an HR background—and this excited me. I remember telling my peers that we already knew HR, so a leader with HR experience was not necessarily what we needed. What we *did* need was a good leader.

Unfortunately, it immediately seemed like Theresa felt she had something to prove. When it was revealed that the HR team had given a terribly low employee engagement score for the third time in a row, she told our team, "If you aren't willing to give a score of ten, why are you even here?" On more than one occasion, she asked me, "Why do your leaders like you so much?" I was baffled by how much it seemed to annoy her that I was well-liked by my business teams. I now know that this had more to do with her own issues and insecurities than mine, but still, it hurt.

Then, the straw that broke the camel's back finally came:

I had spent four days in a city with a group of leaders I had newly started supporting. We'd had a great week full of talent planning, training, and coaching. It had been busy and stressful, but also incredibly fulfilling, and I knew we had done some great work. At the end of the week, the top leader in that market walked me to my rental car and thanked me for my work and presence with the team. I then got the best compliment I had ever received at that point in my career: she told me she now knew what it was like to have a true "HR partner," and that she had never experienced that up to this point.

When I arrived at the airport, Theresa called me. She said she had just gotten off a call with the leader, and that it sounded like we'd had a great week. I was so excited at this moment, thinking I was finally going to get a compliment from my boss. "It got me to wondering," she said, "are you supporting your leaders *too* much? Is that why they like you so much?"

I knew at that moment that I would never win with her.

I immediately called my sister, frustrated, angry, and almost in tears, and told her the story. She said, "I hate to say this, Cara, but… she *hates* you!" We both burst out laughing.

I knew I had to leave. My job and my boss were costing me my health. No compensation or benefits package is worth that. This was mid-October. I gave my notice on January 2. I worked my two weeks, finished my job on a Friday afternoon, closed up my home in Minneapolis, and flew to Roatan the next morning. I had decided it would be my new home.

A Wake-Up Call in Paradise

After a couple of weeks on the island, the gravity of my decision finally sunk in. *OMG, I actually quit my job—a job I loved; a job that was lucrative; a job with one of the best companies in the world—to escape to a Caribbean island. What have I done?*

Prior to handing in my notice, I had hired a coach to help me evaluate whether I was being too reactive, and, if I *did* decide to quit, to help me figure out what I would do next. I didn't have enough money to retire and would ultimately have to work again. So, I needed a plan. My coach recommended that I hold off on planning anything until corporate America had time to "wash off of me." I guessed that would take about four weeks. She said it would be more like three to four months. She was right. After a few months of scuba diving, sitting by the water, and drinking too much, I woke up one morning, made some coffee, and sat on the porch to watch the sunlight fill the sky… and it hit me: I felt *different* inside. Literally. Physically. I could tell that the stress was gone.

I was truly shocked. Before that point, I had not known what it felt like, physically, to be stress-free as an adult. It was exhilarating. (This feeling is what fueled "the great resignation" in the aftermath of the pandemic— we'll talk about this later). The corporate world and all its stress had *finally* washed off me. And by now, I was itching for something to do. So, I went and got a job at Frank's Cigar Bar, a tiny establishment that sells cigars to tourists and mixed drinks to the local expats. I worked Monday and Tuesday from 9AM to 5PM, for $11 per shift. (Not per hour. Per shift. Plus tips, of course, which were generally minimal.) I needed something to do—a purpose—and this did the trick.

Shortly after I started, something strange started to happen: even during those weekly two shifts on a tropical island selling cigars and rum, I could feel (on a much smaller scale, of course) those old nagging feelings starting to creep in: annoyance with some of the customers; frustration with my boss; wishes that I didn't have to work on some of those shifts. One day, while I was walking home from work annoyed and frustrated, I remembered an old adage: wherever you go, there you are.

This "A-ha!" moment was humbling. Very humbling. I realized that although Theresa had had (several) moments of poor leadership, *I* had been part of the problem, too. I didn't have the skill set to deal effectively with that situation. And because of that, I wasn't the easiest person to manage. I didn't always show up in the best way at work. I was often defensive. I expected a lot from myself and the people around me. I was high-strung because I was constantly worried about getting fired, or that someone had it out for me. I had a lot of ideas but little patience when they didn't come to fruition fast enough (or at all).

I wasn't aware of these counterproductive tendencies at the time. For me, they had been overshadowed by my sincere want to be a good employee, and the fact that I enjoyed work overall. Clearly, I had some work to do before I could safely go back into the corporate world.

When I initially quit my job and started living on the island, I didn't know what my next steps would be. If you had told me I would end up being a beach bum for the rest of my life, I likely would have welcomed it. I was that depressed, frustrated, and tired of work and life. I didn't care much about anything. I just wanted out. But as I crawled out of that hole of depression, stress, and burnout, I knew the beach bum life was not for me. I needed to think, plan, and create. I needed to contribute (beyond helping tourists buy cigars and go on dives). But I needed to go back to work in a way that was healthy; in a way that made sense to me.

Rewriting What I Thought I Knew

I come from a medical family that largely believes alternative and complementary care have no place in healthcare. I grew up scared of chiropractors, as they were "quacks." As I got older, I still rolled my eyes a lot when people talked about those topics. I scoffed under my breath at my coaching training when they taught us to ask people questions about where they felt an emotion "in their body." I shook my head when people talked about sound healing and breathwork.

Yet deep down, I've always been someone who's curious about the "woo-woo" things in life—mindfulness, meditation, energy readers, you name it. Over the years, I continued to learn about these "alternative" modalities and ideas. I kept trying out different things. I'm so thankful I did.

It felt like there were two sides to me: the hard-driving HR professional who had earned two master's degrees (in counseling psychology and industrial relations) and who relied on science and proven strategies to accomplish goals and help people, and the hippie who was researching alternative methods to keep me healthy. I was going for acupuncture, trying to meditate here and there, and experimenting with things I could consume to keep me healthy. To this day, my friend Wes loves to remind me of the strange supplements I used to take at my desk. (His favorite was the bee pollen out of a tiny little tube!)

In 2018 I was Googling things like, "How can I work a stressful job without getting stressed out" while diving into the psychology of work. In 2020, I came across a class for coaches based on neuroscience. The pandemic was in full gear, and I had nothing to do, so I signed up. What I learned in that class changed my life (and the lives of many of my coaching clients) for the better. I finally found something that lay at the cross-section of the two sides of me. It turned out there was actual brain research supporting all of these things I had been calling "woo-woo" for years.

I was hooked.

For all of you fellow skeptics out there, trust me when I say I feel you. I am a Capricorn with German ancestry. I'm logical, I'm a planner, and I'm fairly stubborn. I'm also a Gen Xer to the core. I saw a meme the other day that said, "Gen X: the only generation that became 30 at the age of ten and still is 30 at 50," and this describes me perfectly. I had my first "real" (aka, not babysitting) job at 12 years old, at the Dairy Queen right on the edge of our small town. At 12 years old, I was left to close the building up by myself on the nights I worked. I had keys to the place, counted the money, cleaned up, and prepped Dilly Bars for the next shift, all by myself. I've been working in some capacity ever since (except for my 2018 island hiatus). I am practical and results-oriented.

A lot of my generation are skeptical of corporate culture initiatives. Instead, we (over)value self-reliance. At the mere suggestion of implementing anything "woo-woo" in the workplace, we've got one eyebrow permanently raised.

- "What are you trying to trick me into with this culture training? I am *not* drinking your Kool-Aid."
- "This isn't a workplace initiative. People need to figure this out on their own time (and dime)."
- "What's the ROI going to be?"

I, as many others do, used to believe in many of the myths that currently hold leaders and organizations back from investing in wellbeing. I was wrong to buy into such misconceptions. Science backs these practices up. There is a tangible return on investment when you care for people's wellbeing. Culture *does* matter. People need and deserve help from their employers when it comes to their mental wellbeing, and that support can be given in a practical manner.

I did this work while I was building a consulting and coaching business. I implemented facets of what I learned into my individual coaching clients' programs and lives. I took some of the work I had done with teams in my prior life and adjusted it, so it was more impactful and effective. During that process, I saw what happens when people get stronger mentally; when they learn about why they show up the way they do in meetings, with their family, with their coworkers, and with their boss; when a leader leads through a lens of wellbeing and sees the impact that has on their team and how that affects productivity, retention, and engagement.

It was fun to watch those changes take place, and this book puts those learnings into a process that:

- Organizations can use to create a culture of wellbeing that improves productivity, retention, and engagement.

- Leaders can use with their teams to positively impact the employee experience every single day.
- Individuals can use to lead in their own lives differently; to show up at work and for the ones they love with intention.

Here, I present to you a process for how to lead your self well; lead your team well; lead your organization well.

But before I present this process, we need to understand what problem it is that we're solving exactly, and how and why it came to be. What is the cost of a sick and burned out America? We'll explore that next.

Reflect to Retain

Consider your health (mental and physical), your personal life (relationships), and your professional life (work):

What matters to me in each of these aspects of my life, at a soul level? What is my ideal state for each of these? Who do I want to "be" in each of these areas?

How would my daily experience be different if I were living in that "ideal" state?

Why is this ideal state and potential daily experience important to me?

chapter 2

---

the cost of a sick and burned out America

BEFORE WE BEGIN THINKING ABOUT WELLBEING in the workplace, we first need to take stock of the overall problem. We need to know the bigger picture of what we are up against.

Mental and physical health, as a topic and a problem, is extraordinarily daunting. America is sicker than ever, and everyone is paying for it. (Well, most everyone... More on that later.) Individuals are paying for it with their pocketbook, with their daily experience, and sometimes with their lives. Companies are paying for it indirectly (in terms of lost productivity, increased turnover, and decreased engagement) and directly (in ever-increasing healthcare costs). The evidence for these points is hit-you-over-the-head compelling:

- Despite spending nearly twice as much on healthcare per capita and as a percentage of GDP, the US has worse health outcomes compared to *all other* high-income countries.[1]
- In 2022, the US spent $4.5 trillion dollars on healthcare costs. About 75% of these costs went to chronic and preventable diseases, such as heart disease, diabetes, cancer, and obesity.[2]

- Based on data by the Organization for Economic Cooperation and Development, compared to the other 38 high-income countries:
  - US life expectancy is three years lower than the average.
  - The number of avoidable deaths per 100,000 people in the US is about 33% higher.
  - The US has the highest rate of infant and maternal deaths.
  - The rates of suicide in the US are the third highest.
  - Deaths from assault are nearly a staggering six times higher in the US than the nation in second place (New Zealand).
  - The obesity rate in the US is nearly double the average.
  - US adults are most likely to have multiple chronic conditions.
  - The US has among the lowest rates of physician visits and among the lowest numbers of physicians per capita.[3]

Our health crisis is not limited to physical health conditions. Although estimates can vary, there were more than 59 million adults with mental illness in 2022. That is almost 23% of all Americans, or nearly one in four.[4] When we look specifically at the workplace, 46% of full-time American workers suffer from mental illness. This is an increase of 7% from before the COVID-19 pandemic.[5]

We are not alone in the United States. According to the World Health Organization (WHO), the prevalence of anxiety and depression increased by a remarkable 25% worldwide during the pandemic.[6] This makes sense to most of us. During that time, people were isolated from their social networks. They were unable to work, visit family and friends, or be active in their communities. A sense of loneliness, fear of what was to come, and concern about work and school quickly took a toll. Many turned to substances to help them cope (overdose deaths increased by a massive 28.5% during the pandemic),[7] and to add insult to injury, the pandemic severely disrupted people's ability to get professional help to deal with their increased mental distress. Dévora Kestel, Director of the Department of Mental Health and Substance Use at the WHO, summed up the situation: "While the pandemic has generated interest in and concern for mental health, it has also revealed historical underinvestment in mental health services. Countries must act urgently to ensure that mental health support is available to all."[8]

Even now, many people struggle to get care. We all know anecdotally that many still struggle to get out of bed, to deal with the hopelessness that comes from life's daily struggles, to manage the emptiness associated with working for a company or boss that does not appreciate its employees, and to keep up with the frantic pace of daily life. All these factors continue to affect the mental health of many today.

To further complicate the issue, mental and physical health are deeply interrelated. Physical health conditions have been shown to be more prevalent and more difficult to treat when coupled with mental health conditions such as depression or anxiety. A 2023 study in the *European Journal of Preventive Cardiology* showed a shocking correlation between mental health and cardiovascular fitness.[9] It found that adults in their twenties and thirties with a mental disorder (such as PTSD, depression, insomnia, or anxiety) had up to a threefold higher likelihood of experiencing a heart attack or stroke. *Three times the likelihood.* Clearly, separating mental and physical health is an exercise in futility. In the words of Forrest Gump, they go together like peas and carrots.

Unsurprisingly, this mental illness epidemic is showing up at work, and organizations are paying the price for it. Specifically, 55% of those with mental health issues report that their mental illness negatively affects their work. A third of them say that half or more of their worktime suffers when dealing with mental health or substance abuse issues.[10]

Our workforce is burned out.

Burnout: Buck Up, Buttercup

Burnout is the fibromyalgia of the corporate world.

For years, fibromyalgia was considered by many (including those in the medical world) as a "fake" condition. It still is to some. Those with fibromyalgia were dismissed by doctors and family, told it was "all in their heads," and often left feeling dismissed and hopeless.

Fibromyalgia was, and sometimes still is, considered a controversial diagnosis because it's not fully understood. There still is no specific clarity on the disorder. Thankfully, today, it's recognized by most as a very real and debilitating condition. There are even clinics at some of the most prestigious medical organizations in the US fully dedicated to the illness.

Burnout is similar in that it hasn't been understood, and has actually been ignored, by many leaders and organizations for decades.

As a Gen Xer I'm proud of how hard I work. I also used to be proud of the long hours I put in, regardless of the impact this had on my health, happiness, and personal life. I would take my computer on vacation and sit at the tiki bar sipping drinks while working, occasionally taking a few seconds to look out at the ocean (instead of being *in* the ocean). I couldn't imagine going anywhere without my computer. I was annoyed with people who came in late and left early; who (as I saw it) didn't dedicate themselves the way I did.

My work output was important, yes, but the time put in was as well. A few times, I slept under my desk from around 2AM to 5AM, so that the next day, I could continue working as soon as I woke up. (As I write this, I cannot believe that I was ever okay with that, much less proud of it.)

I was burned out—that's a given—but I didn't know it. It was just part of the game, right? It was part of the job. We worked hard, we played hard (but mostly we worked hard). Sure, I was tired and cranky and irritable all the time. Sure, I was constantly ruminating and second-guessing. Sure, I was often reactive and rarely in control of my emotions when things became demanding. Sure, I had a difficult time accepting and hearing feedback. Sure, I never felt "done" and lived with a pit in my stomach from the moment I woke up to when I fell asleep. Sure, I was always tired and running in a million different directions. Sure, I constantly feared messing up and losing my job. Sure, I had a difficult time enjoying my life outside of work. But I didn't take the idea of burnout seriously. No one did. In fact, if you did, that meant you weren't up for the job. We had been programmed to believe that working this way was "normal."

In 2019, the World Health Organization officially recognized burnout as an "occupational phenomenon"[11] having three elements:

- Feelings of energy depletion or exhaustion;
- Increased mental distance from one's job, or feelings of negativism or cynicism related to one's job; and
- Reduced professional efficacy.

What does burnout look like in the workplace?
- Loss of motivation.
- Decline in productivity.
- Difficulty thinking clearly and solving problems.
- Irritability and lashing out at others.
- Shutting down or being defensive.
- Depression and anxiety.

Burnout is therefore not merely a personal problem. It's a problem for the sufferer's colleagues, workplace, family, and friends, and therefore society as a whole.

In a survey by Deloitte of over 1,000 professionals, 77% of respondents said they had experienced burnout at work, and 91% said that having an unmanageable amount of stress at work impacted the quality of their output. Perhaps most notably, nearly 70% said their employer was not doing enough to prevent or address burnout in their organization.[12]

Thankfully, caring about employees' wellbeing is quickly becoming an expectation rather than a nice-to-have. Millennials and Gen Zers currently make up more than 50% of the workforce, and this number is only growing.[13] The success of organizations will therefore soon almost completely rest on the success of these generations. And in a 2018 Gallup poll, these generations listed "the organization cares about employees' wellbeing" as the top quality they look for in an employer.[14] Furthermore, in a 2022 survey, "greater work-life balance and personal wellbeing" were cited as "very important" by 61% of the workforce, compared to 53% in 2015.[15] The tide is changing, and these generations have an expectation for their workplace to care about them as humans.

The tricky thing about burnout is that while employers pay a high price for it (in increased healthcare costs, increased turnover, lower productivity, and lower engagement), the workplace is, by definition, where burnout comes from. It's like they're creating their own dragon to slay. Leaders therefore need to learn how to lead in a way that minimizes that dragon. Should they fail to do so, they'll keep paying the costs. And burnout costs a lot.

The Cost of Burnout

Your business pays for the current mental and physical health crisis plaguing our society today in many ways. Some of these are obvious. Others are not so obvious. You probably know the impact this is having anecdotally. You might even have numbers. Either way, the direct and indirect costs employers face as a result of burnout are massive. To get a full view of the issue at hand (and figure out what we can do about it), we need to explore these.

Healthcare

Healthcare is one of the fastest growing industries over the past decade, with individual and family premiums in employer-sponsored plans increasing between 58% and 63% over that time period.[16] In 2025, US corporate employers will see about a 9% increase in healthcare costs, on top of the 7% increase that occurred in 2024.[17]

What's causing this?

One of the biggest reasons for this increase in healthcare costs is the corresponding increase we're seeing in chronic health conditions such as heart disease, cancer, and diabetes, and the increasing demand for obesity drugs.[18]

But what does this have to do with burnout and your workplace?

Well, have you heard of the Sunday Scaries? What about the Sunday Blues? These terms are used to talk about the anxiety and dread that comes on a Sunday night when employees start thinking about heading back to work. As a kid, I knew that Sunday evenings were a time when we all needed to be good, as my dad was sometimes easily irritable. I always thought this was because of us, or because of the Vikings (if they happened to lose on a Sunday afternoon). As an adult, I now realize that, even though my dad always loved work and his job, part of his irritability was likely due to stress of the upcoming work week.

Here's a fact that shocked me: heart attacks are statistically most likely to happen on a Monday.[19] Suicide and suicide ideation are also the highest on Sundays and Mondays. As reported in a study published in Translational Psychiatry,[20] "negative self-harm cognitions" (e.g., the desire to hurt oneself or die) increase on Sundays and Mondays. These data show the impact that work (even *thinking* about going to work) has on employees' mental and physical health and on the mental health of their household (who are likely also on your company healthcare plan).

When employees are unhealthy, it costs the organization, big time.

Engagement and Productivity

Have you ever come to work with a migraine? What about with the flu, or a cold? Maybe you work in an environment where coming to work while sick is a badge of honor (although hopefully that has lessened after the pandemic). Maybe you feel proud when you come to work no matter how you're feeling. But how productive are you on these days? How engaged are you? Do you do your best work? I'm guessing not. We all know that healthy employees are more likely to be engaged and productive. Now imagine coming to work when you're facing a major health crisis, such as heart disease, cancer, or diabetes. Heart disease and stroke alone cost $156 billion annually in lost productivity on the job.[21] It's almost impossible to be your best self, deliver your best product, effectively serve customers, create, ideate, and imagine when you're sick. Your employees are the same way.

How about mental health issues? In Slack's 2023 global "State of Work" survey, 82% of employees said that feeling happy and engaged at work is a key driver of productivity.[22] It's unsurprising, then, that employees with mental health issues (including burnout) are less productive. They stop work more often, they're often distracted by what's going on in their heads, they're busy rehashing and rehearsing conversations that didn't go well, they're more likely to have lost sleep and therefore be tired during the day, and they're more likely to talk about their issues with their peers throughout the day. In addition to all of these things, they're also likely to get sick. Globally, the World Health Organization reports that 12 billion working days are lost every year due to depression and anxiety, which results in over $1 trillion in lost productivity.[23] Every. Single. Year.

What about presenteeism—those employees who work while experiencing burnout—who *are* physically present, but not at their best? Employees who are physically present but disengaged can cost their employer up to a third of their annual salary in productivity loss. And when you think about your customer-facing employees in particular, the impact here can be staggering: poor customer service can cost your organization millions as customers take their business elsewhere when they have a poor experience with an employee who is struggling.

Sustained, long-term high performance simply cannot exist without employee wellbeing.

Destructive Workplace Behaviors

Burnout shows up in many ways that we tend to attribute to poor employee behavior. Do any of these sound familiar, in yourself or your employees?

- Difficulty completing tasks on time or inability to do so.
- Mood swings or irritability, resulting in lashing out at others or shutting down.
- Depression or anxiety.
- Substance use outside of work hours, to "take the edge off."
- Cynicism about work or the company.

When leaders exhibit these behaviors, the impact is multiplied via a ripple effect that can be very difficult to fix. Employee attitude, performance, and engagement all reflect leadership to some degree. If an employee exhibits such behaviors, the root cause can often be traced back to their leader in some way.

When I was an HR leader, it was far too common for leaders to come to me with these types of behavior issues in their employees. For years, I followed the company's general practice and used whatever tool the company was using at the time. This was usually:

- The StrengthsFinder (how do we leverage the employee's strengths to combat this behavior?).

- A competency model (what competencies is the employee underusing or overusing, and how can we create developmental experiences to help them in these areas?).
- EQi (which attributes do the employee score low in, and how can we develop those?).

In other words, I used to always view the employee as the problem. In my (and the company's) view, it was up to the employee to receive the feedback and fix the problem. This approach can be effective for treating the symptom, but rarely addresses the underlying cause.

Turnover

Keeping employees (especially the good ones) is essential to business success. When a good employee leaves:

- Work suffers as the role sits empty and others try to fill the gap.
- Hiring costs rise due to recruiting, training, and onboarding.
- Productivity dips as the new hire ramps up.
- Institutional knowledge and expertise are lost.
- Other employees question whether they, too, should leave.

Burned out employees are 2.6 times more likely than non-burned-out employees to be actively looking for a job while still in their current role.[24] This fact alone should be incentive enough for leaders to prioritize preventing burnout in the workplace, from a financial perspective. The cost of replacing an employee varies widely based on position, industry, and current climate, but will usually range from 50% of that person's salary (for an entry-level position) to more than 150% (for a high-level or specialized position).

Let's do some simple math here. Let's say an organization has 100 agents or customer service reps, each making about $50k annually. Assuming a conservative estimate of 20% unwanted turnover based on burnout, and assuming a conservative replacement cost of 50% of their salary, this position alone will cost your organization a *minimum* of $500k annually in turnover costs. Conversely, the cost of losing just one executive with a $250k annual salary to burnout could cost the organization $375k!

Burnout costs. A lot.

Workplace Violence

One cost not often considered is that arising from workplace violence.

The term "going postal" has been around since the early 90s, following a series of workplace violence incidents that occurred in post offices starting in 1986. I first learned about this term during grad school, when my professor defined it as someone showing "outbursts" due to excessive stress. This intrigued me. How does someone get to that point?

I had my first (and thankfully only) true concern of someone "going postal" when I worked my first real HR job. I was the head of HR in a medium-sized family-owned business. We had a supervisor (let's call him Dave) who worked the second shift. Soon after I started, he was demoted due to insufficient performance and inappropriate behavior. I was part of that decision-making, and I suspected that he blamed me for it.

As a small leadership team, we would talk about Dave and (inappropriately) joke about who he would come after first when he finally "lost it." One of the owners thought it would be him, because he was the one who communicated the demotion to Dave. The CEO thought it would be him, as he was the (fairly new) head of the company. I thought it would be me, since my office was closest to the front door, and because

Dave had been demoted a few months after I started. Turns out I was right. About six months after the demotion, I had an employee on second shift come into my office and quickly close the door behind him. He told me that Dave had been talking about wanting to kill me for several months, and the previous day, while on a break, Dave had shown him a 9mm he had in the car and shared the details of his plan. Dave knew where I lived (he had followed me home one night), that the house behind mine was on a cul-de-sac, that I went in and out the back door, and that there were bushes he could hide in for the attack.

After a quick investigation, we fired Dave on his next shift. The police were onsite at my office door while we delivered the news. Afterward, they interviewed him, and although he did not say anything to warrant an arrest, they recommended that I not go home for a couple of weeks. "He really, really hates you," they told me.

The officers followed me home and came in while I packed my bags to stay with a friend. They recommended I take handouts to my neighbors with a picture of Dave, his van, and his license plate number asking them to call the police if they saw him in the neighborhood.

The company paid for an alarm system to be put in my home, and our employment lawyer recommended I "watch out" on the days after his unemployment ran out and on the one-year anniversary of his being fired, since those are apparently times when someone is likely to seek revenge if they're still angry. Nothing ever happened, and I was relieved when I heard Dave got another job.

Workplace violence due to stress and mental illness is a real thing. According to OSHA, more than 2 million Americans are victims of workplace violence every year.[25] The Bureau of Labor Statistics reported that there were 454 workplace homicides and over 41,000 nonfatal assaults and intentional injuries at workplaces in 2019.[26] In 2020, a year when most people were not even at work for long, there were still 392 workplace homicides and more than 37,000 workplace nonfatal assaults and intentional injuries.[27] Some of the main causes of workplace violence include employee disputes (such as conflicts between coworkers or between employees and supervisors) and domestic issues (where personal problems spill over into the workplace). Either way, workplace violence costs US employers about $120 billion every single year.

Significant increases in employee absenteeism and turnover occur after workers are exposed to workplace violence, and productivity often decreases, too. Furthermore, employees don't need to have been physically harmed during an altercation to experience psychological trauma, which also costs employers and employees in medical expenses.[28]

Workplace violence costs. A lot.

A Final Note on America's Health Crisis

Employers continue to bear the costs of the mental and physical health crisis. Even those who *do* care about this and want to change it are fighting against some surprising (and strong) forces. But not all is lost, and in order to overcome a problem, we must first understand it. Therefore, in the next chapter, we'll look at how and why we have come to this point, so we can then explore what can and should be done about it.

Reflect to Retain

What are three things I learned from this chapter?

1.

2.

3.

What are three concepts I want to remember from this chapter?

1.

2.

3.

Where do I think burnout is costing me personally? My team? My organization?

What is one thing I'm going to do differently because of what I learned in this chapter?

chapter 3

an uphill battle

JUST AS THERE CAN BE A dark side to every person, there can be a dark side to organizations (even the really good ones). What you may not realize is, there are big industries working *against* your and your employees' health, not always intentionally, but because sick people are customers.

This may feel a little uncomfortable. It may even sound like a conspiracy theory. Bear with me here as we explore our current reality.

- Some industries benefit when people are not in the best of health.
- Some companies create products and services that, when overused or misused, hurt our physical and mental health.
- Some government systems actively keep people unwell because this benefits them politically.

Employers and individuals bear the cost of this. Which industries benefit from your employees being sick? Let's talk about that.

All companies, without exception, need customers to survive. This is Business 101. And when a person gets sick, they become a customer of the medical community, pharmacy companies, and health insurance companies (among others). Therefore, by definition, these industries *depend* on people being sick to keep functioning. Sick people form a huge part of their "sales funnel."

There are three main elements that determine the state of health:

- Genetics (which are inherited).
- Lifestyle (which is comprised mostly of choices).
- Accidents (which are circumstantial).

If something goes wrong in one of these areas, you enter a system that benefits from your illness. You go to your doctor and likely get a prescription (or a few of them), becoming a customer of the medical, pharmaceutical and insurance industries (if you're lucky enough to have insurance). Then, if you're like most Americans, you go home, take your meds, and go back to the lifestyle that created the problem to begin with.

Let's take a look at our average Joe:

Joe works a stressful job. He's got a couple of great kiddos and a spouse, but regularly worries about bills, work, and the state of the world, among all the other things a human has to worry about nowadays. He tries to eat "healthy," but at the end of a long day, he usually wants comfort food, so he grabs some snacks or fast food on the way home, maybe with a beer or two to "take the edge off." He doesn't have time to work out, sleeps poorly, and then gets up and does it all again the next day.

Putting aside any genetic issues Joe may have that we don't know about, we can see that Joe isn't setting himself up for health. Like most Americans, he's putting himself in the path of illness.

Why do we do this to ourselves? And how did we get here?

Big Food

Lifestyle choices create about 75% of the need for healthcare in the US, and one of the biggest factors in lifestyle is the food we choose to eat.

As we saw with Joe, Americans don't often choose wisely—and that's not entirely our fault. Most grocery stores are packed with ultra-processed foods full of added sugar, salt, and fat. From beverages to salad dressings to breakfast cereals—sugar, dyes, and chemicals are in almost every food in the supermarket. They're even in things you wouldn't suspect—like chicken broth, pasta sauce, and "light" salad dressing. The reason these foods make you feel like an addict is because you likely *are* one. And the more addicted you are, the more you buy. You know the saying "bet you can't eat just one?"

We have become the perfect, most loyal customer, and we're getting sicker and sicker because of it. From 2000 to 2020, US adult obesity increased from about 30% to nearly 42%. Obesity-related illnesses like heart disease, diabetes, and cancer are currently among the leading types of preventable premature death in the US.[1]

I took my nieces to Italy recently to celebrate their high school graduation. They had never been out of the US before, and I'd challenged them to try new foods instead of the familiar. (I mean, we were in *Italy*! You *must* eat all the Italian food you can get, right?) At the airport on the way home, one of them asked if she could buy a can of a popular US brand of potato chips. "Of course," I said, knowing this was going to be a surprise for her. She took one bite and looked confused. "These don't taste right." I had her Google the ingredient list for the chips in the US versus those in the EU, and she was shocked. The EU chips had far fewer ingredients. Many additives banned in the EU are allowed in the US.

It could be argued that most of the "food" that Americans consume today is not even really food at all. According to the Oxford Dictionary, food is "any nutritious substance...to maintain life and growth."[2] Merriam-Webster meanwhile defines food as "material...used in the body of an organism to sustain growth, repair, and vital processes and to furnish energy."[3] I'm not sure you could make the claim that cheese puffs and jellybeans "maintain life and growth," they are definitely not considered a "nutritious substance," and it would be hard to prove that they effectively "sustain growth and vital processes."

Is your food even food, or is it mostly chemicals and additives? It's a fair question.

In the US, a food additive must be authorized by the FDA. For this to happen, manufacturers must provide evidence that the additive is safe for its intended use. The catch? There is a long list of ingredients (more than 10,000) that are classified as Generally Recognized As Safe (GRAS) by the FDA that do not have to be reviewed by the FDA before being used in foods, and they are not required to be on the label. This category was initially created for common items like vinegar and baking soda.

How does an additive get on the GRAS list, you might ask? Well, the food or ingredient manufacturer just needs to say it's GRAS. They do have the option of notifying the FDA as such, but it's not a requirement.[4] In 2014, Michael Taylor, former FDA deputy commissioner for food, even said, "We simply do not have the information to vouch for the safety of many of these chemicals."[5] The food companies decide.

Seems a lot like letting the fox watch the henhouse.

There are many steps the FDA could take to make our foods better for us, and thankfully, there have been some small steps in this direction. In October 2023, California banned four chemicals used as additives in food and drink which have already been banned in the EU.[6] In January of 2025, they finally banned Red No. 3, an artificial dye linked to cancer in animals under pressure from consumer-advocacy groups.[7] Possibly, just as it took years for big tobacco companies to be regulated, there will one day be regulation that forces food companies to take American's health into account. But today, the health of Americans is certainly nowhere near a top priority for most of Big Food.

Social Media

The pervasive use of social media platforms has raised concerns about their impact on the mental and physical health of our communities. Numerous studies have shown a correlation between excessive social media use and adverse effects on users with regard to loneliness, depression, and anxiety.[8] Children and adolescents are particularly vulnerable to such effects, especially to cyberbullying, which can lead to suicide ideation.[9] These platforms have been accused of being intentionally designed to encourage addiction through algorithms that keep users scrolling endlessly.[10]

I have a friend who does wisdom tooth extraction for adolescents, and he has seen firsthand just how addicted kids are to their phones. He says it's more common than not for an adolescent to immediately start patting their pockets, looking for their phone, as soon as they begin to come out of anesthesia. The nurse will say, "Hey there, you want to see your mom?" and, in their drugged-up state, the teen will ask for their phone instead.

At the end of 2023, there were 33 states suing Meta, alleging it intentionally designed its platforms in a way that's addictive to teens and that leads to worsening mental health.[11] The problem has become such a public mental health crisis that in early 2024, the city of New York identified social media as a public health hazard and released a formal action plan to combat it.[12] At the same time, the city of New York, the NYC school districts, and the NYC health and hospitals corporation filed a lawsuit against TikTok, Instagram, Facebook, Snapchat, and YouTube. Among the allegations were:

- The platforms targeted school-age children as a core market.
- The defendants had designed, operated, and promoted their platforms to attract, capture, and addict youth.
- These platforms had created a youth mental health crisis.

For these companies, Americans' health isn't the priority—addiction is.

The Medical Community

If you've ever been hospitalized, you likely gained a new appreciation for the work and service of the nurses, doctors, and staff who are dedicated to patient healthcare during your stay there. I grew up being comfortable inside a hospital, as my dad was a hospital CEO. However, I didn't fully appreciate the role and impact of nurses (especially) and doctors until I had an 11-hour surgery that came with a five-night hospital stay and a long road to recovery.

The medical community plays a pivotal role in safeguarding and enhancing the health and wellbeing of our nation. Nurses, doctors, technicians, and researchers work tirelessly to diagnose, treat, and prevent illness and injury. They care for us when we cannot care for ourselves, and they engage in groundbreaking research that has brought discoveries we take for granted today, but at one time seemed like miracles. Some of these are:

- X-rays, to see *inside* the body.
- Antibiotics, to drastically reduce mortality rates from once-deadly diseases.
- Anesthesia, to replace alcohol and a leather strap to bite on.
- Painkillers, to alleviate debilitating pain.
- Prosthetic limbs, to facilitate a fully functional life after serious accident or illness.
- Microsurgery, to enable surgeons to complete intricate procedures, such as nerve repair and vascular surgery, with high levels of precision and accuracy.

The pandemic pushed the medical system and its practitioners within it to the limit. Workers in this industry faced immense pressure and exhaustion, both physically and emotionally. They worked long hours in overcrowded hospitals while having insufficient PPE to protect themselves and their families. They witnessed the suffering and loss of countless patients, which took a toll on their emotional wellbeing and led to extreme levels of burnout. Yet despite all of this, they continued to show unwavering dedication to their work and the health of their community. This selfless sacrifice serves as a testament to their profound sense of commitment to care, duty, and compassion.

Today, the medical community is still bursting at the seams in many areas of the US. There are so many sick people in need of care and not enough staff (of all kinds) and space to treat them. Talk to any nurse, administrator, doctor, or technician, and they will tell you stories of burnout, overwhelm, and exhaustion. Talk to anyone trying to get an appointment for themselves or their loved one, and you are likely to hear a story of frustration and pushbacks.

The individuals who keep our clinics and hospitals going deserve every ounce of respect sent their way. However, there's a dark side to the medical *industry* (as there is with every industry). After all, it *is* a business. Once you're sick and go to the doctor, you're now the medical establishment's customer. You (and your insurance company) pay a lot of money for visits, tests, labs, and hospital stays. Everything has a big price tag, and it's a price tag you're not able to see without a lot of work on your end. When you're a customer, you're at their mercy.

I need an ultrasound twice a year because of my BRCA diagnosis. The deductible on my insurance plan is very high, which means I always know I'll end up paying for this myself. I'm lucky in that I already know this in advance, so I can try to manage costs. Still, to do so, I have to figure out billing codes and call the billing office. To make matters more confusing, the price is different depending on whether I'm paying cash. To make it even *more* confusing, the insurance price is not really the price, because the billing office has different deals with different insurers on the "allowed" price, and they don't always know the "allowed" price until *after* they run it through insurance. So then, I have to make the decision: do I take the cash price (which is usually lower), or do I risk going through insurance in case the "allowed" amount is lower than the cash price? If I guess wrong, then I have to go through the trouble of calling the billing office and having them run it the other (cheaper) way.

Despite the headache, I'm willing to take these steps, and in doing so, I've found the highest price for an ultrasound to be up to 220% higher than the lowest price, depending on where I go, even within a ten-mile radius, *for the exact same service*. It took me a *lot* of hours to figure this out, but it was worth it, because I go twice a year.

However, when you're in the doctor's office and they're telling you that you urgently need an ultrasound to figure out the cause of the pain in your abdomen, you don't have the luxury of time to find that information. And to make matters worse, some practitioners in the medical community get paid more depending on the services provided to you, or what you choose.

Sometimes, doctors are incentivized to sell higher-cost care. My friend Peter works in a pain clinic. He sees patients who come in with back pain, shoulder pain, hip pain, and the like. He can offer them an injection (that pays him about $175) or teach them lifestyle changes (a service that pays him $70, and takes more time). Unfortunately, the system is set up so that Peter is motivated to "sell" you the shot.

Thankfully, Peter has a passion for wellness and loves to help people resolve their pain, not just mask it. This is almost irrelevant, though, because he says that most Americans don't choose the second option anyway. He sums up a "typical" response as, "Give me the pill. Give me the shot. Please don't tell me to exercise, lose weight, and do stretches."

Peter's example is not an exception to the rule. There are countless examples of healthcare workers being incentivized to sell unnecessary surgeries, chemotherapies, physical therapies, testing or bloodwork, and small medical procedures to patients, even in my own personal experience.

- During a regular checkup, an oncologist offered to remove a non-cancerous mole with a string—which a dermatologist would have cut off for about $400.
- I was recommended ulnar nerve surgery that I found out later wasn't necessary—and it didn't work. The pain persists today.
- After that surgery, I was prescribed 76 oxycodone. *76!* I used two, and at my follow-up appointment I was offered a refill.

These examples are not rare—and they aren't cheap. According to a 2022 report by KFF Health News (a nonpartisan, nonprofit news service covering health and health policy), more than 100 million Americans are saddled with healthcare debt, many of them without insurance.[13] This results in dwindled savings, cutting spending on basics, delaying the purchase of a home, and taking on extra work to cover these costs. Even those with health insurance are not in the clear (more on that shortly).

As much as the people of the medical community are there to help, hospitals also need to make money—even non-profit hospitals. To do so, they need customers (patients), and as long as you're sick, you're their customer.

Big Pharma

In 2023, the pharmaceutical industry was valued at $1.6 trillion worldwide, $714 billion in the US alone. That's right: the US accounts for *more than half* of global revenue in pharmaceuticals, spending $600 billion more than the next closest country (China).[14]

An article entitled "Selling sickness: the pharmaceutical industry and disease mongering" in the peer reviewed British Medical Journal outlines how pharmaceutical companies can create their own customers, even when those customers aren't sick. The first line of the article states, "A lot of money can be made from healthy people who believe they are sick." Big pharma sometimes actually *creates* the customer. The article explains how:

- Alliances can be formed between drug companies, doctors, and consumer groups to promote products.
- Illness definitions are expanded and marketed to consumers.
- Normal symptoms are rebranded into "medical problems."
- Pharma companies have funded studies, helped define diseases, and developed extensive financial ties with leading researchers.[15]

In the late 90s, big pharma started marketing directly to consumers through television commercials. I remember thinking it so strange to see commercials for drugs that I could only get from my doctor. In 2022, big pharma spent $1 billion monthly (you read that right—*monthly*) on advertising, urging consumers to ask for a specific drug, sometimes for conditions they didn't even know they had.[16]

Unfortunately, in the name of profit, pharma companies sometimes go to even further, even when they know their product is dangerous. The 2021 Hulu series *Dopesick*[17], based on the book by Beth Macy[18], chronicles America's opioid crisis and how OxyContin was allegedly marketed to create dependence for profit. If you haven't seen it, it's an eye-opening portrayal of what it can look like when a pharmaceutical company tries to "create" a customer base.

My frustration with big pharma is personal:

My mom used baby powder daily. I remember thinking it was a "lady product" because she used it every day. In the now-famous case involving

Johnson & Johnson's talc baby powder, J&J was found guilty of deliberately marketing and selling a product they knew could cause cancer. According to court documents and reports, Johnson & Johnson may have known as early as the 1950s that their baby powder contained asbestos and that this could potentially be linked to health risks, including ovarian cancer. Documents also show that in the early 1970s, J&J failed to disclose to the FDA that three independent tests found asbestos in their talc, one at a high level. J&J consistently denied these allegations and maintained that their products were safe.

The first significant lawsuit came in 2013, when a jury found J&J liable for a plaintiff's ovarian cancer. In 2016, J&J was ordered to pay $72 million in a civil case. Then in 2018, a landmark case awarded $4.69 billion to 22 women who claimed their cancer was caused by asbestos-contaminated talc. As a response, J&J attempted to offload their talc products to a newly created subsidiary to avoid payment. Thankfully, this attempt (along with another in 2023) was rejected by the courts.

Although they were first found liable for selling a product that leads to death in 2013, they didn't stop selling it in the US and Canada until 2020, and globally until 2023.[19]

My mom used J&J baby powder almost every day of her adult life.

She died of ovarian cancer in 2004.

Health Insurance Companies

For employers, investing in wellbeing isn't just the right thing to do—it's a strategic decision. Understanding how the health insurance industry operates is important.

The profit-driven nature of the US healthcare system, as detailed by Elisabeth Rosenthal in *An American Sickness*[20], has compelled insurance companies to use strategies such as denying claims, increasing premiums, reducing coverage, imposing high deductibles, and limiting networks. These undermine efforts to support employee wellbeing.

Even with good benefits, employees face high out-of-pocket costs. High deductibles, copayments, and out-of-pocket maximums are common features of many insurance plans that can lead to significant financial burdens. Even that "free" preventive checkup can come with a surprise bill, due to billing loopholes.[21] George Halvorson, former chief executive of Kaiser Permanente put it bluntly, "People are getting bankrupted when they get care, even if they have insurance." At the time of the KFF Health News report, Americans owed over $195 billion in medical debt.[22]

When people fear medical bills, they delay or skip care. That leads to worse conditions, higher costs, and more stress. Preventive care becomes a luxury most aren't willing to pay for. Productivity drops. Stress and burnout climb. It's a vicious cycle.

Politicians

Politicians often get into their line of work with altruistic intentions. They want to help. However, the influence of corporate interests and the "politics of politics" often muddy the waters for politicians. The reality of the expectations placed on a politician by their party is more complex than it may seem. Once the politician gets the job, the realization usually sets in that to keep their role, they must "play the game." They must raise money for their party and vote on party lines. To accomplish this, they look to corporations to offer significant campaign contributions. They also often make decisions with detrimental consequences for their constituents, in the name of their party. Both of these factors have significant effects on Americans' health.

Corporate lobbyists influence political decisions in the name of their own interests through financial resources, networking, and persuasion.

They try to shape legislation, regulations, and government decisions. One great example of this comes from Minnesota, where Senator Amy Klobuchar used her political influence to classify pizza sauce as a vegetable in student school lunches, to support a frozen food company in her home state. I have a lot of respect for Senator Klobuchar as she later admitted this was a mistake. But still, this example shows the influence that corporations can have on our elected officials, and therefore our nation's health.

This is a problem, because, as highlighted, industries like big pharma and big food often have competing agendas when it comes to public health. According to data compiled by OpenSecrets, the pharmaceutical and health products industry poured more than $372 million—a record amount—into lobbying in 2022, outspending all other industries in that year. Big food and agribusiness also spent more than $150 million on lobbying and donations.[23]

We can't fully blame the politicians. It's part of how the brain works. In social psychology, it's called the reciprocity norm, which states that a person will feel compelled to return a favor they've received from others. This is reflected in our everyday language. How often have you said "I owe you one" to someone? A famous study in the 1970s showed that even being given a simple can of soda made participants more likely to comply with subsequent requests from the giver, compared to those who did not receive the soda.[24] The power of reciprocity is very strong. Big corporations know this and use it to their advantage.

Another complication with politicians is, they are literally "playing politics" in their job. In other words, their role is to put the interests of their political party ahead of Americans' best interests. One example that highlights this is the expansion of Medicaid in 2010, as part of the Affordable Care Act. With this expansion, millions of low-income children and adults would be provided with healthcare, with the federal government covering 90% of the cost and states only covering 10%. This expansion has increased access to care and improved overall health outcomes to millions.[25] Yet ten states have still not expanded care. Why? Politics. In 2012, a Supreme Court decision made it optional for states to participate in the expansion, and these ten states (most Republican-led) have held out. The reason, Tripp Funderburk (former legislative assistant to former Republican Congressman, Bob Livingston) says, is all politics. "Republican politicians are so tied to their party's agenda, that they turn down a 90% federal match to maintain their political purity. They care more about opposing a federal government expansion than implementing policies that are in the best interest of those truly in need."

Politicians can and do negatively impact the health of Americans, including your health and your employees' health.

Why We Are All Sick

To understand why we are all so sick, follow the money.
- Food companies profit when you're addicted to their product.
- Social media profits when you're addicted to their platforms.
- Medical communities profit when you're sick.
- Pharma profits when you stay on medications.
- Insurance profits when you use care—but also when they deny it.
- Politicians profit when they take "donations" from all the above.

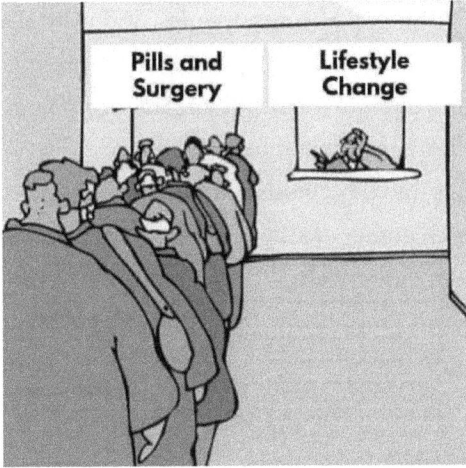

(Image source: The TPG Family[26])

They all get paid when you get (and stay) sick. All of them. They want you in that line.

Alternative health practitioners are trying their best—one patient at a time. They're working tirelessly to help people find their health. They're fighting to make employers and corporations understand that they must spend money on preventive measures that insurance won't cover. They're fighting some players in the medical community and big pharma who actively work against them and classify them as "woo-woo" practitioners because they may threaten their business model.

Please don't get me wrong here:

- Big food feeds the world.
- Social media connects us.
- Medical professionals save lives every single day.
- Pharmaceuticals are a godsend in many cases.
- Health insurance covers a lot of medical visits.
- Most politicians truly want to help.

There are individuals, teams, companies, and institutions within these industries who care deeply about people's wellbeing. These industries and companies are *critical* to the health of America. The problem comes in when huge profits are prioritized over health.

My hope is that one day, these companies will find a way to balance the health of their customers with their pursuit of profit. In the meantime, it's up to you, as a business leader (or an employee) to take care of yourself (and your employees, if applicable) as much as possible.

Reflect to Retain

What are three things I learned from this chapter?

1.

2.

3.

What are three concepts I want to remember from this chapter?

1.

2.

3.

What is one thing I'm going to do differently because of what I learned in this chapter?

PART II

THE SOLUTION

chapter 4

why investment in wellbeing matters

S O FAR, WE HAVE OUTLINED WHO benefits when America is sick. But who benefits when America is healthy?

Individuals, their families and loved ones, and their employers. While it's true there are a lot of forces working against the health of Americans, there is also good news: there's something organizations can, and *should,* do to counteract these forces. There are four key reasons to do so; four key reasons why employee wellbeing is not simply a "nice to have." Let's explore each of these.

1. Profits

Understandably, fiduciary responsibility mandates that company executives prioritize shareholders' financial interests. Anyone who's worked in a company scrambling to make quarterly numbers to appease Wall Street, knows that long-term solutions are often kicked out of the budget, because they need numbers *now*. However, employee wellness is not a quick fix, and this short-sighted approach often means that employee wellbeing is sidelined. Many leaders hesitate to allocate resources to wellbeing, and in the name of profitability, a healthy workforce oftentimes takes a back seat. Yet companies that make the Fortune 100 Best Companies to Work For list outperform the market by a factor of 3.68.[1]

We live in a stress-filled world. Work contributes to that stress, adding to the costly health problem in the US. The National Safety Council (NSC) created a mental health cost calculator to highlight the financial impact of employee wellbeing, measuring absenteeism, healthcare use, turnover, and substance use related to work.[2] They found that the average cost of an employee experiencing mental distress is about $15,000 per year. When you consider that between 40% and 80% of employees experience workplace mental distress in some form, these costs add up—quickly but often quietly. These stats don't even account for lost productivity due to presenteeism or *increased* profitability when employees are thriving.

The NSC (n. d.) has found that organizations see an average return of $4 for every dollar invested in mental health initiatives.

2. The War for Talent

Statistics aside, we know today's employees are looking for an employer that cares about their wellbeing. It's an expectation for many. Prioritizing wellbeing in the workplace is therefore imperative for organizations wanting to dominate the competitive landscape, especially for those with a workforce comprised of millennials and Gen Zers.

Nearly 50% of millennials and Gen Zers report feeling burned out at work—and these generations are willing to change companies and jobs more readily than Gen Xers or Baby Boomers. A 2024 Deloitte study of millennials and Gen Zers revealed that having a good work-life balance is their top consideration when choosing a new employer.[3]

Just as consumers have a choice of where to shop, employees have a choice of where to work, and more and more often, employees are making that choice with their personal health and wellbeing at the top of their priority list. Therefore, if an organization wants to be a winner in the war for talent, they must take note of and provide what's important to these generations. Investing in employee wellbeing is a *strategy* for being a sought-after, highly regarded employer.

3. Social Responsibility

Prioritizing wellbeing isn't just smart talent and financial strategy; it's a moral and social responsibility. Just as companies have embraced environmental sustainability to protect the earth, we must acknowledge our responsibility to safeguard the wellbeing of our employees.

Employees are the heart of any organization. They are your most valuable asset. They dream up the possibilities, bring those ideas to life, build and deliver your product, and take care of your customers. How they feel inside everyday matters.

They are also someone's child. They are someone's mom or dad, sister or brother, friend, niece or nephew, aunt or uncle, or loved one. They are therefore inherently and automatically deserving of responsible care. Caring about how employees feel inside and how they show up every day should be at the top of every leader's priority list. Without your employees, your organization would simply not exist.

Unfortunately, the simple experience of "work" can be incredibly detrimental to the very people building and sustaining your business. In a 2024 Headspace survey, employees reveal just how negatively work is impacting their personal lives:

- 47% say that the majority (or all) of their stress comes from work.

- 77% believe work-related stress has negatively impacted their mental health.
- 71% believe work-related stress caused a personal relationship to end (break-ups, divorce, etc.)[4]

Good leadership can change the world. Its ripple effects are astounding. Think about when you've been treated terribly by a boss. What did the rest of your day look like? Did you go home and:

- Have road rage, cursing out and honking at someone who cut in front of you or was driving too slowly?
- Treat the grocery checkout person in a demeaning way?
- Kick the dog when you came into the house?
- Be snappy and irritable with your kids and spouse?
- Spend the night on your phone or in front of the TV with a beer or glass of wine to "take the edge off" the day?

On the other hand, what did the rest of your day look like when you had a great day at work and were treated with respect, care, and consideration? What was the ripple effect then? Leaders can change the world in ways far beyond what they may be able to see or imagine.

With the increase in gun violence through school shootings, hate crimes, and workplace violence, we should all be concerned about the mental health of our communities. In addition to the impact it has on individual mental health, such violence also has a financial impact on employers, even when the violence happens outside the workplace.

I supported the retail arm of a large technology company when the 2017 Las Vegas mass shooting occurred. At 2AM a store leader on the strip called to update me, and I got on a plane the next day.

I have never seen Vegas like that. Quiet. Empty. Sad.

We had two employees who had been at the concert. One had been shot. Both were horrifically impacted by the experience, as was the entire community. We brought in counselors, held listening sessions, and spoke individually with employees who needed recovery time. We allowed people to stay home for a few days. We gave them the time and space to talk with one another about how they were processing it all.

We also supported customers. We took phones to hospitals so people could call their loved ones (many phones were broken or lost during the commotion). We fixed phones and watches for free (one I saw had actually been hit with a bullet). All of these actions were the right things to do.

This experience showed me something important: employers are in a unique position to positively impact the mental health of this country more than any government, entity, or industry.

- They have the resources to do it.
- They benefit financially from a healthy workforce.
- They have access to employees and can train wellbeing skills.
- They're on the hook for it anyway.

4. You're on the Hook for Employee Health (Whether You Like It or Not)

There is an ongoing argument about whether health insurance should be tied to employment. Whatever you believe, the fact is that right now, in the US, it is. Most employers have to offer health benefits to recruit talent to their organization. But how did this link come to be?

In 1942, the United States was at war. Prices were rising and labor was short. Inflation was looming. To stabilize inflation, Congress passed The Stabilization Act of 1942, and President Roosevelt issued an executive order to invoke the act. In addition to freezing prices, this act froze salaries and wages, including bonuses, gifts, and commissions. What was *not* included was insurance and pension benefits, which were allowed to increase "in a reasonable amount" during the period of the freeze.[5] At this time, employers were in a rough spot where talent was scarce (as many

Americans of working age were either at war or supporting the war effort in some other way) but the need for talent was high.

Sound familiar?

Just as we do today, companies had to get creative to recruit workers. The solution was employer-sponsored health benefits. *Et voilà*: the connection between employment and healthcare was born.

Just like an old-school cassette tape, once you unwind that, it's very difficult to wind back up, as we've witnessed with the ongoing debates about universal healthcare. So, whether you agree or disagree, most US employers are on the hook for healthcare for their employees—and those costs are rising. Instead of fighting it or trying to reduce costs by focusing on your health insurance premiums and offerings, let's try to solve the problem at the root. Besides, there is no reason why any organization should *not* be committed to creating a healthy work environment that protects and builds their employees' mental and physical health. A comprehensive corporate social responsibility strategy should absolutely include a focus on employee wellbeing.

Employers can choose to impact wellbeing and thereby costs incurred by healthcare, absenteeism, presenteeism, productivity, turnover, leaves of absence, and workers comp, or they can choose to ignore it, and thereby contribute to America's health crisis (and reduce their profits).

The Great Resignation

If you're still not convinced that you have a financial, social, and moral responsibility to take care of your employees, I suggest you think back to what happened during the pandemic: many employees refused to go back to work. This was surprising at the time because when everything was initially shut down, people were incredibly afraid of losing their jobs.

"What will I do? How will I support my family? When is this going to end so I can work again?"

There were three basic categories of employees during this time: 1) those who lost their jobs completely, 2) "essential workers" who kept their jobs as they were, and 3) those whose jobs moved to remote work. The "essential workers" were completely burned out, overworked, and at risk of contracting COVID (which was scary at the time, when we knew nothing about it); those who kept their jobs were forced to adapt to a new reality (working from home); and those who (at least temporarily) lost their jobs went home and stayed home for a long time (a huge adjustment). In the US, the government helped assuage some concerns by offering generous unemployment benefits to those who had lost their jobs. This initially did little to reassure people, though. The entire situation felt terrifying, and they didn't know when the pandemic was going to end. All they wanted was to get back to work.

But after several months, a funny thing happened. These people suddenly stopped wanting to go back to work. As restaurants and other "non-essential" businesses started to open up, huge swathes of employees failed to return. Why? Many argued that it was because of the generous unemployment benefits: people were making more money through those than they were at work.

That was part of it. The interesting thing, though, is that when those unemployment benefits ended, people *still* didn't go back, leading to "The Great Resignation."

Employers, politicians, and news reporters were stunned and confused by this phenomenon. Why weren't people going back to their jobs? Why were they suddenly willing to *not* work for a steady paycheck? Why were they suddenly willing to take the risk of entrepreneurship, participate in the gig economy, and live with less, just so they wouldn't have to go back to their jobs?

I knew what was happening. The answer was these employees had opened their eyes. They were forced into the realization that their job was costing them their health. I knew this because it was the same thing I realized three years prior, after leaving my job and moving to Roatan.

The pandemic not only changed the way we operate in the world, but it also highlighted what is important to us. One of those things, for most of us, is our mental health, and for many, it was impossible to unscramble the egg when they realized that their job was a major source of stress that took away from that.

Reflect to Retain

Who else in my organization or family would benefit from knowing this information?

How would I rate my own mental wellbeing right now? What about that of my employees? My family?

How important is my mental wellbeing to me? How about my family's? My team's? My organization's?

chapter 5

mental wellness myths

I N THE EVER-CHANGING POST-PANDEMIC LANDSCAPE, THE importance of mental wellbeing has begun to take center stage in some organizations. Finally, companies are beginning to recognize the profound and financial impact that employee mental wellbeing has on productivity, retention, and engagement. Yet amidst this growing acknowledgment, myths and misconceptions about mental wellness in the workplace persist. We need to understand and debunk these before we can really lay the foundation for a new approach to leading "well."

Mental Wellness is Not the Employer's Responsibility

"This is a personal issue. Figure this out on your own time (and dime)."

When I was in grad school, I had a full-time internship at a massive farm tire factory. On my first day of work, I got a tour of the enormous plant: the giant machinery molding the 900lb farm tires; the incredibly loud machines; the forklifts crisscrossing everywhere; the toxic chemicals being used. Shipping containers came in on a railway through giant doors, sometimes allowing a deer to sneak in and run wildly through the factory!

Imagine if during this orientation, my employer had told me that my safety on the job was my responsibility; that in my free time, I should learn about how to be safe at work; that I should go buy whatever gear I thought would keep me safe (maybe earplugs and steel-toed shoes, "but it's up to you"), take safety courses on the toxic chemicals used in the plant, and Google how to operate the giant machines without falling in and dying (which can happen, and did once during my time there).

Of course, none of this happened. That would be absurd.

Workplaces can pose physical safety risks, whether because of giant machinery or back issues from hours spent typing and looking at a screen. Because of this, employers have a well-established responsibility for ensuring the physical safety of their employees under OSHA regulations. What we (for some reason) don't often acknowledge is that workplaces can sometimes also be inherently unsafe mentally.

Work is a source of stress. It just is. Because of this, employers need to share responsibility for the mental safety and wellbeing of their workforce. By acknowledging this shared responsibility, organizations can contribute to a culture where employees are safe from physical harm and empowered to manage their mental health effectively, improving job satisfaction, engagement, and productivity in the process. It's a win-win.

Health Insurance Offers Sufficient Coverage

"I'm sorry you're struggling. Thank goodness we offer health coverage!"

As previously discussed, access to mental health services, even for those with insurance, has long been a significant challenge for many, and has become especially difficult post-pandemic. Employers spend a lot of resources on ensuring mental health benefits are part of their healthcare coverage, yet persistent barriers still hinder employees' access to them.

The system is difficult to navigate. The lack of transparency and confusion that those seeking help face can deter them from using their health insurance benefits. If they *do* figure out the system, they then have to know in advance that they can afford the appointments. Mental health is not a one-and-done appointment, like treating a cold or infection might be. It's often an ongoing need, with weekly visits over the course of months or more. High deductibles and copays on insurance plans can make care cost-prohibitive for many, even for those with coverage.

If you do figure out the system *and* you can pay the price, finding a provider becomes the issue. There's a shortage of mental health providers which has resulted in long wait times for appointments. People often wait weeks or even months to get an appointment. According to a 2022 survey of over 2,000 companies, when asked about their company's satisfaction with their health plan, "Access to Behavioral Health Care" was the second lowest, only being two points higher than "Overall Cost of Care."[1]

My good friend Sherri's teenage daughter once experienced intense bullying at school and started having suicidal thoughts as a result. Her situation was so concerning that Sherri and her husband didn't feel comfortable leaving her alone at all. Sherri was desperate to help her daughter but struggled to find someone who was taking new clients. Once she was finally able to find care, the therapist wasn't in-network and was therefore required to be paid out of pocket at a price of $190 per session, for several months. Sherri could afford this. Most Americans cannot.

Health benefits are simply not sufficient for addressing the mental health crisis.

Employers Understand Their Employees' Wellbeing

"We're one of the good ones. We truly care about our employees."

In a 2022 Gallup poll, only 24% of workers said they believe that their organization cares about their overall wellbeing. That's not even one in four. Before you start thinking, *Thank goodness we're one of the companies that do care*, consider this: 63% of HR professionals in that same survey said that the company *does* care.[2] Somewhere, there is an immense disconnect. Leaders say they care (and they likely do), but employees don't feel it. This is a problem, because perception is reality. Even if you believe you're doing it right, you may not be.

You cannot always *see* when someone is struggling with their mental health. You have to engage. You have to ask. You have to care.

Millennials and Gen Zers are Just Complainers

"Stop whining and get to work. I had to do it, so you should, too."

This is the equivalent of your parents telling you they had to walk to school four miles away, uphill and in the snow both ways, when they were young. It's deeply unhelpful.

Millennials and Gen Zers watched their parents grapple with long hours, burnout, and lack of balance in a world that prioritized relentless dedication to work. As a result, they've been at the forefront of changing attitudes toward mental wellbeing. Their unique experiences and the world in which they grew up have shaped their perspectives, and they're not shy to ask for what they need regarding their mental health. After seeing the toll their parents' mental states took on their family life, these generations are determined to redefine the narrative about work, so that mental health is valued *along with* financial success, not *instead of*. They watched their parents trade in their health and free time for their work, and they want something different for themselves. Can you blame them?

Some leaders think this means these generations simply don't want to contribute. This is untrue. These generations want to do important work and to contribute to something meaningful. They're just not willing to trade their happiness or life for it.

It's easy, as a Gen Xer, to scoff at them, to blame them, or to tell them stories about "how bad we had it," but I admire their dedication to being kinder to themselves. I feel just as exasperated by the truly lazy people in this generation (and in the other generations), but are the hard workers who merely want to have work-life balance really asking for too much?

I've heard many leaders tell stories about how Gen Zers think they're inherently deserving of a promotion or more money. I also once had a business leader I know and respect (and who has decades of leadership experience) tell me, "People want to be valued. They want to *know* they're valued. There's no big difference between Gen Z and the other generations that came before them. They're asking for 'more' because they just don't understand the game yet."

Conversations About Mental Health Violate HIPPA Laws

"Please don't call your lawyer!"

Once upon a time, as an HR partner, I advised leaders to steer clear of any conversation about mental health. We were concerned about potential legal liabilities or complicated employee relations investigations. We wanted to protect employees *and* the company from anything that could be construed as intrusive at best, or illegal at worst. So, when an employee mentioned they were having anxiety or depression, or that they were struggling with anything mental health related, I was taught to coach leaders to do three things:

1. Tell the employee it was not necessary for their manager to know about their health concern.
2. Provide information about the EAP (employee assistance program) and that they have x free sessions with a psychologist.
3. Ask them if they need an accommodation to get their work done.

There has been a significant shift in this perspective post-pandemic. HR professionals now emphasize that having conversations about mental health, when approached correctly, is imperative to creating a healthy workplace culture. In the years since the pandemic, they have begun to coach leaders on how to have these discussions, check in with employees, steer them toward resources, and navigate sticky conversations.

Conversations about mental health are about creating a space for humans to be human. They are about fostering an environment where employees feel supported, valued, and empowered to bring their authentic selves to work. By opening this dialogue, leaders can proactively identify challenges their employees may be facing and provide necessary resources, thereby reducing absenteeism, presenteeism, and turnover and increasing engagement and productivity in the process.

Of course, it *is* important to tread carefully and to recognize that health diagnosis information must be handled with the utmost privacy and in compliance with regulations. But this doesn't mean these conversations should be avoided altogether.

Policies and Benefits Are the Answer

"We've provided you with great benefits. We've got wellbeing covered."

Many believe that, by offering policies and benefits aimed at alleviating workplace stress, they have given sufficient support to employee wellbeing. While well-intended, this approach often falls short in addressing the complexity of the issue.

While it's true that offering benefits like flexible work hours, work from home policies, healthcare coverage, and child or elder care can be instrumental in reducing some stressors, they can't eliminate them all. Stress is highly individual—what overwhelms one person may not affect another—so a one-size-fits-all solution doesn't work.

Even worse, some policies and benefits are used by employees for the wrong reasons: when offered incentives (cash, PTO days) to participate in wellness activities such as health screenings or biometric checks, some employees simply rush through the motions at the end of the year to cash in on the payout. Employers frequently see that these benefits rarely drive healthy behavior.

To address workplace burnout comprehensively, companies must adopt a different approach—continue to invest in policies and benefits that reduce stressors *while* simultaneously investing in the development of their employees' mental wellness skills. This strategy not only ensures a healthier, more productive workforce, but also fosters a culture of wellbeing where employees feel seen, valued, and empowered.

Wellness Programs Should Focus on Physical Health

"Y'all need to stop eating cupcakes and get to the gym."

Have you ever been part of a "wellness challenge" at work? I have more times than I can count. Here are a few of my favorites:

- Company weight loss challenge: Here, we all stepped on the watermelon scale at work. When the scale did not budge (or moved up a pound or two), we all pointed at each other!

- *"Biggest Loser"* contest with my cubicle row: We each put in $100 on the honor system. At the end of the three months, the "winner" felt too guilty to take the loot as she had only lost two pounds!
- Corporate-wide wellness challenge: An opt-in program where you were weighed and measured, tested on pushups and situps, and assessed on flexibility. Tips and tricks were emailed each week. My friend (who "won" our *Biggest Loser* contest), after being measured after completing the program, proclaimed to our row, "Well, it's official. I'm still one-third butter!"

Many workplace wellness programs focus primarily (or solely) on smoking cessation or weight management, overlooking the connection between mental and physical wellbeing. Mental health is the foundation upon which physical health is built. Have you ever tried to work out, eat healthily, or stop smoking while depressed or anxious? How well do you sleep when you can't quiet your mind? Have you tried to be social with friends when you couldn't pull yourself off the couch? The connection between mental and physical health is obvious and profound.

When people experience high levels of continued stress, anxiety, or depression, it can manifest physically. Sleep is negatively impacted, the immune system is weakened, and susceptibility to illness increases. We then have a hard time making healthy choices as sometimes even going for a walk can feel like an insurmountable task. It can be a vicious cycle.

The interplay between the mind and body underscores the importance of addressing mental health as the cornerstone of wellbeing. When you can manage your thoughts, beliefs, and emotions, you can manage your behaviors in such a way that leads you to physical health.

Wellness Programs Are a Waste of Time and Money

"We don't have time or money to be spending on this woo-woo ish."

As discussed in Chapter 2, the organizational costs associated with the mental health crisis are staggering. As a quick reminder:

- Healthcare costs and insurance premiums are rising at a shocking rate.
- Mentally unhealthy employees are less engaged and productive.
- Employee burnout leads to costly turnover, absenteeism, and presenteeism.
- The National Safety Council (NSC) estimates that 40% to 80% of employees experience "mental distress" in some form. Those employees *each* cost your organization about $15,000 annually.
- The NSC has found that organizations see a return of $4 for every dollar invested in mental health initiatives.

Investing in the mental wellbeing of your employees is always a smart and strategic financial decision.

The Solution

Your organization is made up of your people. It can only be as healthy as the individuals within it. It's time we change the narrative about mental wellness. It's time you show, with action, that you *do* care about your employees' wellbeing. It's time to create a culture where people feel valued, seen, and heard. It's time to foster an environment where wellbeing is prioritized, for the benefit of the company *and* the people.

You may be wondering, *How exactly do I do that?* The answer lies in something you already know how to do: developing skills in your people. Organizations can *teach leaders* how to lead through a wellbeing lens—and teach all employees a wellbeing skill set that can positively impact their whole life.

Imagine the difference an organization could make in the world if all its employees developed a skill set that not only created more productive employees, but also happier *people*.

That's a world I would love to live in. And I believe we can create it.

Reflect to Retain

What myths did I believe about mental wellbeing?

Which ones are prevalent in my organization or with my leaders?

Is there one (or a few) that I still believe to be true?

chapter 6

rethinking the way we lead

WHEN WE JUMP INTO THE FIVE-STEP model, you'll see a few concepts woven throughout. These are:

- Neuroscience basics.
- Intentionality (lead your self well).
- Contributing vs constricting.
- Leadership through a wellness lens.
- Wellbeing as a skill set.

Let's explore each of these, so you'll be familiar with them before we get into the details of the model.

Neuroscience Basics

As I've already mentioned, I'm a skeptic and a questioner at heart. Ask any boss who has ever managed me. As long as I know the "why," I can get behind anything. If I don't, I can't get behind it at all. I had a boss say to me one time, "Cara, just once, can you please do what I ask you to do without asking why?" The problem is, if I don't understand the "why," I question what I'm doing and I become extremely hesitant to spend my time (or the company's time) on it.

This is why neuroscience fascinates me. Neuroscience (brain research) has made remarkable strides in the past 15 to 20 years, thanks to groundbreaking advancements in technology. Because of them, scientists can now delve deeper into the brain's intricacies than ever before.

I'll be bringing in some interesting studies from the classes and research I've done in this space to support your learning. For our purposes here, there are three fundamental areas of neuroscience that are helpful to know as we dive into this book:

- Neuroplasticity.
- The nervous system.
- Default mode network.

Neuroplasticity

Neuroplasticity refers to the brain's remarkable ability to adapt and rewire itself in response to new experiences and lessons and to environmental changes. It's a key factor in skill development, habit formation, and personal growth. You know the phrase "you can't teach an old dog new tricks?" Well, it turns out you can!* It just takes time to change the neural pathways in your brain (this is why it's not a quick fix).

One interesting example of neuroplasticity comes from a famous study of London cab drivers conducted in the late 1990s and replicated in 2000.[1] It provides fascinating insights into the brain's ability to adapt and change.

---

* I must admit that I do not know if you *can*, in fact, teach an old dog new tricks. I haven't looked into that. But, if "old dog" is used to refer to an adult human, you absolutely can.

Researchers observed that these cab drivers, who navigated the complex roadways of London every day (long before GPS), had a larger posterior hippocampus—a brain region crucial for spatial navigation and memory—compared to non-drivers. They found a correlation between the number of years spent as a cab driver and hippocampus size. This study suggested that, as they mastered the streets of London over time, the hippocampus of these cabbies expanded in size. We're not just talking about changes in neural connections here; their brains *physically grew*.

Building on this evidence, a study in 2011 followed the taxi drivers over several years and provided stronger support for a *causal* relationship. The researchers concluded that the brains of the cab drivers grew in response to learning the roads in London. They noted that "there is a capacity for memory improvement and [...] structural changes to occur in the human brain well into adulthood."[2] These remarkable studies demonstrate neuroplasticity: that the brain can adapt and restructure itself in response to specific demands and experiences—even well into adult life.

We can use this knowledge to make changes in our own brains. Think of your neural pathways as roads. Your brain aims to work efficiently, so, when left to its own devices, it will continue to use the same neural pathways over and over again. For example, if you take the same route home every day, you don't have to think very hard. That's why you can sometimes pull into the driveway and not really remember driving home. For your brain to think differently, do differently, and build a new muscle, you must choose a different neural pathway, make mistakes, and practice it over and over. Eventually, your brain will become more comfortable with it (and maybe even change its structure to accommodate it).

The Nervous System

This will be a quick refresher for those of you who have forgotten your ninth-grade biology! Your sympathetic and parasympathetic nervous systems work in tandem to keep you safe, balanced, and (most importantly) alive.

The sympathetic nervous system (your fight-or-flight team) kicks in when you're facing something scary or exciting (think about a big presentation, a fight with your loved one, walking through a dark alley alone at night, or riding a rollercoaster). It orchestrates physiological changes like increased heart rate, faster breathing, and tense muscles, all to prepare you for action. It's meant to help you save yourself (or others) when you (or they) need saving.

The reality is, we don't actually *need* saving as much as we did back when lions wanted to eat us. Yet during times of stress, that system is still activated the same way that it was back in caveman times, even when we don't need to flee and certainly don't want to engage in a physical fight.

An activated sympathetic nervous system is associated with an elevated heart rate, blood pressure, and breathing rate. This "high-alert" status floods the brain with neurotransmitters and hormones (cortisol, adrenaline, and norepinephrine), negatively impacting decision-making, emotional reactivity, collaboration, and strategic thinking. If this state continues over a prolonged time, it leads to chronic stress, which is pervasive in the workplace. This stress response can lead to a range of health problems, including heart issues, a weakened immune system, digestive disorders, autoimmune disease, and mental health problems like anxiety, depression, and burnout. It also accelerates the aging process.

The parasympathetic nervous system is responsible for rest. It promotes relaxation and recovery. It slows your heart rate, relaxes your muscles, and aids in digestion. It allows your body to rest, repair, and replenish. It enables problem-solving, decision-making, and learning new skills. The ability to operate from the parasympathetic nervous system can also protect you from the harmful consequences of chronic stress.

The skills outlined in this book are designed to help you create new neural pathways in the brain and to help you reduce chronic stress via the intentional activation of the parasympathetic nervous system.

Default Mode Network

The default mode network is a network of brain regions that is primarily active when someone is at rest. It's associated with internal mental activities like daydreaming, recalling memories, envisioning the future, and reflecting on emotions. It's crucial for self-reflection, emotional resilience, empathy, planning, creativity, and problem-solving. However, when overactive or poorly regulated, it lends itself to rumination, distraction, depression, anxiety, and an inability to regulate emotions (leading to overreactions or emotional outbursts).

Intentionally managing the activity of this network can improve overall wellbeing. Practices like mindfulness, meditation, and journaling can help one to avoid the pitfalls of over-rumination and actually make downtime a valuable opportunity for deeper understanding.

Intentionality (Lead Your Self Well)

It's easy to become consumed by the demands of the external world while managing teams, overseeing a household, and meeting the expectations of various roles. Amid all this, we often neglect the most fundamental aspect of leadership: leading our "Self" to wellbeing.

Wellbeing is a state where deep inner peace guides intentional outward action. Leading our selves to that state is our number one job.

"Lead your self well" is a philosophy that encapsulates the very essence of genuine wellbeing. It's about being a leader in your life and being a better leader for those you lead (formally or informally). It's about diving into a transformative journey to become the person you were meant to be, as a leader and an individual. It's about learning to put your own oxygen mask on first. Lead your self to wellbeing so that you can lead others to wellbeing. It's the best gift you can give to others: being the best version of you.

This five-step process will give you the tools and strategies you need to uncover your authentic core self, intentionally align your actions with your values, and cultivate the resilience necessary to navigate the challenges of leadership and life, all while protecting your mental wellbeing. You must begin this process, however, from a state of choice. If you're not interested in being mentally well, if you want to tell yourself that you don't need to learn these things, or if you're not willing to commit some time and space to learning and doing, then this process (or any other) won't work for you. You must be intentional about the process. You must be in a state of *choice*.

Contributing vs Constricting

"The trouble is, you think you have time." *

---

* There are differing thoughts on where this quote comes from. Buddha and Jack Kornfield are most commonly associated with it, but I even saw a meme recently in which it was attributed to Kobe Bryant. Many believe it was created based on a longer quote in a book called *Journey to Ixtlan* by Carlos Castenada: "There is one simple thing wrong with you—you think you have plenty of time [...] If you don't think your life is going to last forever, what are you waiting for? Why the hesitation to change? You don't have time for this display, you fool. This, whatever you're doing now, may be your last act on earth. It may very well be your last battle. There is no power which could guarantee that you are going to live one more minute."

Read that again and sit with it for about 30 seconds before reading further.

One common theme throughout this book is the idea that we're always either contributing to the things that are important to us or constricting them. Contributing means "to bring about." Constricting means "to make narrow; to inhibit or restrict." At all times, you're doing one or the other. This goes for our goals, relationships, health, and happiness.

Time is our most valuable resource. Ultimately, when it's gone, nothing else matters, and time is always ticking. There is no way to stop it. I love the line from the song *Breathe* by Anna Nalick: *And life's like an hourglass glued to the table / No one can find the rewind button, girl.* In each of those moments passing by, we're using that resource to either contribute to or take away from the life we want. No activity is ever neutral, because we're constantly trading in time for whatever result we're creating at that moment.

I graduated high school in a class of 77 students. We all knew each other, and during our senior year, each week a few of us were interviewed for the school newspaper. We each had to submit a list of favorites (song, TV show, quote, and so on), and one of my good friends, Kristi, used a quote that said something like, "Life is too short to not give 100% all of the time."

Kristi was the "it" girl in our class. She was (and still is) beautiful, incredibly athletic, smart, funny, kind, and a friend to all. On the flipside (and as you'll learn in Chapter 12), I was in a dark place at this time. I didn't think there was a purpose to life, or any life, for that matter. I was struggling emotionally, albeit quietly. So, that quote annoyed me, even though I loved Kristi. When it came time for my interview, my quote was, "Life is too short to give 100% all of the time." I didn't want life to be taken so seriously all the time. In 18-year-old Cara's view, we all just work hard our whole life and then die.

What I realized later is, you *can* give 100% all the time. You can *contribute* to your life at every moment. It's about intentionality. If I need some down time, then relaxing and watching Netflix (if that's what will provide me with what I need at that moment) *is* contributing to my life. Therefore, I need to enjoy that Netflix time 100% — "give it 100%," if you will — instead of half-watching or half-worrying that I should be doing something more "productive."

Since we're "spending our time" all day every day, we should be aware of whether we're contributing to a full life or constricting it.

In a similar way, your employees are always either contributing to or constricting your results. No activity can be viewed as "neutral," as everyone is getting paid (i.e., using a company resource). If someone is using that resource (getting paid) and not contributing, they are actively constricting your success. Bolstering your employees' wellbeing helps to ensure they are actively contributing to the success of the team and the organization at large.

Leadership through a Wellness Lens

Rick, a friend and former colleague of mine, recently shared a story with me about a customer service employee named Holly who was in an arranged marriage. Holly was a mom to a toddler, pregnant with a second baby, and living with her in-laws. In Holly's culture, part of her role was to serve her in-laws, so while she was working full-time from home with her baby in the background, she was also responsible for all of the household cooking and cleaning for four adults and a child. Her productivity in her job was suffering as a result.

Holly's boss, Andy, came to Rick ready to hold her accountable and put her on a performance plan. Thankfully, Rick was able to step back and look at Holly's situation through a wellness lens. He could see that she was in a very difficult home situation (by her own account), so instead of putting her on a performance plan, Rick and Andy decided to figure out how they could help her.

After talking with Holly and offering support, she decided she wanted to get into a better environment for her mental health. Rick and Andy assisted in getting her into a better living situation and getting some mental health resources. Almost immediately, her work performance improved dramatically. A year later, she was named a "company superhero," an award based on customer service impact. There were over 19,000 submissions for the award, and she was one of the few winners!

Holly had been failing at work, but this was because she was mentally unhealthy, due to her living situation. Had her leaders not approached this situation through a lens of wellbeing, they would have spent hours every week over the next three to four months going through the performance management process, Holly would have likely been fired, and she would have remained in that difficult living situation. Plus, Rick and his team would have had the added expense (in time and money) of replacing her.

It took no more time and no extra effort to approach the situation through a wellness lens. In fact, it saved the leaders' time. It saved company money. It led to them retaining a very valuable employee. It facilitated an incredible experience for Holly's customers. It created a better life for Holly, her husband, her toddler, and her new baby.

I'd say that's a win-win-win.

The lens through which we view our employees changes the way we see them, interact with them, treat them, and lead them in very real ways. What if we looked at our employees as people that matter in the world? People who are likely struggling just to keep it together? What if we sincerely wanted them to be well, so they could perform to higher levels, be truly engaged at work, and stay with the company because the company cared about them? What if our ultimate aim was helping them to have a better life experience?

The path to a culture where employees feel valued, perform at their best, and are incentivized to contribute to the long-term mission begins with leadership through a wellness lens.

This paradigm shift places the mental and emotional wellbeing of leaders and their employees at the forefront of organizational success. In this approach, leadership recognizes that a healthy, thriving workforce is the cornerstone of productivity, creativity, customer service, and innovation. Leaders therefore understand that they must lead by example, prioritizing their own mental wellbeing and supporting the wellbeing of their team. By leading through a wellness lens, these visionary leaders not only drive exceptional performance, but also create a culture where employees can flourish.

Your employees *are* your organization. How they feel inside *matters*. Thankfully, wellbeing is a skill. A skill you (and they) can develop.

Wellbeing as a Skill set

If one day you woke up and wanted a six pack (abs, not beer), you couldn't achieve that in a matter of a few days. It would take some time, effort, a plan, learning new skills, implementing those skills, and dedication. It also may be easier or harder for you than for others, depending on your genetics and how you have treated your body in the past. Finally, it would require consistency. Not perfection, but definitely consistency.

Similarly, cultivating wellbeing is a skill. To learn this skill, you need:

- Knowledge of how you work and think.
- Proven strategies to change ineffective patterns.
- A plan to implement those strategies.

- Time and effort dedicated to implementing the plan.
- Consistency (not perfection).

In a nutshell, you need to learn, and you need to "do." This book provides you with the first three of those bullet points for mental wellbeing, and it provides you with ideas and strategies for how you can go about the last two. Those ideas and strategies won't see you through all the way, though; not without any action on your part. Knowledge is not enough.

I am often a victim of believing that knowledge *is* enough. I read the book, buy the product, learn the details... and end up doing nothing with them.

You. Must. Act.

That action starts with you being willing to inquire within; to ask yourself the questions that lead to you fully understanding yourself (which helps you to understand others). Therefore, the framework in the following chapters outlines The 5 Inquiries. These are five questions that, when answered, will unlock wellbeing, *when coupled with action*.

You must approach this work with radical curiosity, about yourself and others. This can be difficult, and at times, you may need the support of a friend, partner, mentor, therapist, HR partner, or coach as you go through this process. But make no mistake about it, you *can* develop wellbeing as a skill set.[*]

---

[*] As much as the skill set of wellbeing can be developed, there are times when a little extra help is necessary. This book does not take the place of help and support from a licensed psychologist that may be necessary in some instances. If you fear you may be suffering from a serious mental illness or other condition, please consult with a psychologist or your family doctor. Please see the appendices for resources on when it may be helpful to contact a psychologist and some tips on how to do so.

Reflect to Retain

How are you contributing to your life in the following areas? In what ways are you constricting it?

- *Mental wellbeing*
- *Physical wellbeing*
- *Relationships*
- *Work / Team*

What are three things I learned about myself from this chapter?

1.

2.

3.

What are three concepts I want to remember from this chapter?

1.

2.

3.

chapter 7

the 5 inquiries model

THE MODEL YOU ARE ABOUT TO learn will get you in the process of *inquiring, learning,* and *doing,* so you can build a lifelong wellbeing skill set. At the center of this model is you—your Core Self. Being the best version of you is the greatest gift you can give to the people around you. It's the best way to lead your self, your employees, your family, or your organization to wellbeing.

The model is comprised of:

- **THE PHASES**: The step-by-step process that will evoke learning, knowledge, and action.
- **THE INQUIRIES**: Five questions for you to dive into and reflect upon (to facilitate your *inquiry*).
- **THE THEMES**: Topics to explore that help you dive deeper into the Inquiries (so you can *learn*).
- **THE SKILLS**: The practical actions aligned with the five inquiries (so you can *do*).
- **THE CAST OF CHARACTERS:** Those voices within you that govern more than you realize (so you can *know*).

PHASES

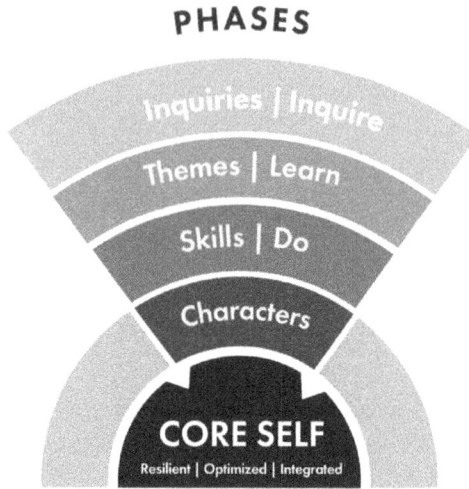

Each part of this book will cover one phase, one inquiry, one character, and various themes and skills.

The Phases

To initially evoke learning, knowledge, and action, we need to *discover*, *diagnose, define, devote*, and *dedicate*. Enter, the phases.

We'll start with the Discover phase. Thoughts, beliefs, and emotions impact how you show up at work and at home every single day. In this step we'll examine and *discover* the beliefs that dominate your inner landscape, laying the foundation for deeper self-understanding. We'll *discover* how to challenge them when necessary and use them to your advantage when appropriate.

Next we enter the Diagnose phase where we'll dive into the origins of these beliefs to *diagnose* how your past experiences created and shaped them. With this knowledge, we'll then identify the strengths and struggles you've acquired that you bring to your work and personal relationships.

Third comes the Define phase. Your purpose and values influence your daily experiences, both within your work and personal life. *Defining* these will help align your actions with who you want to be in the world.

The Devote phase is about who you influence. Your circle is composed of those you count on and those who know they can count on you. We will examine the different circles in your life and learn how you can *devote* your time to support them better and how you can call on them to support you when needed.

Finally, we'll enter the Dedicate phase. Intentionality in your words and behavior is the hallmark of leading your self well. It's necessary if you are to be the person you truly want to be; a person you can be proud of; a person who is mentally strong. This chapter will help you to intentionally *dedicate* yourself to those words and behaviors and to outline how you want to show up for your family, organization, and community.

> *Self-knowledge is the beginning of freedom, and it is only when we know ourselves that we can bring about order and peace.*
> —*JIDDU KRISHNAMURTI*

The Inquiries

Self-inquiry is a process allowing you to explore your past, present, and potential. It's the practice of turning inward and moving beyond autopilot, to rediscover your most authentic self. It's a strategy for getting to know the "you" that lies beyond your habits and stories.

The 5 Inquiries model represents a method by which you can shift your mindset and the way you think. These inquiries are:

1. What do I believe? (The Discover phase.)
2. Where have I been? (The Diagnose phase.)
3. Why am I here? (The Define phase.)
4. Who do I influence? (The Devote phase.)
5. How do I show up? (The Dedicate phase.)

In order to act differently, we must first learn to think differently, and in order to think differently, we must first understand our core self; what makes us tick.

Without a deep understanding of ourselves, we can't live in alignment with our values and intentions. Therefore, we must dive deep into understanding ourselves, our thoughts, and the reasons behind our actions. It's only by unraveling the intricacies of our minds that we can initiate real, sustainable change. The key to mental wellbeing does not lie in quick fixes or external solutions, whether that's a new job or a new partner (or even a Piña Colada on a tropical island!). It can only be found within.

Wherever you go, there you are.

The Themes

Woven into every phase of this journey are principles and concepts that offer focus and depth to your exploration of each inquiry. The Themes provide the intellectual framework for your self-discovery, supporting the learning and knowledge necessary to foster change. You'll learn how these themes are important to the character we'll meet in each phase, uncovering insights that not only illuminate who you *are* but also empower you to create and set intentions to which you can align your actions.

The Skills

While knowledge is wonderful to have, real change lies in "doing." So, in each phase, we'll explore some skills associated with the themes. We will dive into research outlining how each skill interacts with your brain chemistry and nervous system. We'll then look at some exercises and suggestions for how you can implement and practice each skill so you can determine what works best for you.

The Cast of Characters

In each phase, you'll be introduced to a character who plays a key role in the self-talk that occurs within. Each one is already within you, influencing your thoughts, beliefs, and behaviors, whether you're aware of it or not. You'll learn how to listen to what each character has to say, how they show up, and how to intentionally call on them (or quiet them), depending on what you need at the time. You'll also learn to recognize the characters at play in your employees' lives (and in your loved ones' and your friends' lives). This knowledge (along with knowledge of your own characters) will help you to more effectively navigate the difficult conversations and unique situations that come your way.

The Core Self

Together the characters make up what I refer to as your Core Self—the resilient, optimized, and integrated version of you that is capable of showing up authentically and powerfully in every moment. It's the best version of *you*. Core Self has the ability to grow stronger through challenges (resilient), operates in a state of alignment and clarity (optimized), and embraces every aspect of self into a cohesive, balanced life (integrated).

The 5 Inquiries Model

Now that you've been introduced to the key elements—Phases, Inquiries, Themes, Skills, Characters, and Core Self—it's time to see the full picture. This is the complete model: a powerful, integrated system with your Core Self at the center. Every piece plays a role in helping you shift from surviving to thriving, from burnout to brilliance. It's a model for creating long-term wellbeing and performance—for your self and your team. As you engage with each part, you'll build momentum, insight, and practical tools to lead your self and others with purpose, resilience, and authenticity.

THE 5 INQUIRIES MODEL

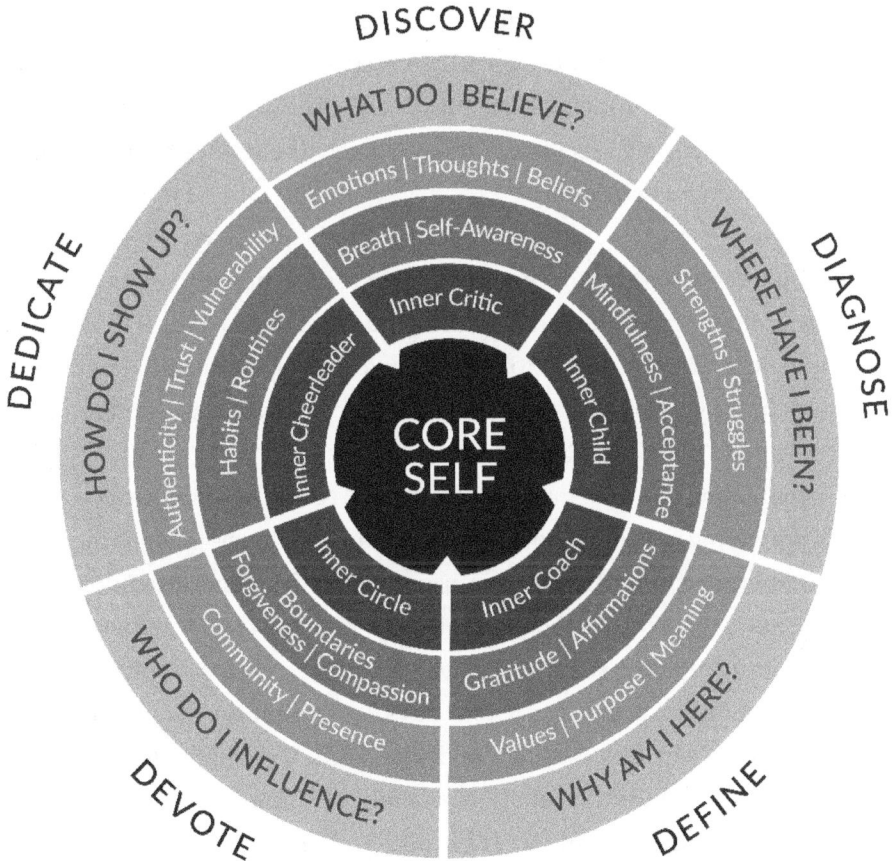

There are two skills that are fundamental to all five phases, and so these will be introduced here, before we fully dive in. Those skills are journaling and somatic exercises. Let's start with journaling.

Journaling

Most of us have kept a journal at some point in our lives, to document events, process situations, or tell our secrets. I, for one, wish I had journaled more throughout my life. I've always known that when I take the time to journal, I feel better. I never knew the science behind it, but I *did* know that it helped me.

I was right. Journaling has been found to help manage stress, anxiety, and depression.[1] Putting pen to paper can slow down the loop in your head, allowing you to better understand what is causing those internal thoughts and conflicts and to come up with better solutions or answers. It helps bring you to the present and make connections, learn, and reflect in a way that "thinking" alone cannot.

Journaling can take many forms, from freestyle writing about a topic, to answering prompts, to a brain dump. Dr. James Pennebaker is a psychologist and lead researcher in journaling. One of his groundbreaking findings is that writing about emotional experiences and traumatic events helps to reduce the stress associated with those events. Writing for just 15—20 minutes a day for a few days led to improvements in mood, reduced anxiety, and even fewer doctor visits.[2] His methods have led to research that indicates that journaling can improve, not only our emotional wellbeing, but our physical as well. This journaling process led to improvements in participants' immune system, by way of reducing chronic stress.[3]

You'll be asked to journal quite a bit throughout this process. Making it a part of your routine doesn't require any special skills, just a commitment to your wellbeing and a bit of time. For now, find yourself a journal or something you'll enjoy writing in. Maybe even purchase a special pen or markers to use. Set yourself up to enjoy this process, as the simple act of journaling will become one of the most powerful tools on your wellbeing journey.*

Somatic Exercises

Somatic work is a therapeutic approach that emphasizes the connection between the mind and body. It helps individuals to become more aware of the physical sensations, emotions, and patterns held within their bodies. Specifically, these practices invite us to listen to and engage with our bodily signals so we can access deeper layers of self-awareness. Whether it's tightening of muscles, shallow breathing, or a flutter of anxiety in the stomach, these sensations contain important messages that can guide personal transformation and wellbeing.

In fast-paced environments, people often live "from the neck up," relying solely on thoughts and mental processes while ignoring bodily signals. However, the body often speaks before the mind does. Tight shoulders might indicate stress long before you consciously realize you're overwhelmed, for example. By tuning into these sensations, somatic work helps us shift from unconscious patterns of reactivity to intentional awareness and choice. Your body is an often-untapped wise partner in emotional and mental wellbeing.

Some of the exercises in these chapters will ask you to "listen to" your body, creating space for deeper understanding. Fair warning: this *will* feel weird for some of you. One client actually said to me, "Cara, this is whack. I couldn't get myself to try it." I encouraged him to try again. He did—and

---

* I'm often asked by clients if they can journal electronically. While I prefer for them to do it by hand (to help slow things down), there are benefits to doing it on a computer or tablet. My preference is purely for you to choose the method that will make you actually do it. If writing by hand keeps you from journaling, then do it electronically (though I still suggest you first try it by hand, to see what works best for you).

he loved it. After doing this work in a coaching session, another client told me it was the most impactful conversation of his career. So, please, play along and be willing to try something new. It may just lead to a breakthrough!

Trust the Process

I know some of you out there may have some resistance to some of the ideas I'll be presenting in the following chapters. For that reason, I would like to reiterate that while the "woo-woo" concepts out in the world have always intrigued me, I'm still a practical person at my core. I need to know "why" they work before I am willing to try or experiment with them.

Now, I am no formal scientist. I am not a researcher in the sense that I ponder a hypothesis and set up experiments in a lab to prove or disprove my theories. I *am* a learner and an *informal* scientist and researcher, however. I love to review studies, absorb information, read books, and listen to podcasts hosted by experts in their chosen field. Then, I become an "experimenter" on myself. I try out the things I've learned. I see what sticks. What makes me feel good? What helps me make desired changes? What is easy to implement and what's not?

I also help my clients practice and experiment on *themselves*, sharing different concepts and modalities. I explain why certain things have been scientifically shown to work, and help them test things out. This is the process I will be facilitating for you in the remainder of this book.

Summary

Some of you may still be skeptical about this approach to the burnout epidemic and America's health crisis. You may question its validity, the time it will require, and its relevance to the workplace. It's true that you could find a million reasons *not* to do this work, and I understand these concerns. Nonetheless, I invite you to embrace the science *and* the business case behind what I'm teaching here. The 5 Inquiries and their corresponding skills are firmly grounded in neuroscience.

If you're thinking this program is not for you because it makes you uncomfortable, I invite you to try it anyway. Being comfortable with discomfort is the pathway to change. In the physical body it's called the hormetic effect: bodily stress given in low doses (whether in the form of high heat, deep cold, calorie restriction, or exercise) actually makes you stronger and healthier. It forces your body to adapt. Constantly being comfortable is not good for us, mentally or physically. I have a friend who calls me "comfort lover," as an affectionate way of gently pushing me when I need to muster the courage to do something I don't really want to do. Don't be a comfort lover!

The stuff in this book took me years to learn. I'm still learning about it today. There are dozens of concepts here that could each easily have full books written about them (most do, actually). Before I wrote this book, however, I realized that my clients needed a place where they could get a base-level understanding of all these concepts. They needed a reference of sorts to point them in the right direction. They needed a place to start.

The place to start is here and with you. You must know yourself. You must learn some new skills. You must inquire within.

Put It Into Practice

At the end of the next several chapters, we'll be doing some exercises to put your learning into practice. These fall into a few categories:

- **REFLECT TO RETAIN**: a place to note a few things you learned or want to remember. At minimum, answer these questions, even if only briefly, before moving on to the next chapter.
- **INQUIRE WITHIN:** thought activities or journaling questions, to help you "Inquire Within" in a deep way.
- **DAILY PRACTICE IDEAS:** short and simple ideas you can do daily, to implement the teachings of that section. Choose one or two of the suggested options to practice daily for 2–4 weeks.
- **WELLNESS WEDNESDAY**: a longer activity to do on a day on which you devote time (at least an hour) to your wellbeing. It doesn't have to be Wednesday; I'll refer to these as Wellness "When-sday" as you can pick any day for wellness.
- **WELLBEING AT WORK:** activities to do with your team. It's often helpful to have an HR partner or coach (internal or external) help facilitate these, so you can participate with your team.

You're learning new skills. In each phase, you are meant to:
1. Inquire.
2. Learn.
3. Do.

Then (and only then) you can move onto the next phase.

You may recall there are two main approaches to navigating this book. If you take the first approach and read it straight through, I encourage you to still answer the Reflect to Retain questions (even if briefly) before moving on.

If you take the second approach and work through the exercises and integrate the practices into your daily routine as you read, spend about two to four weeks on each of the five steps. Each week you should schedule an hour to dedicate to the exercises. Put this time on your calendar now and commit to it. You should also plan on spending 3—15 minutes per day on the Daily Practice tips. This pace and time commitment will allow you to build and solidify your new habits gradually, giving you the time to reflect and adapt. Any skill worth learning takes consistency over time.

Let's go!

PUT IT INTO PRACTICE

Inquire Within

Use your journal to explore one or more of the following questions. Write freely, knowing this is only for you and there are no right or wrong answers. The goal is simply for you to get to know more about yourself and how you're currently feeling as you start this work.

- Reflecting on my current state of wellbeing, health, and relationships: How do I feel, mentally and emotionally, right now? Are there areas in which I'd like to see relief or improvement?
- Consider the concept of leading your self well. What does this mean to me personally? What would be different about my life if I were to fully embrace this process?
- Imagine my ideal self: What traits, habits, or mindsets would I envision this version of me having? Why are those important?
- Does my wellbeing matter to me—truly? If so, why? What am I willing to commit to in order to move the needle on my wellbeing?
- What hesitations do I have about this process? What obstacles or challenges do I anticipate?
- Thinking about my support system: Who can provide encouragement or accountability as I pursue this path to wellbeing?

PART III

———

THE DISCOVER PHASE

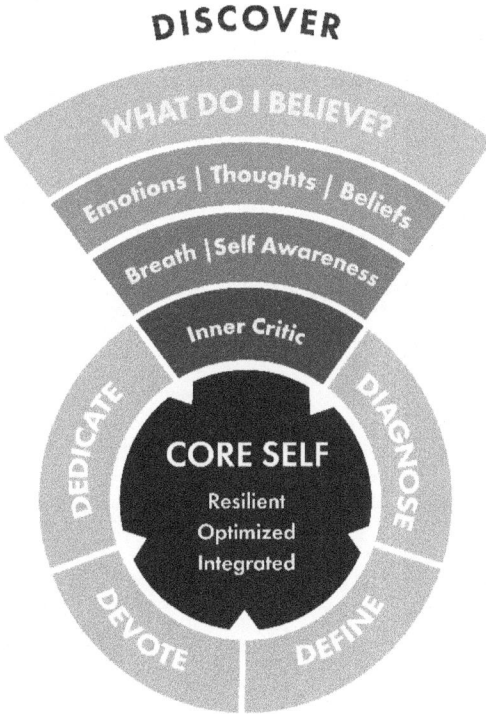

chapter 8

---

what do i believe?

The Phase: Discover
The Inquiry: What Do I Believe?
The Themes: Emotions, Thoughts, and Beliefs
The Skills: Breath and Self-Awareness
The Character: Inner Critic

The happiness of your life depends upon the quality of your thoughts.
—MARCUS AURELIUS

THOUGHTS AND EMOTIONS AND BELIEFS, OH my!
Just like the lions and tigers and bears that frightened Dorothy, the Scarecrow, and the Tin Man in *The Wizard of Oz*, thoughts, emotions, and beliefs have been the hardest thing for me to tame personally.

I grew up in a happy home, but with two parents who could not have had more different ways of responding to stressful situations. My parents had four kids in four and a half years, so I can imagine life at home was a lot, especially when we were small. Perhaps because of this, my dad was known to blow up when things got stressful. He had four very active kids at home, an intense job, and a side business raising a few cattle and pigs on our small acreage, just to make ends meet. My dad could lose it at the drop of a hat if the conditions were right. And my mom? Well, I *never* heard my mom yell. Not once. She always kept her cool (though you knew when she was angry). She always kept her emotions in check, and she knew how to keep her four active kids in line while still allowing us to be free and to play. She would sometimes resort to being defensive or passive aggressive with my dad when they fought, I'm guessing because she wanted to fight too but didn't want to yell (her mom was a yeller, and she deliberately chose *not* to).

Neither of my parents dealt with the emotions that came up in arguments and disagreements healthily. My mom often managed her emotions with food or by being passive aggressive, while my dad managed his with angry outbursts.

Unsurprisingly, I have the amazingly lucky combination of sometimes yelling and sometimes being passive aggressive. You're welcome, friends.

Our thoughts, beliefs, and emotions all impact how we experience this world and how we respond to the situations we encounter daily. Therefore, they very directly impact our mental wellbeing—and they are very much influenced and often defined by our past experiences (which we'll discuss in the Diagnose phase, in Chapter 10). Learning about each of these—our thoughts, beliefs, and emotions—and how they contribute to our mental wellbeing is essential to leading our self well, especially when times are difficult.

The Discover phase is especially important because it helps to create *agency* in our lives. We have agency when we have a sense of control and faith in our ability to handle the things that come our way. This empowers us to shape our destinies, make good choices, and control our behavior.

But what does agency look like?

When my sister visited me on Roatan one time, we traveled to a group of small islands called Cayos Cochinos about 20 miles away in open water. This is an amazing day trip, with spectacular water, reefs, and snorkeling that will take your breath away. However, my sister is apprehensive about a lot of things. She gets nervous quickly and easily. That day, we encountered a small but very strong storm cell on our way to the small islands. It was windy, dark, and raining heavily, but thankfully, the skilled boat captain, Tim, was unflappable. He managed the waves with skill, confidently reassured us with a smile all the while, and chose the best route to get us to our destination safely and swiftly.

Tim had agency. He knew he had control over the situation, and therefore, he was the master of that vessel.

I've been on those same open waters with a captain who did *not* have agency. You could see he was apprehensive; that he wasn't sure if we should continue on or go back. He asked the passengers (who had very little to zero experience) for their thoughts and opinions several times. That was frightening, and I was very grateful my sister was not with me that day!

Agency matters, for you and for the people you lead, and having it is almost impossible if you can't manage your thoughts, beliefs, and expressions of emotion.

How do these work together?

- Beliefs: **deeply held convictions or attitudes** that we hold true about ourselves, others, and the world around us. They're usually based on personal experiences and can also be influenced by culture and upbringing. They influence thoughts, emotions, and behavior, and can shape perceptions of the world.

- Thoughts: **mental processes** that involve the conscious mind and refer to the ideas, images, and words that pass through us. They can be rational or irrational, positive or negative, and can be influenced by beliefs, experiences, and perceptions of what's happening around us.
- Emotions: **psychological states** that manifest as physiological and behavioral responses to the experiences we have. They can be positive or negative, and include happiness, sadness, anger, shame, fear, and joy. Emotions can be influenced by thoughts and beliefs and often impact behavior toward our friends, family, and coworkers. They can also influence how we make decisions and process the experiences around us.

Thoughts, beliefs, and emotions are all interconnected and can influence each other in different ways. *How* they do this can vary depending on the individual, situation, and context.

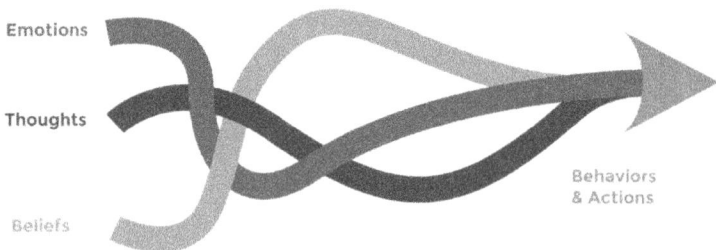

There are theories and debates about which (thoughts, beliefs, or emotions) comes first. While it can be useful to explore the origin point, real wellbeing lies in the understanding that these elements work together as an interconnected system that shapes our behaviors and actions. Once you know this, you can identify where beliefs, thoughts, and emotions are helping you and where they're hurting you. *Then*, you can enter a state of conscious choice regarding how you respond to the situation. This is the goal: to be in *choice* and to *not* be reactive when you encounter stressful situations.

Have you ever gone down the rabbit hole of thoughts, emotions, and beliefs? I have. I still do sometimes. However, it happens much less now that I have learned skills that help me to notice when I'm going down that road. This enables me to effectively challenge my beliefs, thoughts, and emotions and to respond in a way that aligns with my values and who I want to be.

To demonstrate what happens when we do go down the rabbit hole, allow me to share a story from an internal coaching client I worked alongside several years ago:

Amy's team had recently been subjected to reorganization, and she was now reporting to a new leader. Amy had worked there for years, and she now had a new coworker, Jake, who had recently joined the organization. Amy had always been praised for her work, yet she constantly questioned whether she was good enough to keep up with everyone else. She was a perfectionist, and she had a difficult time giving herself a break.

Amy could not figure Jake out. He never seemed to acknowledge her work or give her any positive feedback. What's more, he was very confident, even though he was new to the team. He often spoke up in meetings and talked about how *his* work was contributing to the team's success.

One day, in a meeting with the EVP of their department, Jake talked briefly about a project Amy was leading, but didn't give her any credit. Amy was angry and frustrated at this and suspected that Jake was out to make her look bad in front of others, to position himself for a promotion to a soon-to-be-open role she'd been working toward for almost a year.

During this time, Amy continued to do her work, but she became increasingly annoyed with Jake and was suddenly paranoid about her security in her role. She started to avoid him and wouldn't share information that might help the team (and ultimately the customer), as she didn't trust Jake or want to help him.

One time, she noticed on Jake's calendar that he had more 1:1s with their boss than she did. She saw Jake and her boss at lunch shortly after, and she just "knew" they were talking about the role she'd been hoping to apply for, and that she was slowly being dismissed while he moved in.

Amy quit speaking up in meetings or contributing to projects as much as she used to, and she started to look for roles in other departments and externally. She started having a lot of wine nights with her friends, during which she vented about what a jerk Jake was, how her workplace was a "good old boys club," and how she would never get that promotion.

Eventually, Amy's boss, Brady, noticed her change in behavior and asked what was wrong. Amy wasn't fully honest with him, as she didn't think she could trust him; she told him she was just busy at work and that she was interested in looking at roles in other departments for her "development." To Amy's surprise, Brady was visibly disappointed and told her that he hoped she would stay in her current department. He told her he valued her and would support her in anything she wanted to do. In the meantime, he asked, could she mentor Jake? He said Jake was having a hard time meshing with the team and had a lot to learn. Brady had spent a lot of time with him trying to get him on track, but it just wasn't quite working, and he wanted Amy's expertise to help mentor him. Brady went on to say that Jake had disclosed he was intimidated by Amy's network, skills, and ability to get so much work done in a short time. (Brady was a good leader and had already discussed with Jake that he wanted to ask Amy to mentor him and share what he was working on.)

In that moment, Amy realized that she had completely misinterpreted Jake and Brady's behavior, and that it was not a negative reflection of her work or her worth. Yet she had been ready to jump ship based on a story (a belief) that she had created based on her misinterpretation of others' behavior (and her own insecurities and biases).

Sound familiar?

Maybe the names and details are different, but you likely have, at some point, been convinced of something (feelings or intentions) about someone (probably in your personal circle) that you later found out to be completely wrong.

> *The state of your life is nothing more than a reflection of the state of your mind.*
> —WAYNE W. DYER

You can see how Amy's thoughts (I'm not good enough) and emotions (angry, frustrated, suspicious) created a belief that Jake was out to get her job and was in cahoots with her boss. Once she believed that, the other details (Jake and the boss meeting often, Jake not giving her credit in the meeting, and so on) "confirmed" this belief as true, creating a sense of "knowing" that was completely false, yet was leading her to look for jobs elsewhere.

What would have happened if Brady had not asked Amy to mentor Jake (and unwittingly brought to light the complete inaccuracy of Amy's story)? He would have lost one of his best employees, and she could have ended up in a job she didn't really want, all because of unfounded fear.[*]

The problem was not Jake at all. The problem was the *story* that Amy created *about* Jake.

How does this storytelling happen? And why so often? Let's look at the brain to find out.

---

[*] By the way, Amy ended up getting the promotion, her impactful mentorship of Jake being a contributing factor to this!

The Brain as a Storyteller

Our thoughts and beliefs are associated with neural pathways in our brain. When we think something or reinforce a belief repeatedly, the neural pathways associated with those thoughts and beliefs become stronger, making it more likely that we will continue to think those thoughts and believe that story. It becomes "real" the more we think it, just as a path becomes wider and flatter the more we walk it. One reason this happens is called the confirmation bias.

Confirmation bias is the tendency for our brains to search for, interpret, and remember information that confirms its existing beliefs. It's like your own internal algorithm. Think about your social media feed—Instagram, for example. Once you "tell" Instagram what you're interested in (by stopping at different posts or reels), it starts to "feed" you other things that are similar to those interests, and to filter out content that doesn't align. Once you stop on one cat video, you start seeing them every other post! If, however, you skip past any posts about rodents, you very quickly stop seeing that content altogether. Similarly, once you have a belief (even when it's based on inaccurate information or guesses), your brain will find "evidence" in favor of your belief and will also actively ignore evidence to the contrary.

Once that confirmation bias takes hold, you find evidence for that belief *everywhere*. Our brains naturally pay attention to things that we devote our thoughts, feelings, and energy to.

Let's say one day, you think that you'd like to buy a new red Jeep. This is a distinct vehicle, and you want something that's different. But once you decide you want it (or make the purchase), you start seeing red Jeeps *everywhere*. Similarly, if you hold the belief that "I'm not good enough," you'll start to find "evidence" that "confirms" that. Maybe a coworker says something that bites, or your bratty brother makes a mean comment about your clothes, or your friends talk quietly in a corner and you "know" for sure it's about you. The path (the belief "I am not good enough") gets wider, until you're riding down a superhighway of beliefs based on little more than your brain just trying to be efficient. Unless, that is, you're aware of this and intentionally train your brain to do something different. Answering the question, "What do I believe?" in the Discover phase is paramount to managing these stories.

There is a voice—a character—inside all of us which, if left alone, will create stories all day long about just about anything. Let's meet that character now.

The Discover Phase Character: Your Inner Critic

I would bet you're already at least somewhat familiar with your inner critic. It probably talks to you all day long, and you have likely found that it gets really loud when there is a buildup of energy or stress. You run through your day, so busy and thinking about All. The. Things. To work efficiently, your brain makes up quick stories about yourself or others based on those thoughts and observations—and likes to "talk to you" about those stories. Dr. Ethan Kross, a leading researcher in emotions and self-control, refers to this negative self-talk as "chatter," which can lead to rumination, anxiety, and impaired performance.[1]

What is that voice saying? How does it talk to you (or about you)? What names does it call you? Is it berating? Loving? Does it acknowledge your accomplishments? Or does it only point out the bad stuff? Would you say the things it says to you to your best friend? To a stranger on the street? My guess is that for most of us, the answers to these are not what we wish they were. Your inner critic may sound something like this:

- "You're late for work. Why can't you get your ish together?"
- "You need to work out tonight. You're so lazy."

- "You need to get to the grocery store so you can eat healthier. You're so disgusting for eating that fast food for lunch. Why do you do that to yourself?"
- "If you don't hurry, you're going to be late picking up the kids from practice. A good mom would be there already."
- "Did you hear the tone in his voice? He totally hates you."
- "Your boss is going to be so mad you're not done with this report. Someday, she is finally going to fire you."

And on and on and on it goes.

Your inner critic is a jerk. It tells lies, makes up stories, and leads you down a path of despair where you have no agency. It takes you to the Land of Self-Deception, where your highly inaccurate "but you know for sure they are true" beliefs live—the beliefs that are shrouded in falsehood; the beliefs that take root when they're not kept in check.

Beliefs are different from knowledge, yet many of us get the two confused. The beliefs planted by your inner critic are often not based on fact or truth or anything but your *interpretation* of a situation. And we all interpret things differently.

Once we *believe* something, our brain convinces us that we *"know"* it. Beliefs often lack evidence, yet we are usually so convinced of them—they feel so true—that we can't tell the difference between a belief and us truly knowing something.

In Michael A. Singer's book *The Untethered Soul*, he calls this voice your inner roommate.[2] He describes your inner roommate as someone who lives with you and always has an opinion on what's going to happen next. He says we usually discover that this voice is wrong, yet we "never hold it responsible for the trouble it causes. In fact, the next time it gives advice, we're all ears. Is that rational?" He says it's like living with a maniac in your head.

Think about how you judge yourself at work, or when you're in front of the mirror, or when you're thinking about all the things you should be doing but aren't or that you could be doing better. In these moments, that voice is a jerk. Yet we listen intently, and for some reason, we believe what it says. Wholly.

Imagine if you had a friend who talked to you the way your inner critic does. Would you ever hang out with that person? No, let alone 24/7!

Now imagine what it would be like if you didn't have to take this voice with you every single place you went. Can you even imagine what that would be like? Stop reading now for one full minute and truly imagine it.

There are many words people use to describe this voice. Some call it their inner critic; others their saboteur, gremlin, or inner roommate. Whatever you call it, we all know it well. Some of us have befriended it. Others work desperately hard to push it down deep in an effort to *not* feel it. This suppression doesn't make it disappear—it just changes how it shows up. Sometimes it surfaces as an inflated ego built to "manage" that voice. Other times, it shows up in the form of tension, anxiety, or a physical health issue. When Ryen, a former client, briefly mentioned some difficult emotions and self-talk regarding his childhood, he *really* didn't want to talk about it. When I encouraged him to do so, he replied, "I'd rather just push that back down and let it turn into cancer." We had a good laugh... and then got to work on his inner critic dialogue.

Recognizing the difference between beliefs and facts is crucial for mental wellbeing and having a true understanding of a situation before acting. Problems arise when you allow your unchecked beliefs and thoughts to create emotions that you act upon.

The emotions that coincide with these made-up stories are usually not the good ones. They are the emotions we generally don't like to feel; the ones we often fight against. So, in an attempt to lessen that emotion, you act on that belief by saying or doing something you regret, riding down that superhighway neural pathway where your brain feels comfortable.

Then, you feel sad or disappointed about your actions, and the inner critic creates even *more* things to say about how you messed up.

At some point, there is so much energy around your inner narrative that you actually start to have conversations with another person, with yourself. You become so mad, or so sad, or so stressed, that you "play act" a dialogue with them, without them there, during which you guess what their responses will be and "respond" back to them. In those dialogues, is the person ever responding kindly? No. You imagine the worst, until you get so worked up that you actually get even *more* mad at them and *more* defensive. It's almost like having a dream about someone and waking up angry at them, even though they did nothing wrong.

If you've ever lashed out at someone based on a guess, assumption, story, or belief, and then found out later that you were completely wrong, you know how terrible that can feel. I struggled with this in my career. I was often quick to guess people's intentions and I always just *knew* that I had the story right.

I'm not proud of the way I acted in those moments. Luckily, I had almost always built trust with my coworkers, bosses, and teams before this happened, and thankfully, I usually had the humility to admit when I was wrong and apologize for it when it did happen. My coworkers knew me, my values, and my intent, and were therefore patient with my approach most of the time. But I was not kind to *me* in those moments. I would beat myself up for how I had acted, because I *knew* better. I just didn't have the skills to deal with the situation in those moments.

My boss would often talk to me about this. But it was not something she knew how to help me with. We were not having conversations about where this tendency came from, nor how I could handle these situations differently. (We'll talk about this in Chapters 10 and 11.) No one ever had any advice for me outside of, "Just stop doing it." The good news is that now, I have done the work to recognize when it shows up. I'm not perfect, but I have found the answer, and it lies in the brain. There are science-backed strategies we can employ to be more in control of our thoughts, emotions, and beliefs, and thereby respond to situations and stressors as we *choose* to, instead of succumbing to reactivity. We can intentionally create new neural pathways in the brain, the key word here being "intentionally" (it doesn't happen by accident). Let's explore how.

Reflect to Retain

What stories am I repeatedly telling myself about me or about other people's actions / thoughts / intentions?

What are three things I learned about myself from this chapter?
  1.

  2.

  3.

What are three concepts I want to remember from this chapter?
  1.

  2.

  3.

chapter 9

the discover phase skills

Everything can be taken from a man but one thing: the last of the human freedoms—to choose one's attitude in any given set of circumstances, to choose one's own way.

—VIKTOR E. FRANKL

TO FOSTER A CULTURE OF WELLBEING and balance for ourselves, our employees, or our organization, we must *discover* the way we think. Once we know this, we can be intentional in using thoughts, emotions, and beliefs in a productive way. Before we begin, remember that your brain can change through neuroplasticity; that there are things you can do to make yourself see the world as it is, instead of as your mind is making it up to be. There are skills that can be learned to support you in the quest of managing your emotions, thoughts, and beliefs in order to truly lead your self well. Two of these skills are breathwork and self-awareness.

Breathwork

Breathwork is the deliberate practice of using breath to control and regulate physical and mental wellbeing.

The way we breathe has been scientifically proven to affect our brains and bodies in tremendous physiological ways, whether to increase our attention and alertness or to feel more relaxed and less anxious.[1, 2]

There are two essential components of breath to pay attention to:

- The location of the inhale.
- The length of the inhale compared to the length of the exhale.

Location of the Inhale

You may have heard people talk about belly breathers vs. chest breathers. When you use your diaphragm, you're belly breathing. When you belly breathe, you're using your diaphragm more fully to draw air into your lungs, which makes your belly expand. When you chest breathe, you use your rib and chest muscles more, and your breath is more shallow. To test this, place one hand on your chest and the other on your belly as you breathe normally. Notice which one is moving up and down. For most of you, it will be your chest. Each type of breath has benefits, depending on the situation and need. Here is a simplified summary:

Type of Breath	Belly Breathing	Chest Breathing
How To	Focus on making your belly rise and fall.	Focus on making your chest rise and fall.
How it Works	The diaphragm moves further down as it contracts, allowing the lungs to more fully expand and fill with air.	Muscles of the ribs, chest, and neck contract, lifting the ribcage and expanding the upper lung.
Impact on Nervous System	Activates the parasympathetic nervous system (for rest and relaxation). Lowers heart rate and blood pressure.	Often associated with the sympathetic nervous system (fight-or-flight). Increases heart rate and blood pressure.
Effect	Calm and relaxation.	Short-term energy boost.
Uses	Reduces anxiety. Increases focus and clarity. Regulates emotions.	Immediate alertness. Improves physical performance.

Have you ever watched a baby breathe, with its big belly rising and falling? For the most part, this is how we want to breathe: into our belly. This helps to optimize oxygen exchange, improve energy levels, and reduce anxiety. Simply noticing your breath and moving it into your diaphragm can create a physiologically more relaxed state.

Length of Inhales versus Exhales

Here is another simplified summary:

Length of Breath	Longer Exhales	Longer Inhales
How To	Exhale for a longer count than the inhale.	Inhale for a longer count than the exhale.
Impact on Nervous System	Activates the parasympathetic nervous system (for rest and relaxation). Lowers heart rate and blood pressure.	Often associated with the sympathetic nervous system (fight-or-flight). Increases heart rate and blood pressure.
Effect	Calm and relaxation. Can reduce stress and anxiety and bring greater peace.	Energizing. Can make you feel more awake and alert.
Uses	To calm down (such as before sleep or during a meditation).	To boost energy and focus (before a workout or preparing for a cognitively demanding task).

The information in these tables shows that we can intentionally "set" our mood, alertness, physiological state (heart rate and blood pressure), and mental state (calm or energized) just through our breath. This is a free resource that is *always* available, if we remember to call on it.

There are several techniques for breathwork. Here are a few options.

The Physiological Sigh

The physiological sigh is a breathing technique that can specifically impact your nervous system. The term was coined by Jack Feldman, UCLA neuroscientist, and made popular by Andrew Huberman, professor of neurobiology at Stanford School of Medicine and host of the *Huberman Lab Podcast*.[3] It mimics a long-standing yoga breath technique and helps to calm a person quickly, based on the anatomy of how the chest expands and contracts when breathing. This technique can be used in acute stressful moments to take control of the stress response and turn down that panicky feeling. It can also be used as a daily practice for nervous system regulation that lasts for several hours.

How to do it:
1. Take one deep inhale through the nose.
2. Add another quick inhale through the nose.
3. Follow this with a long exhale through the mouth, with an audible sigh.

For acute stress, repeat this one to three times. For daily maintenance, repeat continuously for five minutes.

Power Breath

This breathing technique is designed to enhance performance by quickly delivering oxygen to your system, to provide a quick energy boost and increase mental alertness. It is often used by athletes but can be adopted in high-intensity situations where maximum performance is required.

How to do it:

1. Inhale deeply through the nose, expanding the chest, with a focus on filling the upper lungs.
2. Pause for a moment, holding the breath.
3. Exhale quickly and forcefully through the mouth.
4. Repeat a few times.

Box Breathing

A combined approach is called box breathing. This rhythmic technique can reduce stress and anxiety, improve mental clarity, and regulate emotions by balancing the nervous system. Its focus is equally on inhaling, holding the breath, and exhaling.

How to do it:

1. Inhale slowly through the nose for a count of four.
2. Hold the inhale for a count of four.
3. Exhale slowly through the mouth for a count of four.
4. Hold the lungs empty for a count of four.
5. Repeat for several minutes.

Final Thoughts on Breathwork

Breath is something often taken for granted. We almost never think about it. It's a tool that can have a massive impact on mental state throughout the day. It's free and available to us *at any time*.

I've found with my clients that after they make breathwork a deliberate focus for a few weeks, it becomes natural for them to notice their breath throughout the day and to intentionally redirect it, bringing them back to center.

There are several other types of breathwork that can be intentionally incorporated to assist in managing emotional states. A list of resources is located in the appendices.

Breathwork is a skill. A skill you can develop.

> *Your thoughts have far less impact on this world than you would like to think. If you're willing to be objective and watch all your thoughts, you will see that the vast majority of them have no relevance.*
> —MICHAEL SINGER

Self-Awareness

Self-awareness is the ability to recognize and understand your thoughts, beliefs, emotions, and behaviors as well as their impact on yourself and others.

Are you on autopilot? Most of us are a lot of the time. The formal name for this is called the default mode network. We briefly touched on this in chapter 6. The DMN is active when we are not focused on external tasks; when we are resting, daydreaming, and letting our minds wander. It serves important functions, but when left unchecked, it can wreak havoc on our thoughts and emotions. It often leads to excessive worrying, rumination, and distressing thoughts. Becoming aware of this mode is necessary to move to higher-level functioning and the ability to see the world as it actually is, not as our brains interpret it.

So, how do we develop self-awareness? Well, there are a few steps:

Become the Observer

We have very much become a society that values thinking, problem-solving, and generally being "in our head." We've lost the ability to be curious about our thoughts and beliefs. We take them at face value instead of asking, "Why do I believe this? What is true about this? What isn't? What do I *know*? What am I *guessing* about?" and we create stories about the things we "know":

- "She's out to get me."
- "He doesn't really love me."
- "I suck at my job, and someday soon, someone will find out."

How can we see our thoughts, emotions, and beliefs for what they really are; as passing thoughts generated by the brain that are not necessarily accurate? The answer lies in learning how to *observe* those thoughts and stories instead of believing them.

I love the movie *Sweet Home Alabama*. Spoiler Alert: Near the end of the movie, Reese Witherspoon's character leaves McDreamy at the altar, saying that she can't marry him. He stops and says, almost emotionless, "Wow. So this is what that feels like."[4] I realize this is Hollywood and most people would *not* respond that way, but it's a great example of how we can *observe* a thought or feeling without assigning emotion or meaning to it in the moment. One way to practice this is to think of thoughts and feelings as nouns.

As you'll probably remember from first grade, a noun is a person, place, thing, or idea. Thoughts therefore fall into this category. A thought is a "thing" or "idea" generated by the brain through experiences, memories, and sensory input. Therefore, a thought doesn't have to be all-encompassing or all-consuming. It's merely a "thing" we can observe, in the same way that we can observe an apple or a seashell or a painting.

Once you start noticing and observing your thoughts and emotions, it's helpful to get to know them. We do that just as we get to know anything or anyone, by getting curious.

Welcome Them and Get Curious

Once observed, it's tempting to fight these thoughts and emotions, to push them down or try to make them "go away." In doing so, you lose the opportunity to learn about them and they'll resurface at some point. Instead, welcome them and get curious:

- Why did this thought show up? What triggered it?
- Is it helping give me some false sense of control?
- Is it based on a past childhood wound (see Chapters 10 and 11)?
- Is it trying to keep me safe? To protect me?
- Is it helping me make sense of something? To problem-solve?
- Is it fact, or is it a story my brain has created?
- What parts *are* factually true and what parts am I guessing about?

The answers lie in your ability to pause and become curious as an investigator, not a judge. What emotion is associated with the thought? Anger? Sadness? Shame? What part of you is angry? Do your best to refrain from immediately assigning meaning to your emotions or thoughts. In *The Untethered Soul*, Michael A. Singer says, "You must be able to objectively watch your problems instead of being lost in them. No solution can possibly exist while you're lost in the energy of a problem."[5]

Another way to cultivate curiosity (and improve self-awareness) is to ask for feedback from trusted friends, colleagues, and loved ones. Reflections from those who know you best can help you to identify blind spots, acknowledge your impact on others, and make adjustments, which can help create healthier patterns.

We *all* have blind spots. If you think you don't, *that* in itself is a blind spot! At work and in our personal lives, there are ways we can show up better that we simply cannot see because our brains are trying to protect us. Embracing feedback from trusted people is the best way to uncover them.

When receiving feedback that you initially don't agree with, act "as if" the feedback is accurate and go to curiosity—investigate. When an investigator gets a tip from a hotline, ignoring it would be irresponsible. The same principle applies here. There may be some truth you just can't see yet. Look for evidence in how it may be accurate or perceived that way by others. Developing a full understanding of the feedback instead of dismissing it allows the ability to reframe these beliefs and thoughts, leading to deeper self-awareness.

Reframe Self-Talk

Once you've observed your thoughts and approached them with curiosity, you can then begin to reframe your self-talk. Changing the narrative in your head takes intention and practice.

1. Notice and identify *patterns* of negative thinking, such as self-doubt, catastrophizing, or black-and-white thinking. Identifying these patterns can help to become more aware of current thinking habits.

2. Once you've identified your negative thought patterns, challenge them: Is there any proof to support these thoughts? Or are they based on assumptions or biases?

3. Challenge your "evidence." How do you "know" this for certain? What competing evidence exists? Remember the confirmation bias. Play devil's advocate; look for evidence to the contrary.

4. Reframe your negative thoughts into more positive and constructive ones. For example, instead of thinking, *I suck at this,* reframe as, *I am still learning and growing, and mistakes are part of the process. What can I learn here?*

5. Develop a habit of positive self-talk (we will talk more about affirmations later).

6. Spend "thinking" time equally. If you still need to think of the worst-case scenario, commit to spending as much time thinking about the best-case scenario, or even a neutral-case scenario. It's only fair to give all options equal space in your head.

Remember When You Have Been Wrong

Another tactic that can help develop self-awareness is to recall a time when you were absolutely certain about something—and it turned out to be wrong. These moments are powerful reminders that thoughts are not fact. Our brains can create convincing stories to protect us from fear, rejection, or uncertainty. Remembering times you've been wrong helps loosen the grip of your current thought or belief—reminding you that certainty isn't always truth.

Let's look at an effective option for how to respond to our thoughts, beliefs, and emotions by thinking of them as a donut. (Stick with me, here...)

Let Them Pass

As the saying goes, we are what we eat. Food is what makes up your cells, and your cells are constantly regenerating and making an updated version of "you." When you see a donut, you can choose whether to eat it or walk past it—whether you make this donut a part of "you"—and you can treat your thoughts (which are observable "things" just as much as a donut is) in the same way. A thought is a thing, and *you* get to decide whether that thing becomes a part of you, or whether you walk past it. Observe a thought just as you would that donut. Ask yourself, "Do I want this thought to become a part of me?"

If you're like me and the donut is in close proximity, you may sometimes have to make the decision to *not* eat the donut several times. The same is true for your thoughts.

When you start this process, thoughts may continue to pop up over and over again, but you can still choose to say no to them. You can choose to observe them and let them pass by without making them a part of you—without assigning meaning to them. It's not easy. It is possible, through intentional work.

When you're in especially difficult circumstances, you may need to make this decision over and over and over again—it may feel like an assembly line of donuts coming at you. When you're in that space, finding a therapist to help you process those thoughts and emotions can be incredibly beneficial. (See the appendices for resources on how to find a qualified therapist.)

> *We become what we think about most of the time.*
> —EARL NIGHTINGALE

Self-awareness is a skill. A skill you can develop.

Leadership and the Discover Phase Skills

As a leader, it's important to recognize the impact that thoughts, beliefs, and emotions have on your own wellbeing and the wellbeing of those you lead. After all, they can and do impact decision-making, problem-solving, and communication. Plus, as a leader, you set the tone for the employee experience. Is it okay for them to acknowledge the tough things in their lives right now? Do they have the space to talk about them if they want to? Are you open to giving them a little time to process their thoughts, beliefs, and emotions? You decide.

In the fast-paced world of leadership, where stress and pressure are constant companions, the skills of breathwork and self-awareness are crucial for creating environments where employees are able to do their best work. Self-aware leaders are less likely to exhibit impulsive reactions and can better maintain composure, manage emotions, and focus on goal achievement. By understanding the role that thoughts, beliefs, and emotions play in the way you see the world and the way you lead, you can better cultivate a positive and supportive work environment that promotes mental wellbeing and fosters productivity and growth. You can help people move through life more gracefully than they do when they have to pretend that everything is okay.

At the end of the day, your employees go home and talk to whomever it is that they talk to (whether a spouse, sister, best friend, or kids) about their boss; about you. You're a big topic of conversation at the proverbial (and literal) dinner table. What do you want them to say about who you are as a leader?

Leaders who lead through a wellness lens by prioritizing their own mental wellbeing and modeling healthy behaviors can inspire and motivate their team members to do the same, leading to a more positive and productive workplace culture. Alternatively, you can do the opposite. The choice is yours.

Summary

The other day, I saw a young woman wearing a shirt that said, "Your anxiety is lying to you." This is true. Your brain is often lying to you. It's making up stories to try to control and problem-solve; to protect you and keep you safe; to work efficiently. The problem is that, as Craig Groeschel said, "A lie believed as truth will affect you as if it were true." Even *Seinfeld*'s George Costanza knew this: "Jerry, just remember, it's not a lie if you believe it."[6] But you are *not* your thoughts. They are simply a "thing" for you to be aware of, notice, welcome, and then let move through you.

We create so many issues by allowing ourselves to believe that our thoughts are who we are. Thoughts are simply thoughts, just like a donut is simply a donut. They are "things" you encounter during the day, and just like you get to decide whether to bite into that donut and make it a part of you, you get to decide whether to make those thoughts a part of your day; a part of your life.

My mom knew this. As she was dying in the hospital, hopped-up on morphine, she doled out some random final advice to the people in her room.

My mom was *not* an advice-giver. Sometimes, I wished she was more of one, and I begged her on many occasions to "just tell me what to do!" Instead, she would plant a seed, ask questions, and let people reach the ideas and conclusions that were best for them. However, at this point in her hospital stay, she apparently had decided there was no time for that.

I was in her hospital room with my aunts (my mom was the oldest of six girls) talking to them about something going on in my life when I said one of my favorite lines at the time: "Ugh, I have issues."

My mom, who was lying in bed, appeared to be asleep, and 36 hours from death, opened her eyes, took off her oxygen mask, and whispered hoarsely, "Cara, your issue is that you think *everything* is an issue. That's your *only* issue." She then put her mask back on and lapsed back into silence. I looked at my aunts with an "isn't she so full of crazy morphine talk?" kind of look. To my incredible surprise, they all looked right back at me, shrugged their shoulders, and nodded in agreement with my mom.

Of course she was right. I had a tendency to make up so many issues in my head. That was my only *real* issue. It would take several more years for that to truly sink in.

> *The best thinking has been done in solitude. The*
> *worst has been done in turmoil.*
> —THOMAS EDISON

DISCOVER PHASE: PUT IT INTO PRACTICE

Inquire Within

Choose two or three of the following journal prompts to answer:

- What does my inner critic say to me at my worst times?
- Once you understand the words it uses, take some time to pay attention to your body. Where do I feel this inside? Is it in my gut? My chest? In my throat or heart? Just notice this feeling created by the voice of your inner critic.
- How do my rumination, worry, or negative thought patterns help me? What purpose have they served? How have they hurt me?
- What thoughts typically go through my head when I'm not being kind to myself?
- How would my daily life be different without that negative self-talk in my head? Be specific here.
- What would be different for me if I intentionally used that voice for positive self-talk? What would that feel like? (Sit for some time

noticing where and how your body would *feel* different if you could do this.)

- o What about for those who interact with me? How would their experience with me change?
- What are at least three positive qualities about myself and how have they impacted me and others positively?
- Where have I been wrong in the past, even though I "knew" something about another person or situation? What was the impact of this "knowing" (and acting on that "knowing")?
- Who do I want to *be* going forward with regard to my thoughts, beliefs, and emotions?

Daily Practice Ideas

Choose one or two options below to practice daily for 2–4 weeks.

- Practice intentional breath (any type listed in this chapter) for three to five minutes each morning for an entire week.
- Set a reminder three times throughout the day for you to sit quietly and breathe deeply for one minute.
- Create a routine for your breathwork. For example, practice once at the top of each hour, before each meeting, every time you get in your car, or whenever you change locations.
- Notice your inner critic's self-talk throughout the day and choose to let it pass through you as an observer, with no judgment. When it arises, simply say, "There you are again," and let it go. Practice this daily.

Wellness Wednesday (When-sday)

Choose one of the activities below to complete on your Wellness Day.

- Journal, without judgment, about your self-talk throughout the week. What did you notice? Were you able to recognize this talk as simply thoughts, and reframe?
- Practice Reframing: Choose one especially difficult moment that happened recently where you noticed yourself telling a story or making an assumption. Ask yourself the following:
  - o What was the situation and my thought or story associated with it?
  - o What evidence do I have to support my thoughts / stories? How do I know this for certain?
  - o Play devil's advocate: what evidence is there *against* it?
  - o Is the confirmation bias at play here? Or am I using any unhelpful patterns such as catastrophizing or black-and-white thinking?
  - o What is a reframe I can use to move from a negative thought to a more constructive one?
  - o What is the best case scenario? What would that be like?

Wellness at Work

- Notice how, at work, your negative thoughts or beliefs impact the way you show up. What's the impact on your work, your employees, or your team? Journal about whether you want that to change. If so, where can you make changes that will make your work more enjoyable or that will make you a better employee or leader, to set you up for success?

- If you are a leader, have a discussion at your next 1:1 with your employees about what thoughts or beliefs impact them. Ask if they would like some feedback on where you see this show up and how it may be negatively impacting them. In case they agree to receive feedback, prepare for this thoughtfully and provide it in the best way for them to receive and use it.
- As a team and with the help of your HR partner or a coach, facilitate a discussion about thoughts and beliefs. Let each individual share (as they feel comfortable) what they've learned about themselves, using the Inquire Within journal questions, and how the team can support them with their own thought patterns. If you have a team with strong established trust, each individual can ask for feedback from others on what they have noticed.

> *Put your thoughts to sleep, do not let them cast a shadow*
> *over the moon of your heart. Let go of thinking.*
> —RUMI

Reflect to Retain

What are three things I learned about myself from this chapter?

1.

2.

3.

What are three concepts I want to remember from this chapter?

    1.

    2.

    3.

What is the one daily practice I will devote myself to as I read the next chapter?

    1.

PART IV

THE DIAGNOSE PHASE

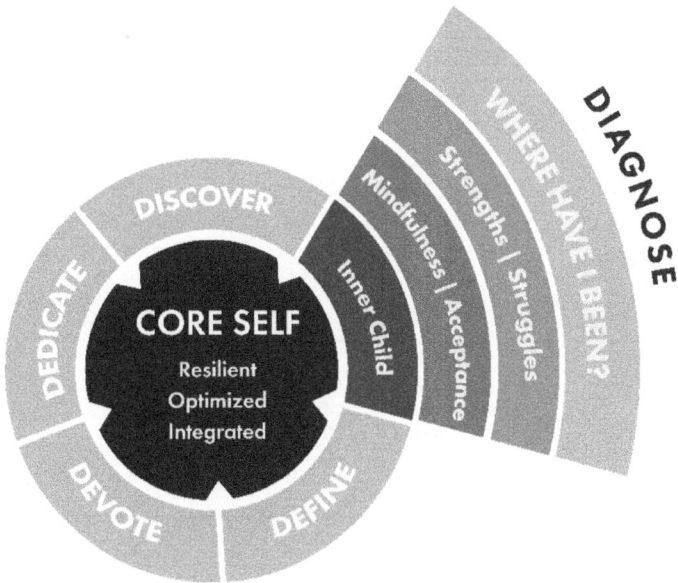

chapter 10

---

where have i been?

The Phase: Diagnose
The Inquiry: Where Have I Been?
The Themes: Strengths and Struggles
The Skills: Acceptance and Mindfulness
The Character: Inner Child

Childhood is what you spend the rest of your life trying to get over.
—SANDRA BULLOCK
(Quoted in *Hope Floats*)

MY MOM WAS THE BEST MOM. Truly. That being said, no one is perfect.

I have a vivid memory from my childhood in which I must have been seven or eight years old. I was in the back of the Suburban on the way to town for something. We lived out on an acreage in Iowa a few miles from anything, so going to town always felt like an adventure. It was something to differentiate those long summer days.

I was a thumb-sucker much longer than is considered acceptable (*much* longer). I tried everything to stop—I was embarrassed of it—as did my parents (somehow, I "knew" it embarrassed them as well). On this particular day, I was in the back seat holding my beloved clown doll my Aunt Leta had made me for my birthday. I loved that thing—it was a source of comfort for me—and that comfort was needed, because I was having a bad day and had been crying. There's a good chance I was also acting bratty and had been whining. I don't remember the exact circumstances—why I was sad, where exactly we were going, who else was in the car—but I do remember my mom's words as she looked at me in the rearview mirror: "Well, one good thing about that thumb, it sure shuts you up sometimes."

I learned something in that moment. I learned to keep quiet when sad.

This memory is burned into my brain and for a long time, I didn't share it with anyone. I knew that to an outsider, it would make my mom seem cruel, when she was anything but. My therapist told me many years later that the reason it stuck out so vividly to me was *because* it was so uncharacteristic of her. So, this story doesn't represent what my childhood was like and what kind of mother my mom was, but it did change the way I saw the world. In that one moment of exasperation from an exhausted mom of four living in middle-of-nowhere-Iowa during summer break with no lifeline of her own, that moment changed me.

Childhood is hard. As adults, we often look at children with envy due to their free time, ability to play, freedom from adult responsibilities, curiosity, and wonder-filled approach to the world and the experiences it has to offer. What we often fail to remember is that this openness and inability to process life's events with a fully functioning adult brain means children create (often inaccurate) stories about the things that happen to them, and these stories form patterns that stick. For this reason, there are moments in childhood that strip the joy from us and stop us from being creative, playful, and childlike; moments that teach us that who we are is not okay; that we need to adapt to someone else's expectations so we can be loved, appreciated, and safe in this world. These moments teach us to hide parts of our personality.

From an evolutionary perspective, we need to be accepted in our circles. As a caveman, isolation meant death, whether from starvation, the elements, or predators, so we have evolved to fit in; to be someone who others won't ostracize or socially reject. To do so, we learn to hide parts of us that others find "bad" or unacceptable. Even if you had an excellent or uneventful childhood, you probably experienced small traumas, events, or circumstances that influence your behavior today, whether it was a quick comment from a loving but exhausted parent (as in my example), a small need that went unmet at an important moment, or feedback from a parent or teacher that was meant to help you grow but instead hurt your open and easily influenced heart at the time. These small moments taught you something, and you carry those lessons with you into adulthood.

I was on the golf course recently with my dad when someone drove past us on a cart. The guy looked annoyed. My dad told me that this man always seemed to be angry about something and that he lashed out at others regularly. "You know, you gotta wonder what happened to a guy to make him act that way," my dad mused. This is exactly the right question to ask.

We all experience trauma in our childhood to varying degrees. The initial Adverse Childhood Experiences (ACE) study[1] attempted to measure just that: the prevalence of adverse childhood experiences, and the impact of those experiences on long-term health. It focused on those traumas, often termed "big T trauma," which include psychological and physical abuse, neglect, substance abuse by a parent or caregiver, and mental illness in a parent.

Fifty-two percent of the participants reported at least one adverse experience. That means that at least one in every two people you encounter has likely endured one or more of these things as a child (though this number is probably higher, as the study relied on self-reporting, and people are not always able or willing to share this kind of information).

The study also found there to be a strong relationship "between the breadth of exposure to abuse or household dysfunction during childhood and multiple risk factors for several of the leading causes of death in adults." The researchers hypothesized (and found) that exposure to these events produced anxiety, anger, and depression in children, which led to later substance use as coping devices, whether alcohol, nicotine, or drugs (Figure 1).

While completely understandable that people would turn to substances to cope, this is, of course, problematic for long-term health.

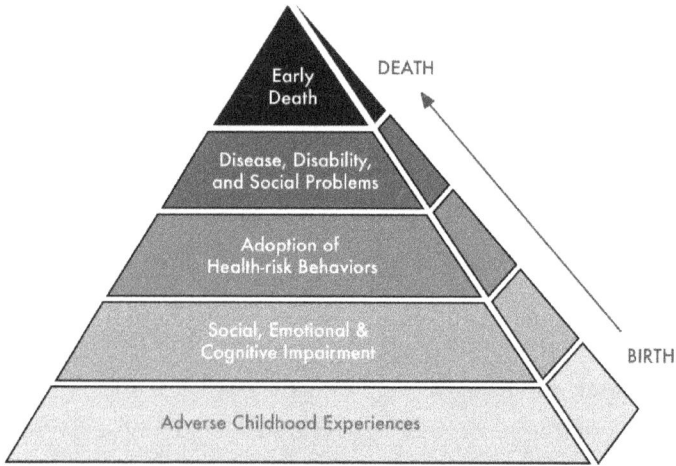

UPDATED ADVERSE CHILDHOOD EXPERIENCES (ACE) MODEL

Adapted from Felitti et al. (1998)

Exposure to ACEs causes psychological pain that, when left unprocessed, travels with you through life. This hurt shows up in different circumstances, and if it's not seen, welcomed, understood, attended to, or resolved, sufferers continue to live from a place of scarcity, defensiveness, and shame. They interpret daily events from the lens of a wounded child; of someone who has been hurt and is trying to survive. From this headspace, the world looks cruel. Words sting. It seems everyone is out to hurt you or trick you or undermine you. You internalize things that have happened and cannot see that others are also acting from their own injuries; that their actions and words are not about you, but them.

This one study examining the impacts of ACEs is just the tip of the iceberg. This topic has been studied by psychologists throughout history, leading to several different theories. Each major theory has a different name for and perspective of the exploration, understanding, and reparation of the hurts we carry from childhood. Carl Jung (shadow theory) calls it individuation; Internal Family Systems (IFS) theory calls it unburdening and integration; attachment theory calls it attachment exploration. Regardless of which (if any) specific theory resonates with you, here are a few fundamental takeaways from this field:

- We each have a challenging (to some degree) side or part of ourselves that formed during childhood.
- This often manifests in behaviors and defense mechanisms that are not healthy and that we're often blind to.
- Uncovering those components of ourselves is essential to self-awareness, growth, effective relationships, and wellbeing.

As much as we might want to believe these things don't affect us today, they do. Figuring out how and altering our behavior (if necessary) is work that is often left to the individual, without them ever being taught how to do so. This topic is often excluded from the workplace with good reason: It's uncomfortable. It's hard to understand. It's vulnerable.

But it's also important.

Understanding yourself and why you show up the way you do in relationships and at work is a critical and transformative step to leading your self well. Knowing who you are, where you came from, and how your past influences your behavior and thoughts today is essential to becoming the person you *want* to be; the person you were *meant* to become; the leader your employees *need* you to be, so you can help them be *their* best. Lead your self well, and you will be able to lead your team well.

The Diagnose Phase Character: Your Inner Child

> *We are problems that want to be solved.*
> *We are children that need to be loved.*
> —P!NK (Lyrics from *What About Us*)

The concept of the inner child is centered on those deep-seated, often-subconscious parts of ourselves that hold the emotions, memories, and experiences from our early years. This work has many names: inner child work, shadow work, trauma work… the list goes on. I personally like to use "inner child" terminology because it humanizes it. Remembering that inside each one of us is a child who was once hurt in some way (and is likely still reacting from those experiences) is a very compassionate lens through which to view life. My friend Brian often reminds me, "We're all just children living in adult bodies."

The inner child represents the part of you that carries the experiences and emotions from your formative years. Those childhood experiences shape our sense of self and our sense of safety, influencing how we perceive the world and others in it. It encompasses the joys, the pain, the trauma, and the vulnerabilities that we experienced as a kid.

Your inner child develops early through interactions with caregivers, siblings, teachers, and our environment. Positive experiences help nurture a sense of safety and self-worth. Conversely, experiences of neglect, criticism, or trauma can lead to emotional wounds that find their way into adulthood. These events, and their effects, are often stored in the subconscious and impact behavior in ways we don't easily understand.

When I start talking about inner child work, I often get dismissive reactions from clients and leaders:

- "I had a good childhood. I don't need to explore this."
- "I wasn't abused. I had food and shelter. I had good parents."
- "Others had it way worse than I did. I don't have the right to feel bad about it."
- "I don't want to dig up things that I don't want to remember."
- "My childhood was a mess. I have no interest in reliving that."

It's uncomfortable. It's hard to understand. It's vulnerable.

But it's also important.

Connecting with your inner child allows you to address those unresolved wounds and childhood unmet needs. The process of acknowledging and validating those experiences creates an opportunity for healing and growth, leading to emotional regulation and self-awareness. It improves relationships with others as well. It's about understanding, in an effort to break free from unhealthy behavior patterns.

You may be thinking: "this conversation does *not* belong in the workplace." You're somewhat right. But the impacts of your employees' inner child are likely present in the workplace anyway. The difficulties from childhood often influence how someone handles conflict, receives feedback, builds relationships, and copes with stress. Acknowledging the influences of your coworkers' or employees' inner child can be beneficial in understanding and improving employee interactions, emotional responses, and overall mental wellbeing.

For example, someone who felt unheard as a child may have heightened sensitivity to being overlooked or ignored in team projects. Someone whose mom or dad left when they were young may have a heightened need for affirmation or be constantly worried that they're going to be abandoned (fired) at any moment. Recognizing these patterns in ourselves and others can help to understand each other better and foster a more empathetic and team-oriented environment, where everyone feels understood and valued. Work environments that acknowledge and support the personal growth and emotional wellbeing of their employees see improvements in team cohesion, employee engagement, and productivity.

So, what keeps us from doing "the work?" Often, our own brains.

Our brains are smart. They work to protect us always, including that vulnerable kid *within* us, and they can come up with some interesting strategies to do so. Some are helpful. Others, not so much. Two interesting strategies of protection are the use of defense mechanisms and the creation of that inner critic we met in Chapter 8.

Defense Mechanisms as Protection

Defense mechanisms are often unconscious psychological strategies used to cope with stress, anxiety, and threats to our wellbeing. They're sometimes healthy and helpful, allowing us to manage stress and maintain emotional stability. When used in excess or to distort reality, they're usually harmful. Understanding these mechanisms can help to understand ourselves better and how we respond to challenging situations. It's also very helpful to be able to identify these in others. This will make you more adept at helping others (loved ones, children, employees, and coworkers) when they're in stressful situations and cannot see the forest for the trees.

Common defense mechanisms are:

- **DENIAL**: refusing to acknowledge the reality of a tough situation. It's a common defense mechanism among individuals who turn to substances to deal with their emotions. When confronted by friends or family, they'll often say things like, "I can quit anytime I want. It isn't impacting my life negatively. It helps me relax and de-stress. It's not a big deal."

- **PROJECTION**: attributing your own unacceptable thoughts or feelings to others. I remember my high school boyfriend *always* accusing me of cheating, and I was so confused about why, until I finally learned that *he* had been cheating on me for months. Classic projection.

- **DISPLACEMENT**: directing feelings of anger or shame onto an easier, less threatening target. It can take the form of kicking the dog, snapping at your coworkers, reprimanding your own direct reports, or yelling at your kids or spouse instead of confronting the source of your anger.

- **RATIONALIZATION**: creating logical explanations or "facts" to justify your behavior or beliefs. People use this to create internal comfort about their decisions, even (or especially) when they know what they've done is wrong.

- **HUMOR**: coping with a distressing situation by responding with humor rather than addressing it directly.

- **SUBLIMATION**: channeling "unacceptable" impulses or emotions into more socially acceptable activities. One of my clients learned to take his work-related anger out on a boxing bag rather than his employees, wife, or kiddos. Another one was into 50-mile trail races. Yet another was a workaholic and proud of it (even though the stress of the job was overwhelming).

- **OVER-INDEPENDENCE:** relying almost exclusively on oneself as a way to protect against disappointment or abandonment—often as a result of learning early on that they couldn't depend on their caregivers to meet their basic needs.
- **INTELLECTUALIZATION:** focusing only on facts and removing emotion when dealing with a difficult situation. In the workplace, this is common when a leader needs to give a tough performance review. Instead of having a "real" conversation about what's happening in the employee's life and their emotions, the leader focuses only on the facts.

What do defense mechanisms have to do with your inner child? Well, ask yourself this: do you identify as an overachiever? Are you a perfectionist? Are you hyper-independent? These traits often mask a deeper wound: your inner child seeking validation and safety through achievement.

For instance, my client Rebecca was a director in a fast-paced tech company. She was successful, often earning promotions and accolades from senior leaders, but she felt like a fraud. Through inner child work, she realized that growing up, nothing she did ever seemed quite good enough for her dad. He was supportive, but he always pushed her to accomplish just a bit more. Now, as an adult, she couldn't stop chasing the next goal, even to celebrate her wins, because "there was always a bigger achievement to attain," if only she "worked harder." Beneath her success was her inner child's need for validation; to be fully loved and accepted. Her achievement and need to do things perfectly were a defense mechanism, to ease the wounding of that little kid.

Do you have an addictive habit? Overindulgence in alcohol, food, sex (including porn), or shopping suggests you are trying to soothe the parts of yourself that you fear are unacceptable. Perhaps your inner child, who may have felt neglected or criticized in childhood, seeks comfort in the instant gratification these habits offer. Engaging in these behaviors can momentarily silence the inner critic and protect your vulnerable self from facing shame or self-doubt.

Do you take pride in how independent you are? Matthew was a charming and successful consultant who had no trouble making friends, building connections, and meeting women. "I have people around me all the time," he said, "but I don't rely on anyone. They always let me down." On the surface, his independence looked like a strength, but it came at a cost. When unpacking his relationships, it became clear that Matthew kept things close enough that he could feel connected, but not so close that anyone could *really* see him. Growing up, Matthew had learned that vulnerability and dependence were risky. For many reasons, his parents were not able to fully protect and care for him. Now, as an adult, he instinctively built relationships with emotional walls just high enough to keep his inner child safe. He would share parts of himself, but never the "full him." This protected him from rejection but also kept him from experiencing the deep intimacy that he truly craved.

Do you often find a "reason" for your behaviors? Antonette was an excellent people-centered leader, and she knew some of her employees were not quite performing to expectations, but she just couldn't muster the courage to provide feedback to her team. She would consistently say, "My team is great and meeting my expectations. The market is just tough right now." She always had a "reason" for why she didn't need to performance manage her employees. In reality she was a people-pleaser, and she learned this in childhood. She had an alcoholic father with whom she'd always to try to keep the peace. This meant that as an adult, she just couldn't bring herself to give tough feedback. Yet she knew it was part of her job to do so. So, she rationalized why it wasn't actually necessary to do so, as a defense mechanism.

The Inner Critic as Protection

The inner critic, who is always brimming with thoughts and beliefs, is not all bad. It actually serves a purpose: it helps us feel like we're in control in a world where we often feel *out* of control. But how does your inner critic and its stories relate to your inner child? Well, the inner critic is formed as a response to the *fears* of the inner child. When your inner child feels exposed in moments of failure, rejection, or shame, it longs to be seen, loved, protected, and accepted. This is the inner critic's cue to jump in to help deal with those emotions, in an attempt to prevent the inner child from feeling disappointment. It attempts to do so in a couple of ways: by keeping us from making mistakes, and by keeping us from being vulnerable.

Let's look at an example:

When we were children, we all wanted to be accepted and loved. I learned very young that the way to do this was to be perfect. To me, this meant getting good grades, doing my chores well, and not being overweight. When I "messed up" (such as if I missed a couple of words on my spelling test, forgot to do my chores, or gained some weight, as pointed out by my grandparents or others), my inner critic stepped in like an over-disciplinary parent. In an attempt to encourage me to "fix" those unacceptable parts of me or keep me from being vulnerable and needing someone's love, it said (and still sometimes says) some pretty mean things:

- "You'll never be smart enough."
- "You're so fat it's disgusting. You should apologize to people for having to look at you."
- "You're never going to amount to anything."
- "You're an embarrassment."
- "You never get things done."
- "Why can't you get your stuff together?"

Again, this voice was trying to *protect* me. Its logic was (is) this: "If I can shame you into doing things that make you perfect, I can make you acceptable and lovable. As soon as you lose some weight, as soon as you don't screw things up anymore, as soon as you achieve that goal, you'll be acceptable and get the love you want." It also told me things to make me believe I didn't deserve the love and acceptance I was looking for, to keep me from being let down if or when I didn't get it.

Being able to recognize how you hide from others and yourself is a key to wellbeing. You must explore. You must be willing to meet your inner child and understand how he or she still impacts your behaviors and decisions. You must be willing to uncover the things that your unconscious mind is trying desperately to hide from you. You must dive deep. You must inquire within. There is a process to do this, which we'll learn about in the next chapter.

One of my favorite movies is *Crazy, Stupid, Love*. In this movie, Jacob (Ryan Gosling) is a very successful businessman. He's got it all: money, a beautiful condo, and a different beautiful woman any night he chooses. He continually distracts himself with success, alcohol, and women. He is self reportedly "wildly unhappy and trying to buy it." But when he meets Hannah (Emma Stone), they end up drinking, laughing, and talking about all kinds of funny and cute topics all night. Jacob finally says to her, "Could you do me a favor? Will you do me a kindness? Will you ask me something personal about myself?"[2] Inside, he wants to connect. He wants to talk about his childhood. In real life, most people aren't brave enough to ask for that, yet we're yearning for someone to ask about us, and then to actually listen; to know us; to see us; to care about us.

This movie also shows us that childhood gives us strengths (not just problems) that we can call on for our benefit. These strengths bring power. In the movie, Jacob's childhood experiences created his drive for success and his ability to keep going through adversity. It also gave him his ability to connect with people quickly and make them feel special. Similarly, although my childhood brought a need for perfectionism and taught me to keep quiet when sad, to yell when angry, and that I was not lovable the way I was, it also brought me so many strengths. I'm someone who never gives up. I'm independent, and I strive to achieve goals. I'm called to help people. I'm understanding when people are emotional (because I get it). I fight for and protect the underdog. I seek challenging things. I'm able to connect with people well and create great relationships.

Get to know yourself. Learn your self so you can lead your self well.

What Do We Do About All This?

I felt horrible writing the story at the beginning of this chapter, because my mom was awesome. She was maternal, patient, kind, wise, thoughtful, and spiritual. (Did I mention patient?) Still, I shared this story for two reasons. First, sometimes people are hesitant to do this work for fear of "blaming" parents. Like me, they have parents they love and respect and for which they hold so much gratitude. Doing this work might make you feel like you're upending memories of your childhood, parents, or siblings. Second, if you're a parent, doing this work has the potential to bring up shame around things you have said and done that may have created hurt in your own children.

It's important to remember that no one gets out of childhood unscathed. No one. Whether it was a parent, sibling, friend, or teacher, a trusted person in your life let you down at a moment that mattered. How you processed this *as a child* influences how you show up as an adult.

We can look at this work not as an opportunity to blame someone, but as an opportunity to learn about ourselves, grow into who we are meant to be, and fully understand and help others. Searching into the corners of our past, shining a light on the experiences that we have long kept hidden, and bringing out the secrets we carry can be a scary process, but also a liberating one. It presents an opportunity for us to get wildly curious about ourselves and others and recognize the strengths that childhood brought (and find ways to harness those strengths).

One of my biggest lessons in this arena came when I revisited an experience I had in second grade. At the time, I was in a small group of "advanced" students for reading class, and during the reading lesson, the four of us would do different activities than the rest of the class. On this particular day, Mrs. Overson had written the same five words on the board for each of us to individually separate into syllables. I struggled, and I was the last one to finish the task. My friend Nicole noticed this, and I can still see her trying to cover up her work so I wouldn't copy it.

Once I finished, Mrs. Overson came to the board to "grade" us by writing our scores on the board. Ben got a star—all five correct. Jennifer, star. Skip Cara. Nicole, star. Back to Cara. She wrote the "-4" so hard on the board that the chalk crumbled under the pressure. I can still see it. She was angry. I don't remember what she said to me, but I know it wasn't kind. I could hear a couple of kids snickering. I ran out of the room and into the hallway-type closet at the back of Mrs. Hauser's adjoining room.*

I wouldn't realize this for decades, but I learned several things at that moment:

- Being wrong in front of other people could demolish my soul.
- Looking like a fool was terrifying.
- I had to be right (perfect) all the time so I wouldn't be publicly humiliated.
- I shouldn't try to do things I wasn't already good at in front of people (it's too risky).

---

* The teachers and parents reading this will be happy to hear that Mrs. Hauser (my favorite teacher ever) was kind and compassionate in that moment. She even taught me a few "tricks" for syllables while we sat in that back closet. A few years ago, I called my childhood friend's dad (a schoolteacher in the same school), thinking that maybe I had imagined the severity of Mrs. Overson's reaction, but he confirmed that Mrs. Overson was, in fact, known to be very mean to kids quite regularly.

The bright side? I also learned to work hard to learn all that I can, to do great work, and that there are some people I can turn to who will help me in a moment of need.

Before I did the work of the Diagnose phase, I was often reactive at work and in my personal life. It was like I could *see* the words, literally, coming out of my mouth before I had a moment to even think about them. I frequently wanted to grab them and shove them back in, but I couldn't: I had already hurt or offended the person on the other end of those words. What was happening in these moments? Simply, my inner child felt at risk, and so I was self-protecting through defense mechanisms. I would fiercely defend myself or my idea, refusing to be "made the fool" (as I saw it) and demanding that my needs be met in an inappropriate way (by being controlling or by complaining, whining, or criticizing). Then, my inner critic would step in and berate me for the way I was trying to defend myself, in an effort to "do better" so that my inner child would get the validation she needed. It was exhausting.

I had a leader tell me once, "You're not responsible for your first thought. Thoughts come into our heads all the time. You *are*, however, responsible for your second thought and your actions." He recognized that I was having some tough thoughts and emotions that were overwhelming, and that I was acting on them without taking the time to think through whether they were accurate. This still happens, albeit rarely, but it's something I continue to work on. Without this knowledge and understanding of how my inner child and inner critic worked together, it was difficult for me to be my best true self.

When we see these behaviors in ourselves and we don't understand where they came from or why they exist, we tend to berate ourselves further. We use our inner critic to punish ourselves for what we have said or done to someone else, or how we reacted in a triggering situation, or how we didn't show up for ourselves when we were challenged.

However, these behaviors, whether arrogance, hostility, lashing out, manipulation, addiction, defensiveness, or playing small, are not defects. They're a signal that there is a hurt that needs attention; to be processed and healed.

The Work

> *No one can make you feel bad if you feel good about yourself.*
> —FRASER C. ROBINSON III (Michelle Obama's father)
>
> *It's your job to do the work to make yourself feel good.*
> —MICHELLE OBAMA

Having the ability to see how past experiences influence current behavior is an important step to leading your self well. It can also lead to the development of healthy coping mechanisms for daily life's stressors. This can help you to feel more empowered and in control of your life and emotions, at work and in the world, and to approach conflict and triggers from a grounded place, rather than with heightened emotion (whether anger, shutting down, or tears). This work can also help you:

- Build better relationships with others.
- Stop emotional meltdowns.
- Bring an attitude of play and fun to your life and work.
- Increase your self-esteem and compassion.
- Improve your creativity and innovation.
- Improve your wellbeing by addressing issues at the root.

You're not alone if you've acted in ways that you're not proud of, whether at work or in your personal relationships. Instead of pushing those moments aside or berating yourself (both of which strengthen your shadow side), there are steps you can take to keep yourself from acting in those ways in the future. If you can start to view your triggers as *opportunities* rather than pain points, it will make this work easier.

This takes some time, and it's not easy. Feelings of fear, insecurity, shame, and doubt can surface. That's okay. Exploring those feelings and observing them as an investigator (not a judge and jury) is key to understanding your self and showing up in your life as the person you are, not as the child who is self-protecting.

Ready to do the work? Let's look at the skills of the Diagnose phase.

Reflect to Retain

What are three things I learned about myself from this chapter?
1.

2.

3.

What are three concepts I want to remember from this chapter?
1.

2.

3.

chapter 11

the diagnose phase skills

JUST AS A DOCTOR SEARCHES FOR patterns and symptoms before making a diagnosis, we must do the same with understanding where our thoughts and beliefs originated and how our strengths and struggles can be used advantageously. There are two skills that will be helpful for you the Diagnose work. These are acceptance and mindfulness.

Acceptance and mindfulness provide the foundation for healing when it comes to our relationship with our inner child. Our past experiences shape who we are today (both the strengths we've gained and the struggles we carry). When we acknowledge and embrace these childhood experiences and the parts of ourselves that grew from them (rather than resisting or judging them), we create space for healing and growth. Acceptance and mindfulness practices allow us to do this work *with* our inner child and inner critic instead of battling against them.

Acceptance

This is a hard one, especially if you like to be in control (hello, my fellow Capricorns!). In addition to childhood experiences, so many things happen that we can't control: the death of a loved one; the choices of other people; a promotion you didn't get; the ending of a relationship you wanted to continue; an accident; world events. If you find yourself fighting a daily battle that you have no hope of winning, learning the skill of acceptance (including self-acceptance) is critical to finding your balance and wellbeing. Luckily, it's a skill you can learn.

Acceptance of our experiences and circumstances can help to regulate emotions, reduce stress, manage pain, increase health outcomes, and increase happiness and life satisfaction. It can also free up the space in your brain that's attempting to change or control situations, events, and people.

Acceptance allows for a sense of agency, which we learned about in chapter 8. It can help us get through incredibly difficult circumstances. In Viktor Frankl's book *Man's Search for Meaning*, he argues that true freedom lies in the ability to *accept* one's situation while finding meaning and purpose within it.[1]

We live in an imperfect world. That, in itself, can create unhappiness. But more unhappiness and frustration are created when we try to control situations and people that we simply cannot, as well as when we berate ourselves for things we wish we had done differently.

When it comes to relationships with others, trying to control every situation often brings frustration, anger, and resentment for everyone involved. When we try to change or control someone else, it's like saying that they're not okay to be who they are, or that they're making the wrong choices. This hurts everyone in the equation. It makes the person feel unseen, misunderstood, and not accepted. Similarly, when you berate yourself for *your* words, actions, or thoughts, you are also slyly telling yourself that it's not okay for you to be who you are or for you to do the things you have done. This also hurts. It makes you feel less-than, unlovable, and unacceptable. Trying to fight these situations while fueled by fear will keep you swimming against the tide. Acceptance is the best way out.

How can you develop acceptance? Here are a few strategies:

- Identify and acknowledge the situation and your feelings. Recognize that you're in a situation that you can't control and wish you could. Remind yourself that it's normal to have emotional reactions to things that you wish were different.

- Find gratitude for what is right in the situation or the person. Usually, not everything about a situation or person is wrong, so what is right? What can you be thankful for?

- Find meaning in the wrong. What is this teaching you? What might this terrible situation lead to that could be positive? Did this situation prevent something worse from happening?

- Do not wait for "closure." Create it. When a relationship ends (whether personal or professional), you may be tempted to seek closure; to want to hear the person acknowledge and apologize for their part in the situation. You're often not going to get this, especially if the person involved is not mature enough to do so, or if they have narcissistic tendencies. These people will rarely acknowledge they did anything wrong. Making the decision to create closure for yourself will help you to move forward, instead of waiting on the actions of someone else to find internal peace.

- Practice radical acceptance. This involves fully accepting a situation, even if (*especially* if) you don't like it. This doesn't mean approving or condoning the situation or person's behavior but acknowledging and accepting what is. It's saying, "I don't like this, but I can't do anything about it, so I'm going to accept it and move on."

- Start small. Just like any other skill, start with the small stuff. Look for small things you can intentionally choose to accept. Accept that your kid didn't empty the dishwasher, or that your boss didn't reply to your email, or that you didn't go to the gym as you had planned. Accept it and move on without letting it get to you.

- Practice the acceptance of something just for *right now*. Sometimes, saying to yourself that you will accept a situation forever is too difficult to do all at once. If you hit that spot, make a deal with yourself that just for today (or maybe even just for this hour), you're going to accept it.

- Make peace with the past. Observe and learn from what you have been through. How did you grow? What did you learn? What lessons can you take to your next job, relationship, or team?

- Embrace choice. Remember you have a choice to accept. It is yours. Make it with intention.

- Move forward. Once you accept what's currently happening, you can move toward what is next for you, based on the reality of the situation and not what you wish it were. Determine what you *can* control, what you *can* do in this situation. Sometimes this is *only* your attitude and thoughts. Start with one small, intentional step to move in that forward direction.

Leadership and Acceptance

Accepting people is sometimes difficult as a leader, especially when someone isn't following through on their commitments or getting their work done.

My first job out of grad school was in an HR leadership position at a big box retail store. This was the first job I could get, and so I took it, even though I was *not* excited about it (my inner child made me terrified of the prospect of never finding a job). I did end up loving parts of the job, but what I didn't love were some of the employees' issues. I frequently felt really frustrated with employees who had problems that annoyed me and took up my day (as I saw it). These employees would come to my office with complaints about the dress code, the fact they had been scheduled with someone they didn't like, or their break times being too early or too late for their liking. What I didn't understand at the time was that while these were "annoyances" to me, they were important to the person. I ultimately realized my attitude was not entirely fair. Yet I still couldn't muster enough patience to handle their complaints compassionately. In other words, I couldn't *accept* that this was part of my job.

Then, one day, I had an idea. I was a new aunt, and my niece, Grace, was my whole world at the time. Shortly after her birth, it dawned on me that at some point, Grace would be an annoying employee (because we all are at times), and when she was, I wanted someone to treat her with love and kindness. I decided to put a 5 x 7-inch picture of her cute chubby cheeks in her purple-and-pink-striped overalls on my desk, facing me, right in the view of the person sitting across the desk. This reminded me that with every employee, I should try to treat them the way I would want Grace's manager to treat her someday. In most cases, this small mindset shift changed the dynamic of the conversation. In the process, it helped me to find acceptance in the parts of the job I hated and the employees who frustrated me.

I've worked with several leaders who came to me as their HR partner looking for a way to get "that one person" off their team. This was usually thinly veiled as a "restructure," or them claiming that the employee would be better on someone else's team. Sometimes, they would outright request that I help "get rid of them." In these situations, I always advised that it would be helpful for the leader to start with acceptance of the employee and the situation (not the poor performance or unacceptable behavior) before they move to employment action. By following the acceptance steps we just talked about (identifying and acknowledging the situation and feelings, finding gratitude for what is right, and so on), a leader can usually see where the employee contributes, where the leader could have done a better job in leading, and what the leader can learn in this situation.

When you lead from this place of acceptance, the next steps, whatever they are, lead to a better and more compassionate outcome for the employee. I have found that practicing acceptance in leadership decisions helps the leader make better choices *and* feel better about those decisions. This means they feel better at night when their head hits the pillow, *especially* when the outcome was termination of the employee.

Acceptance is a skill. A skill you can develop.

Mindfulness

There has been a lot of talk about mindfulness post-pandemic. I first heard about it years ago, when I was struggling with my weight. A therapist recommended mindful eating, and my mindfulness journey began.

The very first time I tried mindful eating was with a raisin: I put it in my mouth and really felt the texture as I bit into it and slowly chewed, so I could notice all the feelings and flavors that came with it. Although I eat my raisins normally now, my mindfulness journey continues today, and it still includes mindful eating. It's a daily practice.

Mindfulness is the practice of focusing your awareness on the present moment and doing this over and over again throughout the day. Its goal is to get you out of the default mode network—out of rumination and storytelling—and into what is really happening right now, without judgment.

Mindfulness is a gentle practice. It's a method for paving new neural pathways, to keep your brain from heading down that well-paved six-lane superhighway of stories and beliefs. As discussed earlier, when we're not

173 | The Diagnose Phase Skills

mindful and when we leave our brains to their own devices, they will find things to analyze, look out for, and figure out. This pulls us away from what is real and present. With patience and awareness, you can teach your mind to be still. When you get there, it is such an amazing feeling that I promise you you'll want to go back again and again.

When we bring mindful awareness to our inner child work, we can gently observe the emotions, memories, and unmet needs that arise without pushing them away. This presence helps us to respond with curiosity and compassion, rather than avoidance or reactivity. Mindfulness also softens the harsh voice of the inner critic, giving us the space to notice its judgments without being controlled by them.

Using mindfulness practices when engaging with both of these characters creates the freedom to *choose* how we work with them.

Jon Kabat-Zinn created mindfulness-based stress reduction (MBSR) as a process in the late 1970s, and he is still seen as the leader of mindfulness today.[2] Through his (and others') research, MBSR programs have been found to improve cognitive ability, reduce stress and anxiety, increase wellbeing, reduce depression, and improve quality of life.[3]

One of the most exciting benefits of mindfulness is its ability to slow brain aging. In a 2019 study using eight weeks of meditation as a practice, mindfulness was shown to increase gray matter volume and cortical thickness. This was correlated with a reduction in depression scores.[4]

In another study in 2020, meditation significantly lowered the rate of age-related gray matter loss in participants, specifically in areas involving mood regulation and the integration of emotion and cognition. Furthermore, in an exciting study in Australia, researchers found that mindfulness training enhanced brain processes in a couple of different ways. First, it increased the brain pathways that process our sensory input, thereby improving subjects' senses; and second, it improved subjects' ability to focus on the task at hand and ignore distractions. Both of these things (high quality sensory input and focus) are important in goal achievement. These findings were immediate and also present during a six-month follow-up.[5]

There are several proven pathways to improving mindfulness:

- **BREATHWORK:** This is one of the easiest ways to practice mindfulness. Focusing on your breath, even for those few seconds while practicing your physiological sigh or doing diaphragm breathing, gently brings you to the present moment.

- **MEDITATION:** While meditating, try focusing on something specific, such as your breath, some sensory input (a smell or sound), or something in nature (like the details of the leaf on a tree). As your mind wanders, redirect it back to that focus, without judgment. You can also practice using guided meditations, which are easily found on Spotify, YouTube, or meditation apps. Guided meditation is great for when you want a little help focusing your attention, or for something specific, like healing, creativity, or energy.

- **BODY SCAN:** Lie back and systematically go through each part of your body, starting with your feet, and scan for areas of tension and discomfort. You then focus on "softening" that body part and releasing that tension. This is an easy process to do at your desk in between meetings in just a couple of minutes (or you can take longer, to really get into it).

- **MINDFUL LISTENING:** Can you recall a time when you truly listened to someone? When you were just deep in their story with them, not formulating your next question or response, or wondering what you were going to do for dinner, or thinking about that email that needs to be sent? Intentionally and mindfully listening can be difficult. Our brains are constantly swirling with input and mental to-do lists. Yet mindful listening is also one of the best ways in which you can bring yourself to the present while simultaneously allowing someone to be seen and heard just as they are.

- **YOGA:** A yoga practice can be a great way to connect your body and breath through movement. Many of us frame yoga as our workout for the day—as a way to achieve toning and calorie burn—but if you set your intention toward mindful connection to breath, you can achieve both (fitness and mindfulness).

- **YOGA NIDRA:** This powerful meditation technique helps you enter a deep state of relaxation while staying awake and aware. It activates the parasympathetic nervous system, helping to improve sleep, reduce anxiety, reduce depression and enhance overall wellbeing.[6, 7]

- **DIGITAL DETOX:** Get off your device! You cannot be mindful while you're scrolling. You know this already. Set aside some time each day to shut off your phone and just "be" in whatever activity is happening in that moment.

Meditation has changed my life, though it took some time for me to embrace it fully. I always thought that I hated meditation, just like I hated running...

In 2015, my friend Kristin talked me into running a marathon. She does them every year, and I decided to go along with her, to check the box, even though I *hate* running. What I learned from that experience is, I actually don't hate running; I had just never run more than three miles before training for this marathon. Turns out that after the three-mile mark, I actually enjoy running (up until about mile 12...). I get into my groove and love the feeling of my muscles doing their thing as I watch nature around me and bask in the knowledge that soon, I will experience the afterglow of endorphins and that runner's high. Yet without the goal of a marathon, I would have never made it past the three miles.

Meditation was much the same for me. I always thought I hated it and was "not good at it," but I just needed more practice. I needed to sit with it longer. I always gave up a few minutes in because it seemed to be making my rumination worse. It still is hard for me to quiet my mind during those first few minutes of a meditation. But then, once I continue to sit and let the thoughts come and quietly go, I reap the rewards. Now, my day isn't the same when I don't take the time for a 10- to 15-minute meditation in the morning. Without it, I'm more anxious throughout the day, I don't sleep as well at night, and I reach for caffeine or sugar to calm me.

Sometimes, we think we know ourselves: what we like; what we don't like; what life will always look like; what is good for us. But then, we change something or try something new, and a whole new world opens up as a result. So, if you've ever said, "I can't meditate," I urge you to try again, even just for the sake of stopping the atrophy of your brain!

Mindfulness is a skill. A skill you can develop.

Summary

The Diagnose phase is not easy. It's not for the faint of heart. It can feel woo-woo and too touchy-feely for a lot of people. It might even scare your HR partner if you suggest bringing this type of work into the workplace. But the impacts of childhood are already in the workplace because they're in each of us, influencing our work and relationships daily. Uncovering and understanding the true "why" behind some of those impacts is therefore a huge step to *really* addressing them for the good of you, your employees, and the organization (not to mention the people in your personal life).

It's a hard journey, but it's worth the effort.

A note to parents (including my dad) and to people who don't want to hurt their parents: there is a tendency, as mentioned before, for parents to look at this work as a process of trying to find someone to blame for their life situation. I can remember that as a bratty teenager, whenever my dad was mad at me, I loved to say to him, "Nature or nurture? You made me *and* you raised me, so basically, this is your fault." I thought I was being clever and funny, and I meant it in a tongue-in-cheek way, but still, there can certainly be a tendency for us to blame others for our actions.

This work is *not* about that. All parents mess up. All teachers mess up. All siblings mess up. All friends mess up. Nobody is perfect, and you can't protect your kid from every person who may say something that hurts them. Even if you could, kids' brains can take *any* situation and interpret it in a way that can become detrimental later in life. Even praise for good grades can get turned into a kid thinking they must be perfect next time (and all the time) to earn that praise again. This work is about finding out why we show up the way we do and understanding it fully, so that we can make intentional choices that make us happier and healthier. It is not about blame.

A note to those of you who have experienced "big T" trauma: if you have experienced a deeply disturbing or life-threatening situation (rape, physical or sexual abuse, emotional abuse or neglect, or a violent crime), this type of work is best done with a therapist. Finding a therapist who is trained in helping people uncover and overcome the effects of trauma can be a life-changing experience. I'm a strong advocate for therapy, and it has helped me to change the way I view the world and the things that have happened to me in my past. I have listed some resources in the appendices of this book to help guide you in finding a qualified therapist, if that's the right course for your exploration journey.

Now that you've learned about acceptance and mindfulness, we can move into the Diagnose phase exercises. These skills will be important to use as you do this work.

THE DIAGNOSE PHASE: PUT IT INTO PRACTICE

I can't tell you how many times I've been in succession planning meetings where leaders will say some version of, "Chris needs to work on his patience. He doesn't bring others along and bulldozes things through, and can't lead effectively because of it. He's had this feedback for three years now. I can't support him for a higher-level leadership position because I don't see it changing." Chris then gets the feedback (again), goes back to his IDP and development tools (a class, a book, Google), and searches for ways to "get better" at patience, without ever really understanding the root. Until he does, he will likely continue to struggle. This exercise is about getting to the root of the struggle. And you must do all four steps.

Please work through this section thoroughly, whether now or after you've read this book. The activities outlined here should take you two to four weeks, and they facilitate a deep process that will be foundational to your wellbeing journey.

This will feel uncomfortable. Embrace the discomfort. Don't run from it (though see the appendices for signs that you need to work with a licensed therapist in this work).

Inquire Within

The following steps will help start the Diagnose phase of your journey:

1. **UNCOVERING**: Identify the specific childhood experiences that shape who you are.
2. **UNDERSTANDING**: Cultivate further understanding of how your childhood influences your behavior today.
3. **IDENTIFYING**: Pinpoint the strengths and struggles created from your past.
4. **MEETING YOUR INNER CHILD**

Set aside some time to go through each of these four steps, whether in one sitting or over the course of a few weeks.

Before you begin:

- Take two to three minutes to breathe deeply.
- Remind yourself that you are choosing acceptance of yourself and others as you work through these exercises.

1. UNCOVERING:

The first step in the Diagnose phase is acknowledging that childhood hurts do indeed exist (in varying degrees of severity) and exploring how they show up in adulthood. This is a necessary starting point.

This step is often ignored in organizations. I get it. It's not something people often want to talk about at work. It can be daunting. Instead, we often start by using an assessment or evaluation of competencies to uncover behaviors that we want to improve upon. But without understanding *where* these behaviors come from, we miss an important piece of the puzzle.

While I've worked with teams and individuals who have shared their findings from this step with coworkers or a leader (and doing so can be extremely helpful to the team dynamics), this is *not* necessary. Knowing it for yourself *is*. Do not skip this step.

To help with this process, think back to your childhood. What are two to four events that happened to you before you were 18 that profoundly shaped who you are today?

Also think about three to five smaller memories that have negative emotions associated with them (such as my example in the car with my mom).

Journal the answers to these questions about each event:

- What was the event?
- What age were you at the time of the event?
- What were you feeling at the time?
- How did that situation influence how you see yourself?
- How did that situation influence how you see the world?

2. Understanding

Spend some quiet time thinking through how these situations affect the way you view yourself and the world around you. Use the following journal questions to further your understanding of how your childhood experiences have helped and hindered you.[*]

Based on the experiences you identified in step 1, answer the following questions:

- What messages about myself did I internalize as a child? How have I carried these into adulthood?
- What emotions or feelings did I have to suppress as a child because of others' expectations (family, teachers, friends)? Are there emotions I have a hard time expressing now?
- What strengths did my childhood experiences give me? Where do I see those, and where would I like to call on them more often?
- What moments of joy and happiness did I have in my childhood? What was I excited about?
- How do I self soothe now? Are my coping mechanisms helpful? What else could I try if not?

---

[*] This is another step that is often shied away from in the corporate world because it's uncomfortable. Do it anyway. Again, you don't have to share what you uncover with anyone.

- Think about a recent situation in which you reacted strongly or emotionally. Trace those responses back to childhood wounds if possible.

3. IDENTIFYING

This next step incorporates what you learned in the first two steps. It should help you to clearly identify the learned behaviors that you exhibit (both positive and negative). This is where organizations often start.

Take a few moments to read the following lists and put a check next to the items you've noticed in your own behavior. Add your own at the end of each list. If you're brave, give the list to a trusted person and ask for their feedback.

Struggles:
- Responds to difficult circumstances in a way that is disproportionate to the situation, whether with anger, anxiety, shame, or sadness.
- Perfectionism or procrastination.
- Chooses unhealthy relationships.
- Low self-esteem.
- Difficulty with intimacy, trust, or vulnerability.
- Needs approval and validation.
- Difficulty saying no and setting boundaries.
- Difficulty hearing criticism.
- Unable to take accountability for actions or mistakes.
- Blames others for things that go wrong.
- Afraid of rejection or abandonment.
- Difficulty trusting others at work or in personal life.
- Identifies as a workaholic.

- Burned out at work.
- Takes frustrations out on others, such as your family, dog, coworkers, or barista.
- Limiting beliefs about capabilities.
- Uses alcohol, screen time, food, shopping, sex, porn, or drugs to "relax" or "take the edge off" at times.*
-
-

Strengths:
- Adaptable to new situations, whether a new boss, a new client, or changing work demands.
- Empathetic to others' situations.
- Strong determination in tough situations.
- Strong work ethic.
- Excellent problem-solving skills.
- Attuned to the "unsaid" things in the room.
- Resourceful and innovative when resources are limited.
- Compassionate.
- Persistent.
- Excellent at time management.
- Humble.
- Grateful.
- Comfortable with conflict.
- Committed to personal growth.
- Stays calm in stressful situations.
-
-

---

* A word about addiction: if you feel as though you may be experiencing addiction to any of the above-mentioned "vices," please consult with your family doctor and/or see the appendices for resources on how to find a therapist.

Defense Mechanisms (definitions in Chapter 10):

- Denial
- Projection
- Displacement
- Rationalization
- Overuse of Humor
- Sublimation
- Hyper-Independence
- Intellectualization
-
-

4. MEETING YOUR INNER CHILD

Meeting your inner child is a way to get in touch with "little you"—to better understand how your childhood experiences impact you, through the lens of the kid it happened to. It often helps to think of your "little you" as another person; as a child who needs care, love, patience, and understanding.

This may feel weird, uncomfortable, or woo-woo if this is your first time hearing about inner child work. As noted earlier, we live in a culture that values *thinking* through a problem rather than *feeling* your way through it. While there are times when thinking is a valuable strategy, this work requires you to *feel* as a way of learning. For our purposes here, it's necessary for you to get out of the "thinking mind" and into the emotional mind, which has access to your emotion, intuition, and creativity.

Clients often resist this work, yet when they finally try it, they find it incredibly profound. Please try again if you can't get there in the first try.

To be clear, this is definitely *not* an exercise for the workplace. You can share, as appropriate, with others on your team as a self-exploration exercise, but when it comes down to it, this is a deeply personal exercise that should be done alone.

Try to imagine your inner child as a separate entity. Your goal is to find out how they are feeling and what they need from you.

1. Lie somewhere quiet when and where you know you won't be disturbed. Take a few deep breaths. Pay attention to the internal sensations you notice, especially the places where you may feel some tension or numbness.

2. Connect to your breath and your heart. You can even put one hand on your heart.

3. Think about the memory of one of the more impactful experiences you identified in the "Uncovering" section and try to put yourself back in front of that situation. Notice what emotions you feel. Try to identify where you feel them physically. Is there a tightening in your chest? Pain in your gut? An ache behind your eyes? Are your legs heavy? Numb? Tingling?

4. Next, visualize the child you were when this occurred. Observe any images that come up. Greet that child and ask them what they're feeling about the memory you have chosen. Listen to what comes up. What do they have to say about that experience? How does Little You feel about it? What emotions do they have? Are they crying? Angry? Sad?

5. If your inner child is quiet, just sit there with them for a few moments. You can visualize yourself hugging them and telling them you love them.

6. Acknowledge what happened to that little kid, showing gratitude and compassion to Little You. You can use words like, "You didn't deserve this. It's not your fault. I love you. Everything is going to be okay. I'm the adult and will keep us both safe from now on."

7. Stay as long as is necessary, until your inner child feels soothed. This could take just a few minutes, or it could take quite a while.

8. Take a few more breaths, returning to the sensations in your body, and see what you notice. Are there places where you're more relaxed? Still tense?

9. Open your eyes and take a couple of minutes to stretch out, come back to the room, and remind yourself that you and Little You are safe.

10. Journal about your experience.

Once you're able to connect with your inner child, it's important to continue to check in with them over the course of the next several weeks or months. See how they are feeling. Reassure them that you're still here and taking care of them and you. Remind them that you are the adult, that you can protect them, and that they don't need to do anything but just "be."

These check-ins can be quick, or they can be long and deep. Regardless, continue to check in. Don't leave them stranded out there!

Daily Practice Ideas

Choose one or two options below to practice daily for 2–4 weeks.

Acceptance:

- Look for two small places where you can practice acceptance throughout the day or week, instead of fighting or getting frustrated about it. For example, if you live in Minnesota and it's winter, just accept the cold without fighting it. If your kid has to be reminded most days to make his bed, or if your husband has to call you every time he's at the grocery store for clarification (even though you've been married and buying the same brand of English muffins for 20 years), accept the situation and respond from a state of choice.

- Choose to practice one "acceptance strategy" from the list in this chapter. Make this a part of your daily routine for one week.

Mindfulness:
- Sit quietly through a guided meditation.
- Do a quick body scan, looking for and releasing any tension.
- Find and follow a short restorative yoga video on YouTube.
- Choose one person to mindfully listen to each day this week, without focusing on your own thoughts or responses.

Childhood Learning:
- Choose one strength that you identified from your "Inquire Within" journaling and remind yourself of this strength throughout your day.
- Choose one struggle that you identified in the "Inquire Within" section and simply notice when it shows up. Don't try to fix it; just notice it like an observer. Where do you "feel" it (gut, heart, legs, etc.)? What was the situation that brought it on? How strong was the feeling? Try to take one deep breath when you do notice it.
- Revisit Little You each day for a quick check-in. Remind them that they are okay and that you are keeping both of you safe.

Wellness Wednesday (When-sday)

Choose one of the activities below to complete on your Wellness Day.

Acceptance:

Choose one or two journal prompts to write about:
- What does acceptance mean to me? What are some things I don't like but I've accepted?

- Consider, when have I felt completely accepted by someone? Who was that? What did it feel like?
- What things have I not yet been able to accept about myself, or find difficult to accept? These could be a situation, circumstance, trait, or behavior. Choose one and look for its root:
  - What do I tell myself about me and that "thing?"
  - What parts of those words are true? What parts are not true? What's the evidence for each?
  - Think back to your inner child: does this lack of acceptance tie back to some belief I generated or experience I had when I was young?
  - What positive behaviors has this "thing" created? What have I learned from it?
  - What would I say to my inner child about it?
- Imagine your most accepting self: What would this version of me think and feel? What would he or she do differently than what I currently do? How can I embody this version of me just for today?

Mindfulness:
- Take 30–60 minutes for deep mindfulness practice, whether meditation, body scan, or yoga.
- Spend 30–60 minutes outdoors, intentionally slowing down to notice the colors, textures, and sounds around you. Breathe deeply and allow yourself to simply *be* in nature. (This is not a time for a workout!)

Wellness at Work

- Working with an HR partner or coach, talk as a team about the strengths and struggles you uncovered while doing the Diagnose phase work. Where do these show up at work? What strengths can the team leverage? Where can the team help with your struggles?

- Find a coworker you trust and discuss some aspects of the Diagnose work. Help each other identify blind spots or defense mechanisms when they show up at work.
- When you find yourself struggling to accept a difficult person or situation, pause, close your eyes, and take a few breaths, acknowledging the person or situation just as they are, without fixing or judging. Ask yourself what is good about this person or situation. Notice what emotions come up and ask yourself, "What can I control right now?" Then shift your focus to your next intentional action.

Reflect to Retain

What are three things I learned about myself from this chapter?
   1.

   2.

   3.

What are three concepts I want to remember from this chapter?
   1.

   2.

   3.

What is the one daily practice I will devote myself to as I read the next chapter?

1.

PART V

THE DEFINE PHASE

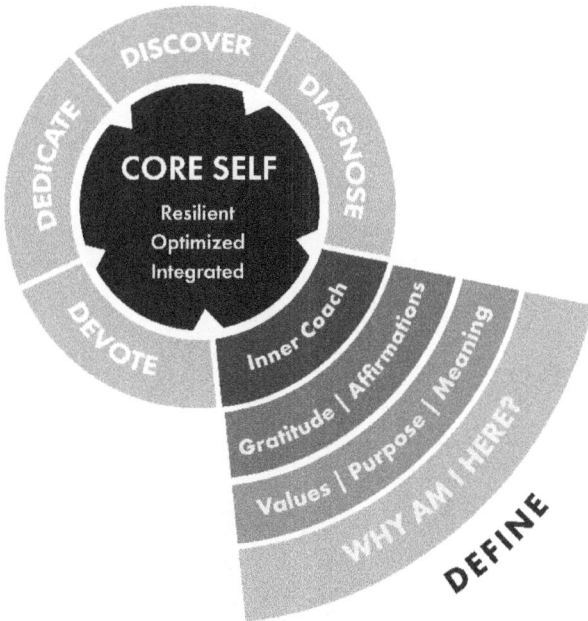

chapter 12

why am i here?

The Phase: Define
The Inquiry: Why Am I Here?
The Themes: Values, Purpose, and Meaning
The Skills: Gratitude and Affirmations
The Character: Inner Coach

Tell me, what is it you plan to do with your one wild
and precious life?
—MARY OLIVER

I HAVE A VERY VIVID MEMORY from my senior year in high school. I was in English class, and Miss Anderson was my teacher (she was amazing). As I have mentioned previously, I grew up in a very small town in Iowa and I graduated in a class of 77. We knew almost everyone in the whole high school, so I always felt comfortable speaking up during class.

I can't remember in what context this conversation started, but during this English class, I asked the question, "What, really, is the meaning of life?" I was not asking this from a place of curiosity, but from a place of anger (this was how I learned to show sadness, as you may remember me mentioning). Earlier that summer, my world had changed.

That summer was supposed to have been magical. My friends and I had big plans, as 17-year-olds often do, including things like hanging at the pool, making money to save for college, and hanging at the pond (or the "pits"). Brandi was one of my best friends at this time, and she had decided to leave Iowa in July to live with her dad in California for our senior year. Let's just say Brandi's stepdad wasn't awesome, and she needed a change. Our friend group was devastated, but we were going to live up the summer until she left.

Brandi was one of those high school girls who everyone likes and also envies. She had an on-again off-again boyfriend, Aaron, who we all thought wasn't good enough for her, but she loved him, so we supported her as best we could.

We were all going to miss her terribly.

We decided that we would all hang together during Brandi's last night in town. We planned on driving around (the only thing teenagers did in my town), sleeping over at her house, and then going with her and her mom to the airport the next day to send her off.

Brandi and Aaron were on "off-again" status at this point, but she still wanted to see him that night. She said she was going to meet us after saying goodbye to him, but she never showed up at the meeting place. This was long before cell phones, so we couldn't get in touch with her.

We waited. And waited. Then, we drove around looking for her. After a few hours, we gave up.

Before going home, I went to my friend Kristi's house. She lived two doors away from Brandi and two blocks from me. As Kristi was walking me home, Aaron's car came around the corner, and Brandi ran out. I said to Kristi, "Keep walking." We did.

When she caught up with us, Brandi was apologetic. She explained that she just couldn't say goodbye to Aaron. We continued to walk away from her, angry. Thankfully, I swallowed my frustration, stopped, turned around, and told her how mad I was that she had blown us off. I told her how much I was going to miss her. I gave her the biggest hug, and we cried. Brandi and I had been through a lot together, including a situation which could have ended the friendship when we were in ninth grade. This had made us stronger, and as I held her that last night, I knew my heart was going to miss her smile and laugh and that bounce in her step. I cried all the way home.

That was the last time I talked to Brandi. About a week later, on July 31, I got a phone call early in the morning from my friend Robin. Brandi and her father had been on a tandem bicycle the night before, and a drunk driver had hit them from behind. Brandi had been killed instantly. Her father was on life support and died a week later.

Words cannot explain what happened to me in those moments. I can clearly remember getting dressed in a daze, emerging from my room, and bursting into tears. My little brother followed me down the stairs, yelling for my mom. "Mom! *Mom!* Cara's crying and I don't know what's wrong! *Mom!*"

My life was forever changed.

Unfortunately, the pain was not over. Exactly one month later, on August 31, my baby cousin Casey died of a heart condition. He was ten days old.

Why? Why would God do this to a baby? To my aunt? Why?

Then, on September 30, my boyfriend's best friend died. He had been at a bachelor party in a town 30 miles away. He was the designated driver and had been driving back home around 3AM when he fell asleep at the wheel on a small Iowa highway. Rod liked to drive fast, so as soon as I heard the news, I knew he had probably been driving recklessly that night. I went to the site with my boyfriend, and we could see where Rod had crossed the center of the road and hit the gravel shoulder on the other side, overcorrected, went into the ditch, and hit the embankment of a country road that met the highway.

Suffice it to say, I hadn't had the greatest summer in the world. Naturally, I was angry, and my question directed at Miss Anderson— "What, really, is the meaning of life?"—was sincere. I wanted to know why we all had to be here, in this place, on this earth, full of death and disappointment and sadness and helplessness. My question was more like, "What's the effing point?" Knowing me, I maybe actually asked it that way! (Sorry, Miss A...)

Miss Anderson tried to answer, and I had a counterpoint to each of her points (I was a good, rational arguer, even at 17). So, she turned the question over to the class. "Who would like to share their thoughts on what the purpose of life is with Cara?"

Someone said it was to glorify God (insert teenage eyeroll here). Someone else said we were here to make other people happy and the world a better place. I responded that if no people were here, we wouldn't need to make them happy, so that argument didn't work. Miss A finally gave up and presented an assignment to the class: a one-page paper entitled "The Meaning of Life" in letter format to me. You're welcome, Jefferson-Scranton classmates.

Oh, how I wish I had kept those papers!

I found myself still asking that question almost 25 years later, when I was trying to figure out how to go back to work as a healthy person who knew how to effectively deal with the stress of a job. Somewhere inside, I knew that finding that answer was part of the solution.

Since then, I've found that the answer to that question comes in three parts:

- Values.
- Purpose.
- Meaning.

The first two I had already been working on with clients and teams for years in my HR and leadership development work. The third one would take some work for me to fully explore.

Once we're able to effectively work through our thoughts and emotions ("Discover") and understand where we have come from and how our experiences have shaped us ("Diagnose"), then we can do some of the fun work: we can start to identify what we value, what's most important to us, and what all the possibilities within this human experience are. Defining these three things (values, purpose, and meaning) is an important next step in leading your self well.

Values

Values are the fundamental principles that make us who we are. They shape our attitudes, actions, decision-making, the company we keep, and the jobs or organizations we seek out. They greatly influence our thought processes and help us define who we are in this world, and how we show up for ourselves and others. They are a compass when we need direction.

Deep down, they're probably the metric you use when you're evaluating whether your life is turning out the way you want it to. When the things you do and the way you behave match your values, life usually feels good. When they don't align, that's usually when things feel... off. In fact, this can be a real source of unhappiness and frustration.

Our values are developed over our lifetime and are influenced by our family, society, cultural upbringing, education, and personal life experiences. They're relatively stable throughout life but can shift and change as we have new experiences and are introduced to new ideas or situations. Generally, such shifts don't involve a complete change in the value, but in how it's expressed.

I've always had a need for and love of freedom and adventure. As a kid, I used to cherish the times I was allowed to walk the mile down to the creek and look for little creatures and treasures to take home (sometimes, the creatures *were* the treasures!). My mom was kind enough one time to house a bathtub full of tadpoles for days (I don't want to think about how that ended).

When Brandi, Casey, and Rod all died within two months of each other, that value became even stronger. I realized life was *really* short and that I needed to go see and do all that I could.

At 19, I took my first plane ride, which was to Germany, to work for the summer. I don't think I stopped being in a state of amazement for ten weeks straight! During this trip, my values of freedom and adventure were in full force, but completely shifted into a desire to experience more cultures and people outside the US.

I also have a strong need for stability. I need a place in the world I call home, and to have enough financial security that I don't have to worry about being able to make my house payment.

It seems like these values (stability and freedom) are opposites, but they're not. I value a balance between the two. In working through my values with a coach, we came up with a name to encompass them both: "stabili-free." I love this. It totally represents me and what's important to me, and I revisit it often.

The link between values and wellbeing is so obvious that it may be overlooked. Studies in the field of positive psychology have shown that when people know their core values and live in accordance with them, they experience greater overall wellbeing and life satisfaction.[1] They are also more likely to get into a state of flow, a term coined and defined by Mihaly Csikszentmihalyi as a state of complete absorption in an activity.

When in the flow state of work or an activity, people are able to push aside distracting thoughts and feelings.[2] Conversely, misalignment between values and actions can lead to frustration and burnout.[3]

Once you understand your values, you can use this knowledge to help make important decisions and to assess whether you're living in accordance with what's most important to you. Moreover, if you're a leader, helping your employees define their values can be an incredible step toward aligning what's important to them personally with the goals of their role and the organization. When this connection happens, you can imagine how much more enjoyable and engaging the work becomes for your team.

Values matter.

Purpose

> *This is the true joy in life, the being used for a purpose*
> *recognized by yourself as a mighty one...*
> —GEORGE BERNARD SHAW

Like values, your purpose shows you the way and provides direction for your life and decisions.

Your purpose is your reason for existing. It's why you're here. It also encapsulates one of those existential questions that's hard to answer but must be figured out if you're to lead a fulfilled life. Your purpose may shift and change somewhat throughout your life, but it's usually a common thread throughout the many eras of your existence.

Contrary to what a lot of people believe, your purpose is not your job. It's your gift to the world and those around you. It's your contribution, and it is as unique as your fingerprint. At first glance, it might look similar to someone else's purpose, but there are differences in the nuances. It's specific to you. It's your personal brand; what makes you tick; what you were sent here to do. Other people will often recognize your purpose even if you don't recognize it in yourself, because it's how you naturally show up in the world. It's often what you get compliments for, and when you do, you may think, *That's not really a purpose as such, or something to be particularly admired for. It's just who I am.*

My good friend Jennifer and I go for walks a lot. I'm lucky to live in a city with an abundance of parks and lakes, and walking around the city lakes is one of my favorite ways to unwind. During one such walk, I remember a conversation in which Jennifer was sharing something she had been struggling with at work, and I was helping her think through it, giving her some ideas on how to deal with her boss. Suddenly, she stopped in her tracks and said, "You're just so good at this. How do you come up with this stuff? You always know exactly the right words." She asked if we could do the *Cyreno de Bergerac* in her next meeting with her boss. I started laughing and told her I had no clue how I knew what to say. It just came to me. Upon reflection, I now know that my ability to coach her through that moment was a reflection of my purpose. That's why it felt so natural: it had become part of who I am as a person. For me, there's inherent joy and happiness in serving others—specifically, in helping others in their tough times. There's a science-based reason for that: having purpose and helping others creates a rush of oxytocin, dopamine, and serotonin, our happiness neurotransmitters.[4]

We're constantly being told who or what we should be by society, our parents, and our friends, but we have a responsibility to find out who we are and what we can contribute, and to then show up in the world as that person. Our individuality is our greatest gift, and so when we can exude that, the rest comes so much more easily. On the contrary, when we don't understand our values or purpose, we flounder, trying to be someone or something else for the world. This means we never fully bring our gifts or our full self to the people around us. Knowing our purpose and living it is essential for personal wellbeing, the success of the workplace, and the betterment of all. I promise you there is someone out there who needs exactly what you bring to the table, whether your knowledge, creativity, expertise, or just your personality. No one else can play your part.

We moved to a different town when I was 11 and, upon hearing the news, one of the women from our church said to my mom, "I wonder who needs you in Jefferson?" I love this philosophy.

The Purpose In Life (PIL) Scale measures an individual's sense of purpose. There's an entire body of research on PIL that focuses on the interaction between the mind and body and how our purpose can affect our health. Findings from this research have consistently shown several factors to be associated with a strong sense of purpose, including higher levels of wellbeing, lower levels of depression and anxiety, better mental health outcomes, and even lower risk factors for heart disease. There has also been increasing research using PIL to assess one's risk of Alzheimer's in later years, with one study showing that those with a high PIL score were half as likely to develop Alzheimer's as those with a low PIL score. They were also 30% less likely to develop mild cognitive impairment.[5]

A more recent study of middle-aged adults published in 2023 showed that higher PIL scores may promote resilience against already-present brain changes. Results also showed greater neural connectivity in some areas of the brain correlated with cognitive performance.[6] A review of the literature on purpose has additionally shown a link between PIL to decreased stroke risk, improved sleep, and lower risk of mortality and frailty in older adults.[7]

Purpose matters.

Meaning

> *He who has a why to live for can bear almost any how.*
> —*FRIEDRICH NIETZCHE*

When people talk about meaning, they're usually asking the question my 17-year-old self put forward in Miss Anderson's class: "Who am I and why do I exist?"

We are meaning-making machines. Our brains are wired for it.

One of the most famous books on meaning is Viktor E. Frankl's *Man's Search for Meaning*. I was required to read this in my humanities class during freshman year of college, and it had a profound impact on me and how I saw the world. Less than two years had passed since those devastating and shocking losses, and I was still asking the question, "What does all of this mean? What's the point?" To make matters worse, I had finally broken up with an abusive boyfriend yet was still blaming myself for what I could have done better. All in all, I wasn't emotionally well. I still owe apologies to my first two college roommates for my behavior back then. Ann and Stacy, if you're reading this, I am so sorry.[*]

In his timeless and inspirational book, Frankl shares his personal experience as a Holocaust survivor in the context of his professional background in psychology and philosophy. He proposes that finding a sense of purpose and meaning in life is essential for human wellbeing and resilience, and that it's possible to find this even in the most extreme and challenging circumstances. While trapped in Nazi concentration camps, he observed that those who were able to find meaning or a reason to keep going were more likely to endure and survive the harsh conditions. This observation led him to conclude that individuals have the power to choose their attitude and find meaning even in their suffering.

---

[*] For the record, I didn't do anything horrible. I was just emotional and, I am sure, difficult to live with. But I digress...

According to Frankl, the pursuit of meaning is the primary force that shapes our lives. He purports that individuals can find meaning through three main avenues:[8]

- Creative value.
- Experiential value.
- Attitudinal value.

Let's look at each of these.

Creative Value

Creative value involves creating work or doing deeds that benefit yourself and the world.

Before I moved to Roatan, I had dreams of living in a place where there was no to-do list. Fast forward to when I quit my corporate job, had been living in Roatan for about three months, and I had started my job at Frank's Cigar Bar. I was yearning for something to be on my to-do list; to be needed; to contribute, even in the small way of ensuring the bar was clean. And it was surprisingly rewarding! This is also when I started studying to become a dive master and volunteering at the SOL (School of Life) Foundation with my chef friend Ed once a week, to help the kiddos of the island with cooking skills and homework. In the absence of the hustle and bustle of corporate life, I needed (and found) creative value.

Experiential Value

Frankl recognized that people can also find meaning through direct *experiences*, particularly through deep connection with others, creating what he called experiential value. He found that higher meaning can be derived from the experiences we have in loving relationships, moments of beauty, or profound encounters with nature or art. He believed that by appreciating life's moments, we can connect with a deeper sense of existence; a more profound dimension of life.

When I was learning to scuba dive, I was sometimes frustrated with how slowly the instructors leading the dives would swim. I wanted to move; to swim faster. Diving taught me to slow down; and to find awe in a piece of coral or in watching nature, like seeing Pederson cleaner shrimp living and "dancing" in a corkscrew anemone. I now love to stop and watch an octopus slink in and out of the coral. I can hover in one place for a *long* time quite happily, basking in the beauty of my surroundings. Through slowing down, I learned experiential value.

Forging deep connections is also a path to experiential value. Deeply knowing another person (whether romantically or as a friend) while allowing them to truly see you in return is a profoundly enriching experience. It involves a true sense of vulnerability that can be like a mirror reflecting your innermost thoughts, fears, and dreams. In this space of connection, there's a profound sense of acceptance, where flaws and imperfections are cherished and even celebrated. It's a feeling of safety and belonging; a place where you can be your most authentic self without fear of judgment. It's a partnership that supports growth and wellbeing — and creates experiential value.

Creating this type of connection can be difficult, as there's risk involved. As we have covered, it can feel incredibly difficult to allow yourself to fully trust in someone else, especially if your past experiences taught you that doing so could put you at risk. When you're busy protecting yourself and your sovereignty and defending yourself against perceived threats, it's almost impossible to create truly deep relationships. You stay close to the surface, never *fully* experiencing deep connection, or you get beyond the surface but just "so" deep, protecting the most precious and difficult parts of you. If this is you, I suggest you go back to

Chapter 11 and revisit the end-of-chapter exercises. The payoff (experiential value) is worth the time and exploration.

Attitudinal Value

The most profound insight from Frankl's work, for me, concerned attitudinal value. He believed that we can find meaning even in the most painful and challenging circumstances. He saw that while we cannot always choose what happens to us, we can always choose the attitude we have toward those events. We can find meaning by enduring the suffering with courage, resilience, and dignity. Our suffering can be used as an opportunity for personal growth and self-discovery.

When I first moved to Minneapolis, I met a woman at work who ultimately became a dear friend. Lori was going through her second divorce at the time, and it was tumultuous. Her soon-to-be-ex-husband could be considered a narcissist, and the marriage was ending in a dramatic fashion due to his cheating, lying, and other demeaning behaviors. I was shocked, angry, and sad when Lori told me the story, but chiefly, I was fascinated by her response: Lori was actively choosing not to give him or the drama her time. Instead, she stayed engaged in her work and other parts of her life. Most people at work didn't even know she was going through a divorce. Of course she had moments of deep grief and sadness, but she didn't let it define her because she made a conscious choice to stay true to herself, hold her dignity, and have faith that this was in her best interests. She found meaning in her struggle and the loss of the relationship. The experience could have flattened her, but instead, she made a conscious choice to use it as an opportunity for growth. She didn't push her emotions or devastation under the rug, but learned and grew from them.

While Lori's story has nothing on surviving the Holocaust, part of the human experience *is* pain. We have all encountered it, and we will all encounter it again. It's how we respond to that pain that determines how and how quickly we come out of it.

The freedom to choose our inner attitude when we have control over absolutely nothing else can lead us to higher meaning, and meaning is important. It's what gets us out of bed in the morning. It's what urges us to achieve things, create and maintain relationships, and seek out fun. It's what helps us define our values and purpose.

Meaning matters.

The Define Phase Character: Your Inner Coach

Values, purpose, and meaning serve as a compass pointing to your true and highest self. This is where the next character in your "core self" comes into play: your inner coach.

By definition, a coach is someone who provides guidance and support in various aspects of life. They're someone who sees you, knows you, and can help you see yourself; someone who guides you to unlock your full potential, even if you're already incredibly talented.

There are countless athletes who are considered the GOAT (greatest of all time) in their sport who have attributed their massive success to the support and guidance they received from a coach:

> *Coach Mills has been a guiding light in my career, helping me to see and reach my full potential.*
> —USAIN BOLT

Bob [Phelps' coach] and I have been through a lot together. He's been a vital part of my success, pushing me when I needed it and believing in me even when I didn't believe in myself.
—MICHAEL PHELPS

All the little things that he [Tom Coughlin] asked of me made me a better player and ultimately a better man ... everything he demands comes from a place of love... He made us all better human beings."
—MICHAEL STRAHAN

I've hired an external coach three times in my career. I've always been incredibly grateful for their support, guidance, accountability, and lessons. One of the things that has been most life-changing has been their ability to help me develop my own inner coach.

An inner coach is an often-untapped resource within each of us that serves as a guiding force to a more purposeful and fulfilling career and life. This internal mentor is deeply connected to our core values and purpose and can help us create meaning in our daily life. They encourage us to reflect on what truly matters by contemplating our talents and the impact we want to make in the world.

Connecting with your inner coach may take some time, but through intentional exercises, you can find this voice. Doing so (and being able to call on them when needed) is an excellent way to work with the inner child and inner critic. Following the guidance of your inner coach, you can better understand and nurture your inner child while challenging the harsh and inaccurate opinions of your inner critic. You can also call on your inner coach to help define your values, purpose, and meaning, all of which provide direction.

Leadership and Meaning, Purpose, and Values

Operating from values and purpose helps us decide what we say yes and no to in our lives. We are inundated with *so many options* for how we spend our resources (time, money, and mindshare) that it can be overwhelming. If you don't have an idea of what's fundamentally most important and why you're here, you'll flounder and waste precious resources on activities, people, and things that just don't matter to you.

Have you known people who flit from job to job, industry to industry, and relationship to relationship searching for something that even *they* can't define? They're probably struggling because they haven't been able to define their values and purpose.

When you hold a value dear to your heart and someone else doesn't find that value important, you may get triggered. Here is an example of how that shows up at work:

Through my own work, I have honed down the values that are most important to me, and two of them are authenticity and transparency. These often go hand in hand. I have no poker face. When someone asks my opinion on something (whether it's a work project or their new haircut), I give it to them. I try to do so respectfully (not always successfully), but I tell the truth. Sugarcoating or saying something just to make someone feel good feels inauthentic or like a lie to me, and my need for authenticity is so strong that I can't do it. Often when someone, in my viewpoint, was not being authentic (whether they were kissing up to the boss, pretending they cared about others, or giving false compliments to ingratiate people with them), I had a difficult time working with them. I didn't respect them, and because of my need for authenticity, I didn't necessarily try to hide it.

What I learned through this work is that other people can value different things, and that doesn't make them bad or wrong. Maybe someone highly values achievement and being complimentary and warm to others helps them to live out that value. Who am I to say that my value is better than theirs?

What I *can* do is notice that the person violates my own personal values and still choose to accept them for who they are (refer to Chapter 11 for more detail on acceptance). I can get curious. I can ask questions about what drives them. I can get to know them a bit better instead of judging them and creating a chasm in a work relationship.

Values are also great because they provide a metric by which to check yourself. When you're feeling off, you can ask yourself, "Am I living in alignment with my values?" Often, the answer will be no. Once identified, it's possible to adjust your behavior and bring it back to what's important to you.

These days, if I spend too much time in the US, I start to get anxious. I feel lost. As my sister once told me, "You're happiest when you're out in the world, Cara." Stabili-free. This value must be honored, or I'm guaranteed to feel "off."

Embedding meaning, values, and purpose into the workplace is essential for effective team leadership and organizational success. I've seen throughout my career that when leaders are able to help employees create a strong sense of meaning and purpose in their work and lives, their employees are more engaged, motivated, and productive. This, in turn, leads to higher job satisfaction and overall wellbeing, which ultimately benefits the organization and its customers.

There are leaders who are great at this, and there are leaders who don't make the time for it. The latter is a mistake, especially in today's environment. Millennials and Gen Zers in particular place a strong emphasis on purpose and meaning in their careers. They are more likely to seek out employers and organizations that align with their values and offer opportunities for them to contribute to society in a bigger way. According to the Deloitte Millennial Survey, 76% of millennials believe that businesses should focus on more than just financial performance and should also prioritize societal and environmental impact (a higher meaning and purpose).[9]

Leaders who understand the values and priorities of these generations are more likely to attract and retain top talent who will work harder for the organization and their customers. In fact, 39% of Gen Z and 34% of millennials have turned down employers that don't align with their values.[10]

Studies have also demonstrated a clear link between a sense of purpose at work and employee performance. A 2021 study summarized in Harvard Business Review found that employees who derive meaning from their work are more likely to stay with their organization, be more engaged, and demonstrate higher levels of performance.[11] Gallup has also found that organizations with higher levels of engagement and a clear sense of purpose outperform their competitors in terms of productivity, profitability, and customer loyalty.[12]

Some of the most profound work I've done with individual clients and teams has been around values and purpose. In my practice, I've found that leaders who are able to navigate the sometimes-"mushy" conversations about what matters most to employees are also the ones who are able to get the best out of their team, and who can rally the team around a purpose that matters to the company *and* to the employees. They take the time to get to know their employees, what they value, how they can align their work with those values, and where individual team members' values might cause friction. It's a "slow down to speed up" strategy. Leaders often want a shortcut, and I advise against this if you're looking for long-term success.

Meaning, purpose, and values at work matter.

Reflect to Retain

What are three things I learned about myself from this chapter?
   1.

   2.

   3.

What are three concepts I want to remember from this chapter?
   1.

   2.

   3.

chapter 13

the define phase skills

The two most important days in a man's life are the day on which he was born and the day on which he discovers why.

—MINISTER ERNEST T. CAMPBELL

(Commonly attributed to Mark Twain)

T HERE ARE A COUPLE OF SKILLS that can help in the Define phase as you find and live out your purpose, values, and higher meaning. These are gratitude and affirmations.

Gratitude

My mom used to say to us as children, "What if you woke up tomorrow with only what you were grateful for today?" This is overwhelming to think about. Right at this moment, I could decide to be grateful for so many things I never even consider:

- Accessible clean water, to fill my water bottle.

- My (fun) water bottle!
- The fact I can breathe easily.
- The fact my heart works.
- Sunshine!
- Vision.
- The ability to think clearly and type.
- Pistachios.
- My big toe (imagine waking up without it!).

How many things do we forget to be grateful for each and every day? Each and every moment?

Gratitude is a transformative process that has the capacity to instantly change our mindset and enhance our overall wellbeing and perspective. At its core, gratitude involves simply recognizing and appreciating the positive aspects of our lives, big and small. In challenging times, there is always something (and someone) for which we can be grateful, and cultivating a practice of gratitude shifts our mind from "lack" and focuses our attention on the abundance around us.

Gratitude produces long-lasting feelings of happiness and contentment via the release of dopamine and serotonin. It also leads to improved mental health and stronger relationships, personally and professionally.[1] Above all, practicing gratitude in all situations can help foster our values, purpose, and sense of meaning, even in difficult times.

Gratitude is a skill. A skill you can develop.

Affirmations

If you're a Gen Xer (or older) and you watched *Saturday Night Live* in the 90s, the word "affirmation" might remind you of Stuart Smalley. Stuart was known for his "show" called *Daily Affirmations with Stuart Smalley*, and his famous tagline was, "I'm good enough, I'm smart enough, and doggonit, people like me!"[2] (If you didn't grow up with the pleasure of watching this live, I highly recommend the sketch with Stuart and Michael Jordan!)

Affirmations are positive statements or phrases that, when repeated to yourself regularly, reinforce a particular belief or mindset. Your cells are in constant communication and the things that you say to yourself matter (as we have discussed). Affirmations are a form of self-talk directed at achieving growth and self-improvement. They are designed to replace negative thoughts and beliefs with more positive ones.

A lot of people scoff at affirmations. I used to be one of those people. But there is real science behind what they can do for you, your health, and your goals. Remember the confirmation bias? If you're smart, you can use this shortcut to your advantage. When you're consistent with your affirmations, eventually, your brain learns to search for signs that will make that affirmation come true. At some point, these signs come to your conscious mind, and you begin to notice things that help achieve that goal, whatever it may be.

My dad has (unknowingly) used this strategy to his advantage his entire life. He may possibly be the most optimistic person I know, especially in terms of his belief in his ability to succeed in anything, whether professionally or in his personal life. My favorite example of this happened on the golf course. He and I used to play in a parent/child best ball tournament every September. One year, on our way out to the course, he said to me, "I think we can win this year." I rolled my eyes. "Dad, neither of us is good enough to win this thing." But he was convinced— "If you have a couple of good drives...my short game has been good...if we each make a couple of lucky putts—I think we can do it." He'd convinced himself there was a path to victory. On hole 11, a par 5 for men and par 4 for women, I clocked one off the tee right in the middle of the fairway. (I actually won longest drive for that shot.) And my dad? Well, he put it in from about 130 out. A double eagle! Now we didn't win the tournament—but when you affirm that you can do something, your brain helps find a way to make things happen!

Affirmations have also been shown to increase activity in the areas of the brain used for self-related processing, meaning they can help buffer against painful or negative information. A review of the research on affirmations shows that they help us:

- Decrease stress, rumination, and anxiety.
- Perceive critical messages with less resistance (hello, performance reviews or constructive feedback!).
- Increase feelings of hopefulness.
- Boost problem-solving.
- Prepare you for meetings by calming nerves, increasing confidence, and improving chances of a successful outcome[3].

There are a few simple steps you can take to develop and use this skill effectively:

- Identify your goal or desire to see positive change.
- Create statements that are positive, concise, and specific.
- Use vocabulary that resonates with you personally.
- Implement a consistent affirmations practice (your brain needs time to integrate these messages).
- Repeat these statements aloud while visualizing the outcomes.

My mom somehow also knew the importance of affirmations. She was a fourth-grade schoolteacher, and at the beginning of every year, she would provide her students with a handout entitled "Think Positive," which had ten statements. It was an old-school mimeographed copy that she printed, colored, and then laminated for each student. Every day, after they had said the Pledge of Allegiance, my mom would make the entire class read those statements—the positive affirmations—aloud.

One day when my mom was in the hospital, I went out for lunch and when I returned, she directed me to an envelope where she had written some things down. "Are these notes for your funeral?" I asked. They were. In the bottom corner, she had written the word "handouts." I laughed. "Handouts?"

She said, "Well, I *am* a teacher. There are some things I think everyone needs to have." The "Think Positive" handout was one of them. We honored her request, and there were dozens of former students at her funeral who were so happy to get another copy. *

About 12 years after she passed away, a friend forwarded a story from the Des Moines Register to me. It was about a lawyer with a practice in Des Moines. She had the "Think Positive" handout (her original from fourth grade) framed in her office next to her law degree. She talked about how it changed her life so much that she gave it to each of her clients and requested they read it every day while working with her. My mom's legacy living on…

Positive affirmation is a skill. A skill you can develop.

Actively doing this work around meaning, values, and purpose may seem hokey. It may even embarrass you at first and as a leader, you might question the value of this type of work. What I would say to this is, aside from a bit of extra time spent on journaling and exploration, it requires no additional work whatsoever. It merely involves doing what you already do every day, through a different lens. I, for one, have seen values and purpose work change teams and individuals in the workplace. I encourage you to explore this side of yourself and your team, even if it feels uncomfortable.

---

* You can download a copy of this original handout using a link in the appendices.

THE DEFINE PHASE: PUT IT INTO PRACTICE

Inquire Within

Choose one of the topics below and spend 30–60 minutes on the exercise.

Cultivate Your Inner Coach:

Find a quiet place where you can spend at least 30 minutes alone.

Start with three deep breaths using any breathwork technique you choose, as long as the breaths go into your diaphragm and include longer exhales than inhales. Close your eyes and imagine your inner coach. What do they look like? Is it a person or an image? A she or a he? Or neither? How do they communicate with you? What do they know about you? What are the best traits you have that they can see? (This is *not* a time to be shy. Your coach sees the very best in you.)

Ask your coach:

- What guidance do you have for me in terms of identifying my values, purpose, and meaning?
- How can I align my actions with my values?
- What advice do you have for me so I can lead my self well?
- How can I be kinder to and more supportive of my self and the people in my life?

Journal about what you learn in this "dialogue." Notice any sensations you feel as you connect with your inner coach. What's happening in your chest, heart, and gut? Do you feel lighter anywhere? Heavier?

Identify Your Values:

Clarifying your values is *not* best done by selecting them from a list. Although that can be helpful, starting with a list leads to a sort of "vote" on what society has told you is most desirable or socially acceptable, rather than identifying who you really are and what's important to you. Values are observable. You live them. The best way to identify them is therefore to examine situations where you felt your best and uncover the values that are already there. Begin by taking some time to journal about the following:

- Identify one of the happiest times of your life. What were you doing? Who were you with? What factors contributed to this happiness?

- Identify some of the proudest moments of your life. Why were you proud? Who shared the moment with you? What factors contributed to this feeling?

- Identify some of the most fulfilling times of your life. What need or desire was fulfilled at this time? How and why did the experience give your life meaning? What factors contributed to this fulfillment?

- Beyond the basics (food, shelter, water), what *must* you have in your life in order to be fulfilled? (Partnership? Travel? Creativity? Music?)

- Think about a time when you were angry, frustrated, or really upset. What were the circumstances? What made it so maddening? What factors contributed to these feelings and emotions? What did you do in response to this situation? In hindsight, would you have done anything differently? (In this example, you can look for values that were *not* being honored by yourself or the other person, or values that were completely ignored or blatantly violated.)

After journaling about these experiences, think about what values are associated with each of them. Considering your answers to the previous questions and what you already know is important to you:

- List the values identified that are most important to you. Feel free to combine some values if it helps you to clarify what they mean for you—for example, "learning/growth/expansion." You can also make up a word from other values (as I did with "stabili-free"). There's a list of values in the appendices if you need some help.
- Prioritize these values by ranking them 1—10 (I know this is hard) and score how satisfied you currently are with how each of these is showing up in your life.

Value / Value Combination	Value Ranking	Current Satisfaction

Create Affirmations

Create affirmations for your own personal goals. These can be related to work, physical health, mindset, how you interact with your family and friends, personal learning goals... whatever is important to you.

Here are a few sample affirmations I use in my daily practice:

- I manage my emotions, thoughts, and beliefs so I can see the world as it really is, not as my mind is making it out to be. I welcome opportunities throughout the day to practice this skill.
- I try new things without fear of embarrassment. This is necessary for me to grow and implement new learnings. I feel transformed by the new skills I master through practice.
- I am highly focused and productive when I'm working with clients and building my business. In this space, I make decisions and accomplish tasks efficiently and effectively.
- I am in tune with my body's needs. I listen to my body with love and care and treat it with kindness and respect.
- I take action every day to nurture my body, physically and mentally.
- When practicing acceptance of something: I accept that [this situation] is not exactly as I wish it were. I trust that life unfolds as it should, even when I don't understand it.

Create a list of three to ten affirmations to use in your daily practice.

Daily Practice Ideas

Choose one of the practices below and practice it daily for 2 – 4 weeks.

- When you notice you're irritated, angry, sad, or annoyed about something, call on your inner coach to help you through the situation before responding or reacting. Ask them:
  - Is one of my values not being honored here?
  - How can I communicate that (if appropriate)?
  - What can I do to bring that value to the situation right now?
  - How do I want to show up in this situation?

- Practice gratitude. Make it a habit. Find something you do in your everyday life (such as walking to meetings, getting in your car, or using the bathroom) and use those times as a reminder to think of three things you are grateful for at that moment.
- Create a morning or evening affirmation practice for 2 weeks.

Wellness Wednesday (When-sday)

Choose one of the activities below to complete on your Wellness Day.

- Think about a person for whom you are grateful. What have they done to contribute to your life? How have they made you a better person? Write that person a letter and send it to them or call them to say thank you.
- Do you have a decision to make? Think through that decision using your values.
  - o Identify your options or choices for the decision.
  - o For each option, take your top ten values from the Inquire Within exercise and project how that option would support each of your values (using a 1–10 scale).
  - o Evaluate your scores as you make your decision.
- Spend some time working on finding your purpose. You can start with answering the following questions. Then, write a statement that encapsulates your sense of purpose, even if it's still evolving.
  - o What did I learn about myself and what strengths and abilities did I hone through my childhood experiences (Chapter 10)?
  - o What activities or interests bring me the most fulfillment? What specifically about those activities makes me feel fulfilled?
  - o What are my values? How do they tie into my overall purpose?

- o What activities or subjects am I passionate about? What do I gravitate toward learning or doing in my free time?
- o What skills and talents have I picked up? What is the one thing I am "known" for? What makes the people around me say, "You're so good at X"?
- o What impact do I want to have on my family? My community? The world?

- Spend some time thinking about how you can cultivate more meaning in your life through the three avenues to meaning defined by Viktor Frankl:
    - o **CREATIVE VALUE:** Where can you create work or do something for yourself and the world? Could you do some volunteer activities? Could you mentor someone?
    - o **EXPERIENTIAL VALUE:** Where can you deeply appreciate life's experiences? Could you find time in nature? Plan an adventure (large or small) to a place you haven't been? Spend intentional quality time with someone you love?
    - o **ATTITUDINAL VALUE:** Where can you find meaning through your attitude and perspective in challenging times? Can you look for humor when faced with a frustrating moment? Can you reframe the situation by asking yourself, "What can I learn here?"

Wellness at Work

Values:

Take some time to help your employees identify their values. You can assign the "Identify Your Values" exercise in the "Inquire With" section as pre-work and talk about it as a group or in your individual 1:1 meetings. Notice where your employees' values align and where they might conflict with each other. Openly talk about how the team can honor every person's values during the workday. (My experience has shown that this work is best facilitated by a coach or an HR partner, so the leader can be a participant in the room and further foster trust, authenticity, and buy-in.) Once you have had this conversation, work with a coach or your HR partner to facilitate a team session to create a team purpose focused on what the team wants to accomplish together over the next 6—12 months. Identify how this will help the customer, the organization, and the employees themselves. Start by brainstorming with the team:

- Why do we exist? What can this team do that no one else can?
- What would make us excited about participating on this team?

Gratitude:

Express gratitude at work. Don't do this in a weird and awkward way by making people go around the room and say something they are grateful for, or by asking each person to thank everyone formally. Simply make it part of the way you show up. If you consistently do so openly and with gratitude, your team will follow your lead. I have seen it happen!

Inner Coach:

As a coach to your employees, help them find their own inner coach by walking them through the "Cultivate Your Inner Coach" subsection. Ask them to reflect on these questions and share with you (as they feel comfortable):

- What they learned about how their inner coach sees them.
- How their inner coach can help them with this specific work/project/work relationship.
- How you can support them from a place of working *with* this part of them.

Reflect to Retain

What are three things I learned about myself from this chapter?

    1.

    2.

    3.

What are three concepts I want to remember from this chapter?

    1.

    2.

    3.

What is the one daily practice I will devote myself to as I read the next chapter?

    1.

PART VI

THE DEVOTE PHASE

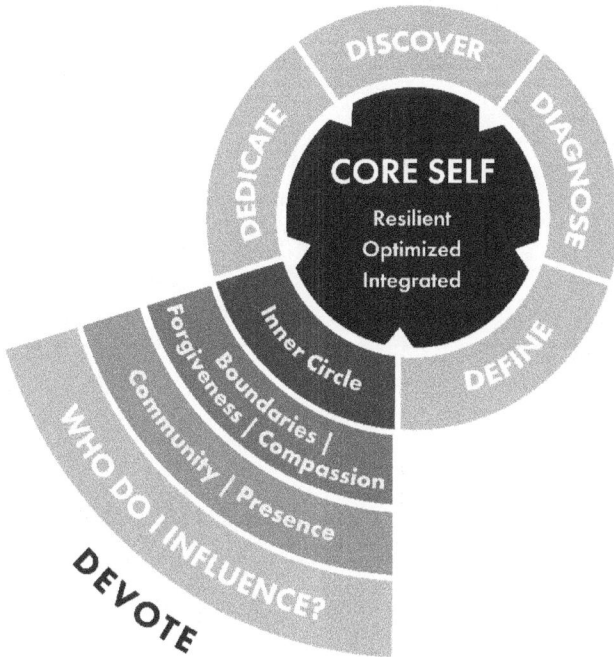

chapter 14

who do i influence?

The Phase: Devote

The Inquiry: Who Do I Influence?

The Themes: Community and Presence

The Skills: Forgiveness, Boundaries, and Compassion

The Character: Inner Circle

A NYONE IN MY LIFE HAS LIKELY heard me refer to them as part of my "team," whether my friends, family, coworkers, or partners. I live my life thinking about my relationships as my teams, even if just a team of two. I often start friend group texts with, "Hey there, team!" There is something about being a part of a team that stirs the deepest emotions within me. It conjures a sense of connection that hits my soul. These are the people with whom I share my experiences, aspirations, and celebrations. I also share my frustrations, sad times, and concerns. Therefore, throughout this chapter, I will refer to the various groups of people in our lives as our "team," "community," or "circle."

The Devote phase is about answering the question, "Who do I influence?" It's crucial to truly understand your impact on the people, or the teams, in your life (and their impact on you) if you are to lead your self and your team well. This is where the focus in this process begins to move from you to others.

Community: The People in Our Lives

We walk through life interacting with and influencing people in big and small ways all day long, from those we live with and the strangers we pass in the car to our coworkers and employees in our offices and on our Zoom calls. These interactions either contribute to or constrict our daily experience. Abraham Maslow identified "belonging" as a fundamental human need, just above food, water, shelter, and safety.[1] We *need* people and connection.

One of my favorite movies is *The Shawshank Redemption*. I love the scene where Andy (Tim Robbins) locks a guard in the bathroom and plays opera music over the loudspeaker in the yard, and the prisoners all stop and listen. It's a beautiful moment. But Andy pays a steep price for this: he's thrown in solitary confinement.[2] There's a reason why solitary confinement is such an effective form of punishment: we need connection to survive, as Maslow said.

There are four categories of people that make up our circle and provide us with connection and a sense of belonging. These groups and individuals are important to identify when we're thinking about how we influence and how we are influenced by others.

- **OUR ORIGINAL TEAM:** the family we were born into or raised by, including extended family and close family friends. This team greatly shapes our early experiences, values, and beliefs. It's our first social network, and it hopefully provides us with a sense of belonging and teaches us how to love, cooperate, and handle conflict.

- **OUR WORK TEAM**: comprised of our coworkers, peers, employees, bosses, contractors… all the people we come into contact with because of our work.
- **OUR COMMUNITY TEAM**: the people we know or interact with because of where we live. Some of these are people we know personally, such as our neighbors, doctor, hairstylist, or car mechanic. Many of them are strangers, such as the man we pass in the grocery store, the terrible driver on the road, the unhoused guy on the corner, or the cashier where we shop.
- **OUR CHOSEN TEAM**: team members who exist in varying degrees of "closeness," but every member has something in common: we care about them to some degree, and they care about us. We *choose* them. This team (especially the members who are closest to us) is very important. This is our "inner circle." Our family is often part of our chosen team but doesn't have to be.

The Devote Phase Character: Your Inner Circle

Your inner circle is a select group of individuals who hold a special place in your life. This circle is invaluable as the emotional bonds formed with these people provide numerous benefits for your mental wellbeing. There are two important aspects of this circle: (1) how you show up for and help them and (2) when to call on them to help you. If you're reading this thinking, "I don't need anyone," remember that ultra-independence is often a defense mechanism and a learned response to childhood wounds. I'd encourage you to revisit chapters 10 and 11 to do some exploring into the root of that characteristic.

There are several benefits to being a part of the teams in your life, especially your inner circle.

- **SHARED EXPERIENCE:** Whether in the form of a six-month work project, 18 years of raising a child together, exploring a new country with someone, or simply sharing eye contact and a smile, we go through our days, weeks, and lives sharing big and small experiences with those around us. Shared experiences strengthen our sense of belonging and activate brain regions associated with social connection and reward, releasing oxytocin, the feelgood chemical.[3] When a certain event takes place in a social context, the brain's memory systems engage more effectively, enhancing memory formation and recall, making the memory more vivid and long lasting.[4]

- **SAFETY IN THE FACE OF ADVERSITY:** Being human comes with some degree of pain, but you don't have to face those challenges alone. Ideally, you can rely on your inner circle for emotional support, encouragement, and guidance.

- **GROWTH AND DEVELOPMENT:** Those with different skills and perspectives challenge us to expand our own perspectives and skills. Have you ever played a game or worked on a team with people who were more skilled than you? What happened? Probably, you improved. Your inner circle can also help you see your blind spots, so you can cultivate better self-awareness (see Chapter 9). When you work with someone collaboratively, you engage in joint problem-solving and knowledge integration, leading to an enhanced understanding of the subject or situation.

The teams in our lives are sometimes there for the long-haul and sometimes specific to a time or experience in our lives. One of my favorite teams lasted for exactly 100 days: my "team" when participating in a bicycle ride across America with almost 300 other people. This was when the Internet was dial-up and before cellphones were common, so all we had was each other.

I wasn't a cyclist. I was just very young and thought the ride sounded like a cool experience. So, I signed up with big intentions to train.

I didn't. At all.

As a result, I relied heavily on that team (who were initially strangers) to help me, especially in those early days. I didn't know how to change a flat tire, I didn't know that I needed a tarp for my tent (thank you, Jay, for giving me your extra one), and I didn't know how to fix my seat when it popped off after I couldn't get my feet out of the pedals quickly enough and I fell over on day 1 (true story—I still have the chain link scars). Nearing the end of the ride, I no longer needed help with those things, but I did need emotional support. On day 82, I remember wanting to throw my bike over the guardrail and hitchhike home.

At the end, I didn't want to celebrate with anyone but them. Our shared experience, our achievement through sustained adversity, and the way we grew individually and as a "family" was something rare. Without this team, I would never have made it.

Unfortunately, being a part of a team isn't always sunshine and rainbows. What happens when your teammates don't step up during challenges and setbacks? What happens when they're not able to contribute with action, or even comforting words or a fresh perspective? In these situations, being a part of a team can feel like an enormous risk, and for some, a huge responsibility. How or whether people show up in their teams (in work and life) will very much depend on how their family "team" influenced them growing up and how they have experienced team dynamics in the past. The person who must do everything on their own, the person who can do *nothing* on their own, the employee who needs everyone's collaboration, the employee who doesn't care what anyone else thinks… all of these players can be detrimental to your team's (and workplace's) success.

If you grew up not trusting your family (your original team), you will likely have a very difficult time being vulnerable with others. You may have learned early on that it's risky to count on others, or that you have to carry the burden of teammates who aren't able to contribute emotionally, physically, or financially. If you find this to be your experience, I recommend you go back to Chapter 11 and do some deep work on understanding yourself and the influences from your childhood. You may also deeply benefit from talking with a professional to help you unlock this understanding. Refer to the appendices for some resources for finding a qualified therapist.

Loneliness and Connection

> I used to think the worst thing in life was to end up alone. It's not. The worst thing in life is to end up with people who make you feel alone.
> —BOBCAT GOLDTHWAIT
> (Quoted by Robin Williams in World's Greatest Dad)

What happens when we don't feel like we have a team? Very often, loneliness sets in.

Let's be clear here: being *alone* and being *lonely* are not the same thing. I've lived alone for most of my life, but I am rarely lonely. Being alone means being physically by yourself, and this can be an excellent time for self-reflection, relaxation, and personal growth (not to mention completing most of the exercises in this book!). Being lonely, on the other hand, is an uncomfortable emotional state caused by a lack of meaningful social connection. It often involves feelings of sadness, emotional isolation, or a desire for companionship. You can be lonely in a crowded room, even if you know everyone there. You can be lonely in a committed relationship. Superficial connections do not alleviate loneliness.

While being alone can be a great source of growth, being lonely can lead to very negative outcomes. In fact, loneliness has a profound impact on both mental and physical wellbeing, so much so that, in June of 2022, the American Medical Association officially recognized loneliness as a public health issue.[5] The World Health Organization (WHO) quickly followed suit in November of 2023, launching the Commission on Social Connection to address loneliness as a pressing health threat and to create solutions to combat it.[6] Loneliness was not created during the pandemic, but it certainly exacerbated it.

Not only does loneliness impact our personal experience, but it also changes our brain. Neuroscience shows that lonely people report less trust (and act in less trusting ways) and show high levels of depression symptoms.[7] In addition, there are real health, and therefore cost, implications of loneliness. These include an increased risk of premature death from *all* causes, 50% increased risk of dementia, nearly 30% increased risk of heart disease and stroke, and higher rates of depression, anxiety, and suicide.[8] And, of course, there are business impacts. A staggering 62% of employed adults consider themselves lonely. That's *more than half of your team*. Lonely employees miss work almost six times more than employees who are not lonely and are nearly twice as likely to quit their job within the next year.[9] They are even self-reportedly less productive.[10]

Connection matters. Cultivating and nurturing your team matters.

Nurturing Your Team

Simply being on a team does not mean we automatically reap the *benefits* of being on a team. To do so, we must *nurture* that team, and nurturing takes intentionality. My favorite way to think about the people in my life is through the metaphor of a garden:

- Some have strong roots, and you know they will be there forever.
- Some are here to brighten your day for a short season.

- Some are easy to care for and need little attention; others require a daily dose of water.
- Some nourish you; others you choose to nourish.

Furthermore, the nutrients in a garden's soil are limited, just like the energy you have available to devote to the people in your life. The *time* you have available to tend to your garden is limited, just like the time you have available to tend to your team. The more you tend to one plant, the less time you have to tend to others.

There are also weeds. The weeds in your garden take nutrients from the soil and from the plants within it. Identifying and dealing with weeds is important because of the damage they can do. While some weeds look beautiful, this is just a deception.

In the landscaping outside my porch, there are a few plants amid some beautiful ground cover. Last summer, I largely ignored my landscaping, as I was devoted to writing. Due to my neglect, I watched as a giant thistle continued to grow past the short wall and past the windows of my porch. It started to sprout beautiful purple flowers, and I was in awe that something considered a weed could be so beautiful.

We had an incredibly dry summer that year, so I went for a couple of months without mowing the grass. When I finally did, I noticed my landscaping for the first time and was shocked. This four-foot weed with the gorgeous purple flowers had killed all the ground cover I had planted within a two-foot radius and left a sad circle of brown, dead, flattened leaves in its wake.

The lesson here: there are people in your life who masquerade as gorgeous flowers but are sapping your nutrients (your energy and time). They often show up as toxic relationships—the ones you know you need to end but have a difficult time doing so. The more weeds there are in your garden and the less willing you are to get them from the root, the more nutrients they will take from the plants that matter. And a weed's roots often run deep.

Nutrients (your personal energy and time) are not unlimited resources; you must choose where and how you spend them. Choose wisely. As Aristotle and Taylor Swift (what a combo!) both said, "A friend to all is a friend to none." When you spread yourself too thin, the people who do matter the most to you, whether your partner, child, friend, or coworker, are not given the time and energy they need to sustain the relationship. It's therefore important to be extremely intentional about who you give your energy and time to. Making the difficult decision to choose *not* to give your resources to someone is essential to devoting your time to those who truly matter.

Presence

If you're a parent or if you have been very close to a child as they've grown up, you know how important presence is.

As a child, my niece Marta Mae had a beautiful way of pulling me back in when she wanted my attention and I was distracted. She would come over and put one hand on each of my cheeks, get really close to my face, and tell me her story or ask for what she wanted. She *demanded* presence, and she deserved it. The truth was, I always *wanted* to give it to her, but sometimes, I needed that reminder when I was distracted by work or personal things happening in my life.

Her approach was so precious. Kids just ask for what they want.

Being present in the lives of the people we care about is a fundamental aspect of building and maintaining meaningful relationships, both personally and professionally. I can remember sitting on the sofa at my sister's house once in 2007 (when smartphones were still somewhat new) and responding to a work text that came through while we were talking.

She said to me, "That's so rude. You're having a conversation with someone else while I'm sitting right here." This moment was so eye-opening, because she was right.

Unfortunately, today, this is not the anomaly it was then. It's just how we live. We're consistently *not* present. Even my sister has adopted the culture of answering texts on her devices while we're together.

Presence means being fully engaged in what we're doing in each moment. By now, many of us have learned that "multitasking" is often just the brain jumping from one task back to another, which is mostly incredibly inefficient. Having the discipline to stick with one thing—the most important thing at that moment—makes a difference. It improves communication, teamwork, and productivity at work, and it creates shared memories and strengthens bonds in our personal lives.

The best place to start when practicing presence is mindfulness. Meditation, mindful listening, breathing exercises… all the skills we discussed in Chapters 9 and 11 can bring us into the present moment. Setting boundaries with technology and carving out specific time for our loved ones and employees can also foster the benefits of presence.

Cultivating Teams at Work: Leadership and Belonging

The approach I'm about to share with you does not reflect traditional "team building" as you likely know it. I'm not recommending trust falls and truth trains! This approach is about getting you to understand three things:

1. The impact that loneliness has on your business results is huge.
2. Work life and home life cannot be separated.
3. (Therefore) Cultivating your work team will have far reaching impacts past the walls of your organization.

When employees don't feel like they belong, they experience insecurity about their jobs and their place on the team, hindering creativity, performance, innovation, and engagement. On the other hand, when workers feel like they belong, the organization reaps the rewards. In a large study by BetterUp, feelings of belonging were associated with a 56% increase in job performance, a 50% drop in turnover risk, and a 75% reduction in sick days.[11]

Connection and meaningful relationships with coworkers are a cornerstone of belonging. I can remember my time in HR at a Fortune 50 company where we used Gallup's engagement survey. The item "I have a best friend at work" was one of the top indicators of engagement and performance across the organization.[*]

Furthermore, research shows that bosses directly affect the level of work-family conflict and satisfaction an employee experiences at home.[12] This is not a responsibility to take lightly. Your words and actions matter. If you're a people leader, how you show up for your team can negatively or positively impact other areas of their lives (and their partners' and children's lives). You're either contributing to their overall wellbeing or constricting it.

The health of your employees and their families can be changed for the better when you care for your team.

Connection matters.

The Solution

What hinders us from showing up for the people in our circles in the way that we want to? How can we nurture our inner circle and other teams? The skills in this Devote phase will help you do just that. They will enable you to live in line with your values while simultaneously honoring

---

[*] To all of my former BFAWs: I miss you!

the people in your life. But let me warn you in advance, they are not for the faint of heart.

Reflect to Retain

What are three things I learned about myself from this chapter?

1.

2.

3.

What are three concepts I want to remember from this chapter?

1.

2.

3.

chapter 15

the devote phase skills

DEVOTING YOURSELF TO THE PEOPLE IN your life is easier said than done. Relationships go through messy and difficult times. Learning the skills of forgiveness, boundary setting, and compassion can make those difficult times easier to get through when they do occur.

Forgiveness

Forgiveness is not easy.

I once had a boss who could likely be classified as a narcissist. While under her leadership, I was asked by a high-level leader in the organization about my ideas for a reorg that was happening. I didn't agree with how my boss was going about it, and I (very politely and professionally) offered my opinion to this leader when he asked me for it. My boss never said anything to me about this conversation, and I assumed the leader hadn't shared my ideas with her. Turns out I was wrong.

During my performance review several months later, my boss took the opportunity to knock my score down for this reason (she said this in our meeting but did not actually put it in the review). At the time, I worked in an organization where my position was granted stock every year, and during this performance review, my boss also denied my stock grant, stating my performance was not as good as the previous year. Instead of speaking with me directly and professionally, she opted for revenge—revenge served cold. That decision cost me well over $100k over the course of the following years, which is a *lot* of money to me.

I was angry with this boss for *years*. Although I thought of her rarely, that anger was always lurking somewhere in my body. My anger wasn't about the money anymore. I just didn't care enough about her to try, because I didn't see her as a "good person" overall. It was literally while I was writing this book that I was finally able to forgive her, and it felt like a huge exhale.

She was the only person left in my life who I hadn't been able to forgive. I told myself that she was a terrible person and didn't deserve it. I created this story based on the "evidence" that I hadn't really seen much good in her even outside this situation. I'm guessing she had long forgotten about the incident. Refusing to forgive her kept it as a part of *my* story, however.

When someone hurts us, we have a few different options:

- Ignore it (this often leads to festering and resentment, which manifests in other detrimental ways).
- Find forgiveness and acceptance.
- Exact revenge.

> *Revenge is sweet and not fattening.*
> —Attributed to ALFRED HITCHCOCK

Sweet, sweet revenge. What is it that makes us plot and plan and sometimes seek out vengeance?

What's interesting (and a bit frightening) about revenge is that planning it out actually activates the pleasure centers of the brain.[1] Part of this is, of course, biology. From an evolutionary standpoint, it shows others that you're not vulnerable prey and will actively defend yourself against predators. In today's world, your brain wants you to exact revenge because it's a way of making things "fair" again. So, in a way, the desire for revenge is actually normal. (Phew…) Still, revenge-plotter, beware…

> *If revenge is sweet, why does it leave such a bitter taste?*
> —ANGELA ELWELL HUNT

How do we feel *after* revenge is carried out? Well, that picture is not so sweet. I'm guessing most of us have been in a situation where we've gone through with an act of revenge (most of them small) and then felt terrible the next day. That's because our pleasure centers don't generally stay activated *after* the act of revenge. In fact, people often report negative moods almost immediately after exacting vengeance. Putting a coworker down in front of others with a perfectly timed passive aggressive zinger, or cutting someone off in traffic who did the same to us two minutes prior, or stealing the favorite hoodie of an ex-boyfriend who wronged us, usually sounds like a great idea and feels good… for just a moment. Then, the bitter taste sets in, and we're left with thinking about our character, who we are, and how we operate in this world.

So, what is another option?

Forgiveness.

Forgiveness is an intentional choice to *actively* let go of anger, resentment, and the satisfaction that comes with planning revenge. It's not a free pass. It's not justifying the injustice or pretending it never happened. It *is* for *you*; for your health and sanity. It's accepting the apology you may never get. Sure, it's a gift you give to a person who may not deserve it, but mostly it's a gift you give yourself.

When we ignore a hurt, it generally doesn't just go away. We regularly revisit it, at a cost. We get lost in the pain and emotion, often losing precious time to rehashing and rumination that could be spent on positive things. Not to mention, reliving the pain leads to increased stress hormones that run through the body and often result in unhealthy activities or substance use to numb the pain.

Difficult life experiences actually provide you with an opportunity to practice the skill of leading your self well; to live in line with your values; to experience difficult emotions and situations and to consciously choose to respond as the person you want to be. Your character is built (and revealed) in the tough times, not the easy ones. Each time you've been put in a place where you needed to forgive has been an opportunity for you to practice living as your highest self; to practice leading your self well.

Many view forgiveness as weakness. The opposite is actually true. It's much easier to harbor anger, resentment, bitterness, and blame than it is to forgive. Forgiveness takes strength. As Mahatma Gandhi said, "The weak can never forgive. Forgiveness is the attribute of the strong."

The more intolerable the hurt, the harder it will be to forgive, but practicing forgiveness can have powerful health benefits. Observational studies and even some randomized trials suggest that forgiveness is associated with lower levels of depression, anxiety, and hostility, reduced substance abuse, higher self-esteem, and greater life satisfaction.[2] In examining the brains of people who choose to forgive (in a research setting), functional MRIs showed that the choice of forgiveness was associated with positive emotional states and activation of brain networks associated with empathy, compared to non-forgiveness.[3] Studies have also shown that forgiveness, as opposed to chronic anger, lowers stress levels, resulting in decreased risk of heart attack, improved sleep, decreased pain and blood pressure, and lower risk of diabetes.[4]

> *The sweetest revenge is to forgive.*
> —Attributed to JEROME ISAAC FRIEDMAN

So, how do we forgive?

One of the problems with forgiveness is that it's an active process that's not always achieved on the first go and usually isn't linear. Often, you must decide to forgive many times, or frequently remind yourself that you have chosen forgiveness over anger, resentment, and revenge. It's how Jerry describes a breakup in an episode of *Seinfeld*: "Breaking up is like knocking over a Coke machine. You can't do it in one push. You gotta rock it back and forth a few times. *Then* it goes over."[5]

There are full books written on forgiveness. Most resources will give you some practical steps to move toward forgiveness. I'll summarize the most common ones here.

1. Affirm your intentions for forgiveness, starting with you. Remind yourself that this is an act of love and a health decision for *you*. Forgiveness will help your mind, heart, and body heal. It's an opportunity to build resilience and practice being the best version of yourself.

2. Remember that there are many reasons why people hurt us. Try to understand those. Was the hurt unintentional? Was it inflicted because you hurt *them* in some way? Did they have something else going on in their life that made them act in a hurtful way?

3. Recall a time when you needed someone else's forgiveness. Give the forgiveness you would have liked to receive at that time.

4. Assess whether the "hurt" happened because you had different expectations of that person. Often, anger and hurt feelings result from unmet expectations. Do you feel hurt by this person because they didn't do what *you* wanted them to do?

5. Forgive with no expectations. Don't expect the person to change or be grateful for your forgiveness (if you even decide to share it with them). Don't expect the relationship to be repaired. Don't expect that you'll immediately feel better. Simply forgive for yourself, with the knowledge that you're making the best decision for your highest good.

6. Reflect on the events that happened, how you felt, and how the situation has affected you since, including your own anger and hurt. Recall these instances as an observer of the events. Notice the emotions that arise and journal about anything that comes up for you.

7. Find compassion for the person you are forgiving (even just a small amount). Have you been in their situation before? Do they have a traumatic past, or a hard time showing up for the people in their lives? Did they hurt you in an attempt to honor someone else?

8. List a few ways in which the hurt may have helped you. Could there be a deeper lesson for you here? Did it prevent something worse from happening? Did it build a resilience in you that you would not have otherwise?

9. Decide to forgive and seal this with an action. Share it with the person, if appropriate (without expectation), or with a trusted friend. If you're someone who aligns with ceremonies, write a few lines about the hurt or a letter of forgiveness to the person and set it on fire (responsibly, of course). Even standing in front of a mirror and declaring that you have forgiven someone can help you move forward.

Forgiveness is usually seen as situational; as something one chooses when a specific "wrong" has been done to them. But we can also cultivate forgiveness as a part of *who we are* and *how we show up* in our various teams.

One way to do so is through a "forgiveness day." It looks something like this:

As an experiment, for one day, internally extend a sincere olive branch to everyone you encounter who does or says something that rubs you the wrong way. This could be the person who doesn't hold the elevator, the guy who cuts you off in traffic, your teenager who lashes out at you because *they* forgot to do their own laundry, or your coworker who makes a snide remark. Forgive them all, just for a day. See what that feels like as you're falling asleep that night. If you're feeling brave, you can even choose to forgive that person you have not been able to forgive— just for the day. You can go back to resentment and anger tomorrow if you want, but for today, choose to forgive them.

> *The practice of forgiveness is our most important*
> *contribution to the healing of the world.*
> —MARIANNE WILLIAMSON

Forgiveness is a skill. A skill you can develop.

Boundaries

Boundaries are guidelines that protect our emotional, psychological, and physical wellbeing in our relationships, including the relationship with ourselves. They define how we want to be treated and what we accept and reject based on our needs, values, and priorities. Boundaries foster healthy and respectful interactions, and they serve as a commitment to self-care. Those who care about you will respect your boundaries, even if they don't fully understand or like them.

We're always setting boundaries, intentionally or not. Our words, actions, and reactions signal to others what behavior we find acceptable and what we don't, and in turn, we teach people how to treat us. I implore you to do this with intentionality.

When our boundaries are passively ignored or actively violated, this can trigger the brain's stress response system, leading to anxiety and stress. On the contrary, well-defined, healthy, and protected boundaries provide a sense of safety and control, promoting mental wellbeing and preventing future resentment or conflicts. Setting and upholding boundaries is not easy, though. It requires us to say no even when it's uncomfortable to do so; even when we want to say yes; even when it means the end of an important relationship. This is why many of us shy away from setting boundaries intentionally. It's a skill that gets easier with practice, and without holding firm boundaries, others may dictate them for you, undermining your health, relationships, and career in the process.

Boundaries are essential for mental wellbeing, but they can be misused if not grounded in self-awareness and respect for others. In their extensive research in boundaries, Drs. Henry Cloud and John Townsend discuss how overly rigid boundaries can stem from past fears or insecurities, hindering the development of healthy relationships.[6] Healthy boundaries focus on self-regulation, not controlling others.

Simply labeling a desire or preference as a boundary doesn't necessarily mean it's healthy. When the term is used to dictate the behavior of *others*, it's generally not healthy. A healthy boundary is about what *you* will do to protect your wellbeing if someone acts in a way that isn't healthy for you. For example, telling someone "You can't do this because it violates my boundaries" is very different than saying, "If you act in this way, I'll leave the room." Boundaries aren't ultimatums, they're meant to foster understanding and respect.

Because of this tendency to label something as a "boundary" in an effort to control another, getting to the root of your need for a boundary is extremely important. Boundaries should be reasonable and

249 | The Devote Phase Skills

communicated calmly. If your boundary isn't open to discussion, or is given in a disrespectful way, it may actually be a preference or a coping mechanism, not a healthy boundary.

When used in unhealthy ways, boundaries can cause resentment and harm to relationships.[7] Before setting a boundary, examine your own needs, values and emotions. Understanding the purpose for the boundary, your true emotions about it, and whether it's reasonable and fair is essential to ensure you're not setting a boundary as a coping mechanism to deal with an insecurity or fear.

Setting effective boundaries starts with having self-awareness around your true need for the boundary. It's about honoring your needs and values. It involves identifying your needs, wants, and limits in your relationships, and then communicating these clearly and consistently to the people in your life. And just as we all know you can't make an empty threat to a toddler, you have a responsibility to uphold the boundaries you set. Protect them by addressing violations respectfully and implementing consequences when appropriate.

If you've tried everything to set boundaries and they are continually being ignored, it may be time to walk away from that relationship or job. This can be difficult. It takes courage. It takes intention and consistency. But it also results in creating the space to lead your self well.

> *When someone shows you who they are, believe them the first time.*
> —MAYA ANGELOU

There are two essential parts of honing the skill of setting boundaries that often get overlooked. The first is setting and respecting boundaries for your treatment of *yourself*. This includes creating standards for how you talk to yourself, how you show up in conflict, what habits and routines you devote yourself to, and how you approach your physical and mental self-care. The second often-overlooked aspect of boundaries is respecting the boundaries of others. When a loved one or a coworker sets a boundary, it can feel like they don't care about you. Practicing acceptance and compassion (which we will talk about in a moment) and managing your thoughts and beliefs can help you to honor someone else's boundaries when these feelings arise, even when it means you can't have things exactly the way you want them.

Setting boundaries is a skill. A skill you can develop.

Compassion

> *If we could read the secret history of our enemies, we should find in each man's life sorrow and suffering enough to disarm all hostility.*
> —HENRY WADSWORTH LONGFELLOW

A skill that can help tremendously in forging the ability to forgive is compassion. Compassion is that gentle pull within each of us—the string—that reminds us of three things:

1. We are all connected.
2. We all struggle at times within this human experience.
3. We can choose to help each other through those struggles.

I often remind leaders who are dealing with tough employees, "It's hard being a human. We're all doing the best we can with it." I really believe that. I don't think that many people go out in the world on a daily basis and decide they want to hurt others or themselves, or that they intentionally want to create more pain and suffering in the world.

Compassion is a bit different from empathy. Empathy is the sharing of emotions with another person. When they feel joy, we feel that joy right there with them. When they feel pain, we feel that pain. Compassion, on the other hand, is not about feeling "with" the person as much as feeling "for" them. Compassion is about relating. It's about really *seeing* someone. It's about paying attention to others and showing up with curiosity, in a dedicated attempt to understand what their experience is like for *them*. It's taking their word for how they're experiencing their feelings.

In theory, compassion should be somewhat easy. At our core, we're wired to care for others, and evolutionarily, we depend on it. However, it often is *not* easy. As we have already discussed, our nervous system makes us more reactive, anxious, and quick to judge when we're in a stress state, and in that heightened state, many factors can create an environment where being compassionate is difficult:

- **IMPATIENCE**: Being curious and compassionate takes time.
- **DISTRACTION**: With all the things going on in our heads, it's sometimes very difficult to put them aside and truly listen to someone.
- **COMPARISON**: We have all felt at times that our own pain or problem is so much worse than another's. However, the pain of others is complex and full of emotions and history we likely know nothing about. This is why asking them about it and taking them at their word for their experience is essential to extending compassion.
- **JUDGMENT**: Do you know someone who is always complaining? Someone for whom the sky is always falling? Someone who seems to always have something going wrong (and needs to tell everyone about it)? Having compassion for this person can feel difficult, because they demand so much emotional energy from others. It can be easier for your efficient brain to dismiss them as needy, unaware, clingy, or annoying.

Research shows that compassion in the workplace matters. It's been shown that compassionate leadership behaviors significantly improve employee wellbeing.[8] This impact is possibly due to the effect compassion has on our brains: giving *and* receiving compassion both trigger positive feelings in the reward centers of our brains. It benefits both the giver and the receiver.[9] It can also take us from fight-or-flight to our rest-and-digest mode, and, as we know, this is the goal of our work here. Showing compassion to others can boost your own self-esteem, and receiving compassion can combat loneliness and depression. Compassion has been shown to have a number of benefits for both psychological and physiological health. With positive effects on mental health, emotion regulation, and interpersonal and social relationships, it is clear that developing compassion can have significant and far-reaching benefits.[10]

As with any of the other skills in this book, compassion can be learned, as evidenced by observed increased neuroplasticity and feelings of positive affect following compassion training.[11] Stanford Medicine even offers a class called "Compassion Cultivation Training" for physicians and psychologists.[12] Honing the skill of compassion requires intentionality, consistency, and practice. Here are some ways in which you can increase your ability to show compassion:

1. **RECOGNIZE OTHERS' SUFFERING.** Remember everyone is going through something, even those who you "know" have it all together or whose life is "easier" than yours. Most people do a great job of hiding their pain. One clue that someone is suffering is if they exhibit anger. Anger is almost always a cry for help; a sign that someone is suffering in some way.

2. **ACKNOWLEDGE THEIR SUFFERING AND TAKE IT AT FACE VALUE.** Rejecting another's experience, making it out to be not as bad as they perceive it to be, or thinking that it's not as intense as your own suffering takes away from your ability to show compassion.

3. **ACT.** Be intentional about looking for places where people need compassion and where you can help. Oftentimes, listening to someone is the only "act" necessary. Practice your mindful

listening from Chapter 11. See them. Acknowledge their pain and struggles.

4. **PRACTICE LOVING KINDNESS.** Loving kindness is an ancient Buddhist practice about giving "universal friendliness" to yourself and others. One practice that I use to change my mood for the better almost instantly is internally offering a quiet sentence of loving kindness to random strangers throughout the day. Whether it's the woman walking her dog past my house (or her dog!), the delivery driver with my Amazon box, or the barista at my coffee shop, I say something internally like this: "I wish you a beautiful and peaceful day and hope that you find joy in your heart today." I know it sounds ridiculous, but I challenge you to try it!

Another way to cultivate compassion is to realize that your brain is designed *not* to be compassionate most of the time. There's a bias our brain engages in to help us think efficiently. I remember learning about this in college; it's called the fundamental attribution error, which relates to our tendency to attribute others' behavior to *who they are* rather than the situation they're going through. I learned this early, and the hard way.

I was 17 and working the drive-thru at a fast-food joint in our small town. It was a busy Saturday, and the person ordering couldn't decide between a cheeseburger or a chocolate shake. I quickly grew annoyed as she went back and forth, holding up the line ("They're completely different foods! Does she want dessert or a meal?") before finally deciding and pulling up to the window. I stood at the window waiting to see what kind of idiot could not make this decision, and my stomach sank when she pulled around the corner. It was Patrice, the wife of my boyfriend's best friend. They had been married a few months before he died in that horrible accident I told you about earlier. I was so ashamed that I had even *thought* of her in a demeaning way, and I was *so* grateful I hadn't said something snarky to her while she was deciding.

I realized very quickly that I can never truly know what someone is going through. It's far easier for the brain to think, *She's an idiot*, or, *He's a terrible person*, or, *She's so lazy*, rather than, *Maybe her husband just died tragically*, or, *Maybe his dog is really sick*, or, *Maybe he just lost his job and is paralyzed with fear*. I didn't know about the fundamental attribution error back then, but it was sure hard at work in my busy brain. I *did* know, acutely, that *I* was the problem in that situation, not her. I have never forgotten that moment.

Even our closest friends and family are likely to have situations they're struggling with that they're not sharing with you. Paying attention to this bias can go a long way in cultivating compassion for those you encounter daily, whether friends, coworkers, family, and strangers. Remember, we are all connected.

Compassion is a skill. A skill you can develop.

Note to Self

> *Love and compassion are necessities, not luxuries.*
> *Without them, humanity cannot survive.*
> —DALAI LAMA XIV

One of the most important aspects of forgiveness and compassion is extending them to yourself. You simply cannot be mentally strong and healthy when you're busy beating yourself up and refusing to forgive yourself for mistakes you've made. You are human. You make mistakes. Learning how to take care of yourself when you do so is essential to leading your self well.

Self-compassion has been linked to improved coping skills, emotional intelligence, goal mastery, and happiness.[13] Additionally, self-compassion and self-forgiveness help protect our inner child from our inner critic. As we know, the inner critic is likely loud and incessant, and your inner child needs protection from that voice. You can practice self-compassion and self-forgiveness by tapping into your inner coach, aligning with your values, and using some skills that you have already learned:

- Recognize your thoughts as simply thoughts, not reality. Don't fight them; just acknowledge them as you would experience a wave or a cloud rolling by (or that donut). Chapter 8.
- Mindfulness meditation. Do a guided meditation specific to self-compassion and self-forgiveness. Chapter 11.
- Breathwork. Practice some of the breathwork methods we spoke about in Chapter 9 to bring your nervous system out of your fight-or-flight response and into rest and relaxation mode.
- Talk to yourself as you would to a friend. What would you tell your best friend? Your child? Your niece?
- Acceptance. Acknowledge and accept that you're human and make mistakes sometimes, and that you will continue to do so throughout your life (it's a part of being human). Chapter 11.
- Affirmations. Write an affirmation about self-compassion and self-forgiveness and add it to your daily affirmation practice. Chapter 13.
- Call on your inner circle for help. Don't try to suffer through.

Summary

Our circles or teams are a very important aspect of our lives. According to research by Dr. David McClelland of Harvard University, your "reference group" (the people with whom you spend time) significantly shapes your behaviors, aspirations, and overall success.[14] How you treat those around you (with forgiveness, compassion, and boundaries) and how they treat you can be the difference between:

- Mental wellbeing and mental distress.
- Your team's success and your team's failure.
- Leading your self well and leading your self into chaos, frustration, and despair.
- Improved business results and lowered productivity and engagement.

Choose your inner circle wisely and with intention, and then trust it. Lean on it when you need help. Support it when its members need help. Your future, and theirs, depend on it.

THE DEVOTE PHASE: PUT IT INTO PRACTICE

Inquire Within

Choose one of the categories and spend 30–60 minutes on the inquiries.

Your Inner Circle:

- Who are the important people on my chosen team? My work team? My community circle? What actions do I take to ensure they feel loved and cared for? Who are the weeds (who may be disguised as flowers) that may be detrimental to my wellbeing?
- What am I devoting my free time to? Am I spending it on the people who matter the most? Or am I spreading myself too thin? Am I giving someone too much and not setting boundaries around my time?
- Are there weeds in my circle? Are there friends, family, or co-workers who are not contributing to my life in a positive way;

who are not healthy for me? What are the reasons I'm keeping them in my life? Are those healthy reasons? Where do I need to make changes here?

Forgiveness and Compassion:

- Who have I not yet forgiven for a situation in which I was treated poorly? What's holding me back from forgiving them? (Practice the steps of forgiveness provided earlier in the chapter.)
- What would be different if I could show up in forgiveness more proactively in my relationships?
- What do I need to forgive myself for? Where do I need to provide myself with more compassion and understanding?

Boundaries:

- Where have I set effective boundaries? Where haven't I? What were the consequences for each?
- Where do I need to set better boundaries: At work? With my partner? With my other personal relationships? With myself?
- Evaluate these areas where boundaries are important. Do I have boundaries in these areas? Do I need to create some?
    - **PERSONAL SPACE:** Define areas or times when you want or need personal space and privacy. Communicate this to your family.
    - **PERSONAL DEVELOPMENT:** Set aside regular periods of time for physical and mental self-care.
    - **FINANCES:** Establish spending limits and guidelines (as an individual, part of a couple, or a family member).

- o **RELATIONSHIP NEEDS:** Communicate your needs and wants regarding emotional support, communication, and quality time. Ask about your partner's.
- o **WORK HOURS:** Set start and end times to your workday. Communicate them to your boss and coworkers.
- o **VACATION TIME:** Commit to using your vacation time in a way that allows you to disconnect and recharge.
- o **FEEDBACK:** Communicate boundaries on how you give and receive feedback, ensuring it's respectful, timely, and constructive.

Daily Practice Ideas

Choose one or two options below to practice daily for 2–4 weeks.

- Create affirmations based around forgiveness and compassion and add them to your daily affirmations list.
- Be a good stranger. Find one stranger each day to whom you silently offer compassion or loving kindness, or choose one day on which you will do this to every stranger you encounter.

Wellness Wednesday (When-sday)

Choose one of the activities below to complete on your Wellness Day.

- Choose one Wellness Wednesday to turn into a day of forgiveness. On this day, offer forgiveness as your first response to every person you interact with. At the end of the day, journal about the experiment. What worked? What didn't? How do you feel? Exhausted? Relaxed? Frustrated? Serene? How did it impact your day overall?

- Do a deep dive into a relationship in which you know you need to set better boundaries. This could be your relationship with your boss, partner, kid, or a good friend.
  - Sit and "feel" into what the relationship feels like now (not what you *think* about it; what it *feels* like).
  - Make a list of your needs, desires, and limits in that relationship and make a plan for how you will communicate them to this person.
- Create a list of boundaries for yourself and others. Be realistic about this. What self-talk, behaviors, and actions will you accept and not accept from yourself? How will you treat yourself as you work to honor these boundaries (remember your skills of acceptance and self-compassion)? How will you communicate these boundaries to others, in words and actions?

Wellness at Work

- Think about where you may be disrespecting someone else's boundaries, even if the person has not explicitly said this to you. How can you find out what they need?
- If you manage people, ask what is important to them. Open a conversation about boundaries and find out where their work currently supports their boundaries and where it currently hinders them. Together, problem-solve those places where your employee feels like a boundary is being crossed.
- Consider whether you're currently holding a grudge against someone at work for a wrongdoing from the past (whether recent or long ago). Walk through the steps of forgiveness remembering that forgiveness is for you and your mental wellbeing, that it's an

act of self-care, and that it doesn't always follow a one-and-done model. You often must choose it every day until it "sticks."

- Brainstorm how you can better connect with the people in your work team. How can you make them feel seen and heard (refer to the mindful listening section in Chapter 11)? How can you make them feel important? Where can you ask for their advice or support? How can you showcase their contribution to the team? Can you create connections simply for the sake of connecting, such as by asking about family, interests, and what is happening in their life?

Reflect to Retain

What are three things I learned about myself from this chapter?
   1.

   2.

   3.

What are three concepts I want to remember from this chapter?
   1.

   2.

   3.

Which one daily practice will I devote myself to as I read the next chapter?
   1.

PART VII

THE DEDICATE PHASE

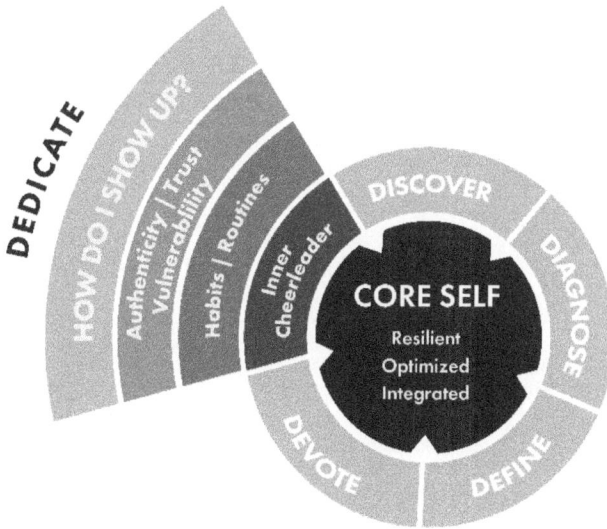

chapter 16

how do i show up?

The Phase: Dedicate
The Inquiry: How Do I Show Up?
The Themes: Authenticity, Trust, and Vulnerability
The Skills: Habits and Routines
The Character: Inner Cheerleader

ALLOW ME TO BEGIN THIS PHASE with a tale of two leaders. I have supported retail field leaders at a couple of different points in my career—actually, in my first and last corporate jobs. Retail field leadership is a tough business. It's demanding and challenging with a dynamic and fast-paced environment. It's forward-facing with customer issues, it relies on headquarters setting your operational processes, and there are often staffing and people-related challenges. Leaders are tasked with achieving ambitious sales goals and margins while managing tight payroll budgets and an employee base with traditionally high turnover. They work long and irregular hours, rarely have weekends off, and are often required to put in extra time during holidays, when friends and family are usually taking time off. The job often takes a toll on one's ability to find balance. That being said, it also forces you to become a type of leader you just cannot learn to be anywhere else. Some of the best leaders I've met have been through retail field leadership—as have (unfortunately) a few of the worst.

One important tenant of retail field work is the employee engagement survey. Part of this survey is an assessment of the leader by their direct reports. As an HR leader supporting retail field teams, my job often centered around these surveys. I would frequently coach and train leaders where gaps were identified in them.

One year I supported a store leader (we'll call him Damien) whose direct reports didn't like, respect, or value him—mostly for good reason. He took a lot of time away from the store, barked orders, rarely listened to employees, acted one way in front of the district leader and another when it was just him and his team, thought his ideas were the best, didn't follow through on his commitments, berated people in front of others, and had his few favorites (and made them known).

It was early in my career, but I've always been very direct, so I tried to coach him on these things without outing the leaders who came to me in confidence, frustrated with his leadership. But he wouldn't listen. When the survey results came in, they were as I had expected: across the board, his assistant managers had told the truth about what it was like to work for him.

He called me into his office, showed me the results, and asked me what to do. "You tried to warn me. You've talked to me about these things. I didn't believe you. What do I even do with this?"

To be transparent here, I think in that moment, he was more worried about what *his* boss was going to say to him (and whether he would lose his job) than what his employees thought. Regardless, he had come to me in humility and asked for help, so we put a plan together based on authenticity, vulnerability, and trust. The following week, Damien sat at the head of the leadership meeting table and started the meeting by reading out each and every one of the comments the team had written about him. It was not a short list, and it was harsh. They had not held back. Then he said, "I'm sorry. I've let you down. I didn't know you felt this way about how I lead. I want to do better." He then scheduled a meeting with each person, in which he asked what he could do to be a better leader. He was present. He listened. He followed through on the promises he made. He explained why he had to say no to some of their requests. In other words, he pivoted in his leadership style and behaviors. Most importantly, Damien won the trust of his team back.

This took a while. Consistency over time is required in situations like this. He also had a few setbacks. But he learned and grew into a better leader from that experience.

Fast forward about 15 years, and I was the HR leader for several stores in the retail division of a different company. There was a store leader in one of my markets whose assistant managers were really struggling with his leadership style. He took a lot of time away from the store, barked orders, rarely listened to employees, acted one way in front of the district leader and another when it was just him and his team, thought his ideas were the best, didn't follow through on his commitments, berated people in front of others, and had his few favorites (and made them known).

Sound familiar?

I also tried to coach this leader—to share with him some of the concerns I had heard from his team—and he also did not listen. In fact, he went to *my* boss to complain that I was not performing in *my* job effectively. When the employee experience survey came around this time, it showed similar responses to Damien's. This leader's response (we'll call him Mitchell) was the opposite of Damien's response. Mitchell went to his team, as a group *and* individually, and berated them for their responses. He said they were ungrateful for the fact that they were working for such a great company. He actively and admittedly decided to put one of them "in the desert" for a few weeks—meaning, he gave him the silent treatment.

It was bad. The situation turned into an employee relations investigation that did not end well for Mitchell.

What we can learn from these two stories is that how a leader shows up is critical. It can significantly influence the culture and therefore success of a team and organization. Being intentional in how you choose to show up matters.

If you've followed the process in this book up to this point, you've already done the groundwork. You've started to truly get to know yourself: how your thoughts and emotions show up on a daily basis; how your past influences you present; what your values and purpose are. You have thought about who's in your circle, how you want to treat them, and how you want to be treated by them. It's now time to put all of this together and dedicate yourself: how will you show up in this world? How will you lead your self well? How will you lead your team well? How will you lead your organization well? How will you lead your family well?

In my 20-plus years spent supporting leaders in several industries, including big and small companies in both the public and private sector, I have found that leading with three qualities can be the key to creating a team where people thrive and do their best work (and have fun while doing so). Those three qualities are authenticity, trust, and vulnerability. I've also learned, through coaching personal and business clients, that these three qualities are just as effective in creating space in your personal life for you and others to thrive; for you to lead your self well.

Authenticity

Authenticity, in the workplace and in our personal relationships, is essential for collaboration, engagement, and employee wellbeing. It's about being genuine, honest, and true to oneself while interacting with colleagues, employees, and superiors. It's about not pretending to be someone you aren't or conforming to norms, and embracing your unique qualities, thoughts, opinions, ideas, and values. Authenticity can play a pivotal role in creating an inclusive environment, as it gives your team permission to also show up as their authentic selves.

One of my favorite stories about authenticity in the workplace seems small in its lessons, but it isn't:

I was supporting a brilliant but tough VP at a corporate office (we'll call William) who was known to be hardcore. He was not down with the "mushy" stuff, and he said things as he saw them, directly. He would not spend the company's money on lunch for the team during all-day meetings, as "our customers don't owe us lunch just because we're in a meeting," and he was vocal about not celebrating people's birthdays. He was all business all the time, and he looked the part. I was scared of him for the first six months I supported him!

During an all-staff meeting of the entire department, each of the five VPs were asked to provide an interesting fact about themselves. During breaks in the meeting, the facilitator would read out one fun fact and ask the group of about 300 who they thought had written it. William's fun fact was that he was a barefoot water skier, and we were *all* shocked when the facilitator revealed this. I would have never, ever guessed this about him. At our next 1:1, William said to me, "You wouldn't believe the number of people who have stopped into my office to tell me they were so surprised by my fun fact." He smiled while he said it. William rarely smiled at work. This small glimpse into William's personal life started a great conversation about authenticity and how people want to know their leader as a person, at least somewhat; that showing a personal side of us—our human side— helps to connect with employees, and them with us. It makes work easier, performance conversations more effective, and feedback more welcoming.*

Authenticity contributes to healthy work cultures by promoting trust and meaningful connections and reducing workplace stress. In such an environment, employees are more likely to speak up, share ideas, and provide feedback, leading to greater innovation.[1] Organizations and leaders that exhibit and encourage authenticity have been positively related to motivation and wellbeing.[2]

Trust

Do you trust your leader? Your teams? Do your employees trust you? How do you know if they do? What about the people in your personal life? Are you able to trust people naturally, or do you make them work for it?

"Trust" is a word that's thrown around a lot, but what does it really mean to trust?

Trust is a cornerstone of all relationships. It plays a pivotal role in shaping the quality of our connections. It fosters intimacy by creating a sense of safety. In our personal relationships it encourages open, honest, effective communication and creates a safe container where thoughts, feelings, and needs can be more-easily expressed.

When trust is present, it reduces anxiety and uncertainty, allowing us to relax and be our authentic selves with others. This is essential for the development of truly close relationships.

---

* As an aside, this was the hardest leader I've ever supported, from an "earning respect" perspective. He made my job tough. He viewed HR as a sort of necessary "evil" and was not interested in HR as a partner. But we stuck with it—both of us. About ten years later, he asked me to come and work with the consulting company he had cofounded on a big, several-year-long project. I was surprised and honored that he felt that strongly about my work.

Good leaders know that a culture of high trust leads to engagement, higher productivity, better collaboration, and increased retention. Good leaders also know that lack of trust are detrimental to the success of any team and, ultimately, any organization. But leaders have a hard time knowing where to start with building trust. It's elusive. It can sometimes feel like you either have it with someone or you don't. But it's buildable, and it's important to do so. Paul Zak, founding director of the Center for Neuroeconomics Studies, found in his research that compared to low-trust companies, people at high-trust companies report 74% less stress, 106% more energy at work, 50% higher productivity, 13% fewer sick days, 76% higher engagement, and 40% less burnout.[3] It seems worth figuring out.

Trust is made up of many components, and there are different models available that define the intertwining factors determining whether we "trust" someone. Those factors, as defined by RHR International, include:

- **AFFECTION:** Do you like and care about the other person?
- **COLLABORATION:** Can you effectively work together?
- **CONFLICT:** Do you have faith that if you face conflict together, you'll be able to work through it effectively?
- **TRANSPARENCY:** How comfortable are you with revealing your ideas, thoughts, and feelings to this person?
- **PREDICTABILITY:** Is this person consistent in how they treat you, or are you constantly walking on eggshells?
- **COMPETENCE:** Do you have faith in the person's ability to do their job effectively and contribute positively to the team?
- **RISK:** To what degree can this person threaten your success or cause you emotional pain? (The more the person can hurt you, the greater the risk.)[4]

Addressing each of these factors in your relationships can improve the level of trust you earn from the people in your life.

Establishing trust requires intentional effort. It rarely occurs by happenstance. Leading by example is the best place to start. When you behave consistently over time, others can build their faith in you and thereby offer trust in you. Open, honest, and transparent communication with those in your circles about what's happening in the relationship or the organization is crucial. Keep your promises (and proactively explain to your team when you simply cannot). Hone your conflict resolution skills. Address issues quickly without letting them fester. Be respectful during conflict. Using the skills of compassion, forgiveness, self-awareness, and gratitude (as outlined in earlier chapters) can also help create more trust in your relationships.

What happens when trust is broken? Each of us, at some point, is going to let someone down. It's part of being human. When trust is broken, rebuilding it takes time, patience, and consistency, as demonstrated by Damien's story. His managers didn't automatically grant him their trust. He needed to continue to show that he was leading in a different way, because violating trust creates a wound, and wounds take time to heal. You can't put a Band-Aid on one and expect it to be fixed the next day. It takes time and care, and sometimes a lot of it, depending on the depth of the wound. If you introduce further hurt before the healing is complete, you have to start over.

Rebuilding trust must be an intentional activity; one that people (and teams) work on together.

Consistency over time is crucial.

Vulnerability

Vulnerability is one of the most powerful yet misunderstood elements of human connection. It helps foster trust and authenticity. Similar to forgiveness, it's often perceived as a weakness, but is, in fact, a profound expression and source of strength. It requires us to reveal our authentic selves, and it allows us to foster deeper, more meaningful connections both in our personal lives and in the workplace.

Dr. Brené Brown, a leading researcher on vulnerability, describes it as "uncertainty, risk, and emotional exposure." In her book *Daring Greatly*, she emphasizes that embracing vulnerability is essential to building resilience, promoting creativity, and ultimately cultivating trust within relationships and organizations.[5] By opening ourselves up to others, we take down the walls that inhibit genuine connection, and this allows us to truly "show up" and experience life and our connections more fully.

Neuroscience research offers insights into why vulnerability can feel so difficult to embrace. Being vulnerable opens us up to social threat. When this happens, brain scans light up just as they do when exposed to a physical threat. We move into that fight-or-flight space where heart and respiration rates increase and problem-solving abilities greatly diminish.[6] What's really interesting is that a study in 2018 found that, during the vulnerable process of feedback, the person *giving* the feedback feels equally as anxious as the person *receiving* it.[7] It's no wonder most of us have some fear of showing vulnerability: our brains are trying to protect us from a perceived threat.

In the workplace, vulnerability is increasingly seen as a critical leadership skill. Leaders who demonstrate vulnerability foster psychological safety, making it easier for employees to express ideas, share feedback, and take risks without fear of punishment. According to Amy Edmondson, a Harvard Business School professor known for her work on psychological safety, employees in such environments are more likely to engage, innovate, and support one another. Vulnerable leaders pave the way for authenticity and psychological safety in the workplace, modeling behavior that encourages teams to bring their whole selves to work.[8] This openness not only enhances and strengthens organizational resilience, it can foster greater innovation, faster transformation, and improved revenue growth.[9]

However, vulnerability must be approached with intention and balance. Brown warns against what she calls "floodlighting" — sharing too much, too soon, or without appropriate context. True vulnerability is not about indiscriminate sharing; it's about thoughtfully exposing aspects of ourselves in such a way that builds trust and demonstrates authenticity. When we share purposefully, we create a foundation for trust that can support honest conversations, difficult feedback, and shared learning experiences. In personal relationships, this kind of vulnerability deepens intimacy by fostering mutual understanding and respect.

Showing vulnerability may feel uncomfortable at first, but as with any new practice, neural pathways can help rewire initial responses to this, making it more comfortable over time. Taking small steps to being more open will help deepen those pathways.

Embracing vulnerability is a choice to be seen, heard, and valued for who you truly are, and to invite others to do the same. In a world where authenticity is increasingly valued in the workplace, the courage to be vulnerable is not just an asset; it's an essential skill for fostering meaningful relationships, effective teams, and resilient organizations.

The Dedicate Phase Character: Your Inner Cheerleader

Now that we have discussed the importance of authenticity, trust, and vulnerability, I would like to introduce the final character within your core self who has a powerful and positive voice: your inner cheerleader.

This character is always there, ready to encourage you through life's tough moments; to help you do the things you don't want to do and to celebrate with you when you accomplish them. Tapping into this voice can help you push through obstacles and self-doubt. Your inner cheerleader can congratulate you after a strenuous workout, pat you on the back after having that tough conversation, and celebrate with you when you get that promotion. The key here is to remember that this voice is a part of you, and it wants to be heard and to be helpful.

Your inner cheerleader is a great voice to counteract the voice of your inner critic. When you feel self-doubt or lack of motivation, call on your inner cheerleader. They want to help and to celebrate with you!

One way I use my inner cheerleader is by solidifying, reinforcing, or validating a healthy choice I made for myself. For example, as I make my way through the parking lot to my car after the gym, it's quite common for me to say something (yes, aloud) like, "Nice work, Cara. I know you did *not* want to do that, but you freaking rocked it. You see how good you feel right now? Remember that tomorrow, girl, and get back at it."

Summary

You have already learned about and (hopefully) practiced most of the skills that will help you create authenticity, trust, and vulnerability in your life. The skill in this Dedicate phase that will bring all of these together is creating habits and routines. Let's explore this next.

Reflect to Retain

What are three things I learned about myself from this chapter?

1.

2.

3.

What are three concepts I want to remember from this chapter?

1.

2.

3.

chapter 17

the dedicate phase skills

We are what we repeatedly do, therefore, excellence is not an act, but a habit.
—WILL DURANT, paraphrasing ARISTOTLE

I LOVE THIS QUOTE ATTRIBUTED TO Aristotle. It reminds me of, "You are what you eat." The idea behind it is so basic that we sometimes dismiss it, but it's true: you are what you do. Doing something repeatedly makes you more likely to do it again, until eventually, those behaviors become automatic and effortless. They become who we are.

That's the good news and the bad, because this isn't only true with the habits and behaviors we *want* to form; it happens with *all* of our repeated actions.

It often feels like bad habits are so much easier to form than good ones. Unfortunately, I've had a lot of bad habits at various points in my life, whether procrastination, ruminating about my ex, scrolling through social media (also when I'm procrastinating), wearing comfy clothes all the time, or reaching for food when I'm bored or stressed. Notably, I have never had to "try" to develop these.

I also have a lot of good habits, including skipping the snooze button, taking an early morning quick walk daily, brushing my teeth at least twice a day, eating veggies during every meal, and taking my supplements. Each of these, contrary to my bad habits, took some intention to create.

Habits are beneficial for your brain and how it operates. Your brain loves patterns and predictability, as this allows it to conserve mental energy and free up cognitive resources for more complex and creative tasks. Habits therefore provide structure and routine that can reduce stress and anxiety.[1] Positive habits also give you a sense of agency and empowerment, leading to increased psychological resilience in response to stressful events.[2] These rarely come easily, however. They take intention, and they often require getting rid of old habits.

Part of the problem when attempting to rid yourself of old habits is trying to simply stop cold-turkey, without acknowledging that when you do this, you're working against your brain. Remember, your brain prioritizes efficiency, so once you create a habit, it will be easier and easier to continue down that pathway. Creating new pathways (habits) is therefore difficult at first. You're essentially creating a new highway from scratch when another one is already paved and ready to use, and your brain is *always* going to want to take you down that comfortable, paved road.

Embrace the hard. Change rarely comes without effort.

Learning how habits work can help with the process, so let's explore that.

Habits often follow a "cue, routine, reward" loop. A cue triggers a habit, you perform the routine, and you receive a reward. To change a bad habit, you must address this loop.

For years, I had a habit of immediately throwing on my best cozy pants and grabbing something comforting to eat when I arrived home from work. Food was my drug of choice. This caused me so much shame for years, and unfortunately, it became a strong habit for dealing with work stress. We could say my habit loop went like this:

- **CUE**: Walking through the door at the end of the day.
- **ROUTINE**: Eating something delicious and carb-loaded.
- **REWARD**: Pleasurable taste and lowered stress.

This came up with my therapist when I was in the throes of it. I was frustrated with my inability to not eat crap food right when I got home after a hard day. The difficulty was, as I told her, *it worked*. It felt and tasted good, and, more importantly, within five to ten minutes of me eating whatever it was, I felt calm. I remember telling her I wished I was a drinker instead. Somehow, that seemed more acceptable and less embarrassing. Which do you think sounds more acceptable to say to your friends: "I had such a stressful day that I went home last night and had two glasses of wine," or, "I had such a stressful day that I went home last night and ate two donuts"? Neither are good for us, but no one wants to admit the latter.

The first step to breaking a habit loop is recognizing that it's there (self-awareness). Then, you must address each component of the loop:

- **CUE**: Understand the cue (the trigger) and determine if you can change it. If not (I still had to go home every day), recognizing this cue as a trigger will help you to anticipate and manage it.
- **ROUTINE**: Replacing the habit with something else is much easier than simply eliminating the habit altogether. Choose something that provides a similar reward or addresses the need that the old habit fulfilled.
- **REWARD**: Try to identify the underlying reward and modify it, if helpful.

For my food issue, I came up with a plan: replace the food with alcohol. One drink. My therapist was not a huge supporter of this idea and made me promise that if it turned into more than one, I would tell her. The next week, she asked how it was going, and laughingly told me she had not been able to write in her notes that she recommended I start drinking to deal with stress, so instead, she had written something like, "Discussed other alternatives for stress reduction efforts." Anyway, I ended up ditching the alcohol plan. I knew it wasn't a good long-term strategy. I ultimately replaced it with a cup of tea and a short breathing exercise. Over time, the problem disappeared. I no longer felt that trigger when I walked through the door.

Habits can come in a lot of interesting forms. For example, I've learned for myself that unhealthy relationships can be more about habit than wanting the person in our life. We can get into the *habit* of having someone to call, lean on, help, or provide support, even if that person isn't good for us or even if we don't really enjoy having them around. If we're not present and paying attention, we can stay in a relationship for too long out of habit, and when that relationship ends, part of the difficulty may actually be in breaking the "habit" of having that person in our life.

One of the best things I've learned to do is to not beat myself up for my habits. It's easy to create negative self-talk when you've just eaten a whole pint of ice cream and are considering going to the store in your cozy pants to buy another. However, shaming and blaming hurts more than it helps, though understanding *why* your brain wants you to have that ice cream is important. Here's what's been going on when I've been in the ice cream rabbit hole:

- My stress was the most pressing thing at that moment, so some sort of salve was necessary, and my brain knew it.
- My brain was taking the easiest and most familiar path to No Stress Land, so it could be free to work on other cognitive tasks.

I therefore could not, logically, be mad at my brain. It was trying to help me in the most efficient way possible. So, please don't beat yourself up when you take that path. Commit to paying attention to the *reasons* you want to do the familiar, and interrupt with a different activity. When you *do* choose to do the habit you don't want to have anymore, commit to getting on the unpaved road *next* time, knowing it will not feel nearly as easy as doing the familiar and comfortable.

A few things will help to do this:

- Remind yourself of your "why" (your motivation).
- Link this with one of the values you identified as being important to you in Chapter 13.
- Remind yourself of the strengths you developed from your childhood (Chapter 11). How can you use those strengths to help you?
- Bring forth your inner coach and inner cheerleader.
- Anticipate the upcoming cue. When I was trying to break the habit of eating comfort food when I walked in the door, I had a Post-It in my car that read, *Set your intention,* as a reminder to decide, before I got out of the car, what I was going to do in those first ten minutes at home.
- Affirm out loud what you will do instead.
- Be kind to yourself and learn from your "relapses." (In full transparency, I had one last week. Ice cream is my kryptonite!)

Forming Wellbeing Habits and Routines

Through my own wellness journey, I realized there were a lot of things I wanted to do in my day to promote my mental wellbeing—so many that the list felt overwhelming. As a perfectionist, I wanted to do them all. If I did that, though, I would spend my entire day on those activities. My coaching clients often feel the same.

For those of us with kids, demanding jobs, a house to maintain, and/or friendship and family commitments, how do we find time for wellbeing?

Simply, we have to make choices, and creating habits helps with that. I've found these tips to be effective with my busiest of clients:

- **FIND YOUR WHY**. Without really knowing and "feeling" this, it will be easier to let it slide. Take the time to journal about why something is important to you.
- **HAVE A MORNING ROUTINE.** Hal Elrod wrote a book called *The Miracle Morning*, which presents an awesome construct for starting your day off with habits that set you up for success.[3]
- **VISUALIZATION**. Visualize your ideal life or goal achievement and the positive emotions that will come with that.
- **DEFINE YOUR IDEAL SELF.** Make statements about who you want to be and remind yourself of that. Examples could be, "I'm a healthy person," or "I'm a caring and effective leader." Throughout the day, ask yourself, "What would a healthy person do?" "What would a caring leader do?"
- **HABIT STACK.** Add new habits to something you automatically do or an activity you like. Choose one "wellness activity" to do while watching a show you enjoy. Do a two-minute wall sit while brushing your teeth. Do balance challenges while heating up your coffee. Recite your affirmations on your commute.
- **REFRAME.** Focus on positive outcomes. On the days I struggle to get to the gym, I remind myself, "You're 30 minutes away from a good mood."
- **CONSISTENCY OVER INTENSITY.** Choose a consistency "rule" that makes sense for you. I hate cardio interval work, so a consistency rule I have set for myself is that I must do it for just one song (even though my real goal is 15 minutes).
- **SET YOURSELF UP FOR SUCCESS.** Plan and prepare. Meal prep, set out workout clothes the night before, or turn on the Netflix setting that does not automatically play the next episode.

- **HAVE A NIGHT ROUTINE.** I find that Nighttime Cara can make or break Morning Cara. I wash my face and brush my teeth right after dinner (I hate that routine, and delaying it often delays my bedtime), set out my workout clothes, and do a quick three- to ten-minute pickup of my home before I go to sleep.
- **CHOOSE YOUR ENVIRONMENT.** Find a focused environment for work so your brain knows it's time to work when you're there.
- **REWARD YOURSELF** for carrying out the habits you're trying to implement. This could be a massage for every tenth workout you complete, or a movie on the weekend if you've completed your morning and nighttime routines each day that week.
- **HABIT TRACK.** Track habits without being too rigid. Commit to not missing more than one day. Find an accountability buddy to stay on track.

One of the best pieces of advice I've heard about habits came from a friend and former colleague. Karl Bradford is the author of the book *Maximum Performance* and an avid marathoner, while I, as I have said previously, am *not* a runner. I'm not built like a runner, and I didn't like running. The year I decided to run that marathon, I asked for his advice as I was frustrated that I wasn't getting any faster. He looked at me and simply said, "Cara, if you want to run faster, you gotta run faster."

I laughed. It was so true. Somehow, I had expected myself to just miraculously become a faster runner if I kept getting out there. But the facts were, I was never *choosing* to run faster. I was just hoping it would happen.

Intentionality is key.

Creating habits and routines is a skill. A skill you can develop.

Summary

I want to finish this chapter with a story about a cockroach.

One thing that's important to me is flexibility and mobility. I want to be able to move and explore and adventure for as long as possible, and flexibility and mobility are paramount to fulfilling that desire. My goal is for my muscles to automatically use the correct recruitment patterns to keep me injury-free in my daily life, especially in times when I'm not paying attention or I need a quick response. Here's the thing about that work: it's not fun for me. At all. Still, I work on it. Consistently. As a result, it's become a habit.

About a year ago, I was in my Roatan condo when I came out of the bathroom to see a cockroach above the front door, near the ceiling. It was giant and *disgusting*. Luckily, I have learned a strategy for killing those super-fast sons-a-guns:*

1. Have your DEET spray in one hand and a flipflop in the other.
2. Spray the thing to slow him down.
3. Smash him with the flipflop.

I pulled up a chair to get close enough to spray him. The chair was in between the wall and the end of the kitchen island, with very little wiggle room. When I sprayed the cockroach, I realized he was the flying kind, and he flew out from the wall and landed on my right foot. *Ew!* I have no clue what exactly happened next, but I jumped away from him, somehow contorted my body, hit my leg up against the island counter… and landed on my feet.

I have no idea how I did this. I would pay money to see video of it.

---

*Disclaimer: I do not kill many living things—basically only cockroaches and mosquitos. Please see Chapter 15 on forgiveness if this makes you think of me as a bad person!

I ended up with a giant bruise on my right shin and knee, which is a blessing, really. It could have been (*should* have been) much, much worse.

I'm almost certain that my body knew how to move in the right way and handle that situation safely because of my consistent habit of stretching and mobility work. There was no other explanation. We are what we repeatedly do; so I was mobile and nimble. My body knew how to move correctly through that split-second situation because of my repeated habit. My habit saved me from injury for certain. (And yes, I got the cockroach in the end. Poor little fella.)

We've all heard the quote, "Death by a thousand cuts," but I like to say, "Success by a thousand acts." We see the outcomes of our habits on a lag measure—we don't see them every day—but they eventually add up. In the book *Atomic Habits* James Clear reminds us, "Every action is a vote for the type of person you wish to become."[4] Those habits, when intentionally created and repeatedly practiced, turn you into the person you want to be, for your family, your employees, your friends, your organization, and, most importantly, your self. So, your question is: How do I show up?

You can begin answering this question by defining the person you want to be for your different circles and for yourself. Once clear on that, defining how that person would show up on a daily basis in authenticity, trust, and vulnerability is the next step. Then, if Aristotle was onto something and we are, in fact, what we repeatedly do, defining and developing habits that align with that vision will set you on the path to leading your self well.

THE DEDICATE PHASE: PUT IT INTO PRACTICE

Inquire Within

Spend 30–60 minutes on the following journal questions:

- How would I define my ideal standards in all the facets of my life? Write these in "I am" statements. For each of these, identify why it's important. For example:
    - I am a healthy person.
    - I am authentic and trustworthy with my partner, family, and work circles.
    - I am a woman of value who cares for herself.
    - I am honorable in the way I treat other people.
- How would my life be different if I were living in accordance with those statements? What do I have to say "no" to in my life to be doing that?
- How do I want to show up in authenticity, trust, and vulnerability at work? At home? What would it *feel* like if I could make small changes toward this way of being? What would feel different if I could become more comfortable with it?
- What habits do I have that support who I want to be? What habits are getting in the way of that?

Daily Practice Ideas

Choose one or two options below to practice daily for 2–4 weeks.

- Choose one bad habit you have and try to replace it with something else for two weeks.
- Choose one good habit you want to start and use one of the hacks given earlier in this chapter (such as habit stacking, using your environment, setting up appropriate rewards, or tracking) and start doing it.
- Choose one of the other skills in this book and tie it into something you do every day. For example:

- ○ **GRATITUDE**: When I make my morning coffee, I will find three things for which I am grateful.
  - ○ **AFFIRMATIONS**: When I brush my teeth, I will silently repeat three affirmations.
  - ○ **COMPASSION**: When I drive my car for the first time each day, I will send loving kindness and compassion to the people I pass by (or someone in my life).
- Think about your future self as you go through your day. What can you do in the morning to help your "afternoon self?" What can you do this week to help your "next month self?"
- Create a morning self-care routine. Start small: take 10−15 minutes and choose to do a gratitude walk, stretching routine, guided meditation, or affirmations.

Wellness Wednesday (When-sday)

Complete the following activity on your Wellness Day.

- Take today to think through how you show up in authenticity, trust, and vulnerability with the people in your life. Ask: how well am I doing so far this week? What can I do with the last few days of the week to show up the way I want to (for my circles, my teams, and my self)?

Wellness at Work

Exploring Trust:
- Choose one person at work who you trust and one person you don't fully trust (so you can practice learning why and how trust is created). These people can be on your team, a leader, or a peer.

Answer the questions associated with the components of trust in the previous chapter to identify why you do or do not trust them.

- o **AFFECTION**: How much do I care about the other person?
- o **COLLABORATION**: Can we effectively work together?
- o **CONFLICT**: Can we face conflict and have faith that when we do, we'll be able to work through it effectively?
- o **TRANSPARENCY**: Am I comfortable revealing my thoughts, ideas, and feelings to this person? Is the feeling mutual?
- o **PREDICTABILITY**: Is this person consistent in how they treat me, or am I walking on eggshells around them?
- o **COMPETENCE**: Do I have faith in the person's ability to do their job effectively and contribute positively to the team?
- o **RISK**: To what degree can this person threaten my success or cause me emotional pain?

- If you're brave enough (and if appropriate), have a conversation with the person you don't trust about the component(s) that you identified as having led to the mistrust. Share ideas on how you can improve your trust. (I highly recommend preparing for this conversation with a coach, trusted HR partner, or mentor ahead of time.) You can also have a conversation with the person you *do* trust, talk to them about why, and thank them for the ways in which they have shown up for you. Be sure to ask them for feedback on how you're doing on the components of trust.

- Once you have done this, flip this exercise around and ask yourself, "Can my team trust me?" Try to answer the questions as they would. Make a commitment to improving one component in how you can be trustworthy.

Exploring Authenticity and Vulnerability:

- Create opportunities for people to share stories about themselves, especially those that highlight their personal or professional strengths and struggles and how they are trying to grow. Build these pieces into regularly scheduled meetings or into offsite business meetings or workshops. (Collaborate with your HR partner, coach, or external consultant to create these experiences so you can fully participate and thereby model authenticity and vulnerability, instead of leading the activity.)

- Be transparent about your mistakes, failures, or needing help. Openly admit when you've made a mistake or when you need help with something. This is a powerful way to show vulnerability and to create safety for others to do the same.

Reflect to Retain

What are three things I learned about myself from this chapter?
  1.

  2.

  3.

What are three concepts I want to remember from this chapter?
  1.

  2.

  3.

What is the one daily practice I will devote myself to as I read the next chapter?

    1.

PART VIII

DELIVER

chapter 18

when is my time?

DO ANY OF THESE SOUND LIKE things you or your employees say?

- "I take a week off, and within one day of being back, I feel like I never left."
- "What does it matter? I'm so far behind I'll never catch up."
- "What's wrong with me? My fuse is short. I'm frustrated. All sorts of things are right, so I can't quite figure out what feels so wrong."
- "I'm battling with the idea that I can't do this forever, but I feel trapped."
- "I'm making a great living and I'm working remotely, but I'm still not happy."
- "I feel like I'm winning the rat race, but I'm still a rat."
- "I want to go on vacation, but that will mean doing an 80-hour week before and after. I'm at my breaking point already. I can't do that."
- "Does this place even need me? Am I appreciated? Am I going to do all this work only to be told I'm not good enough and get cut?"
- "It's Wednesday and I haven't cried yet this week, so that's good."

- "I wake up every night at 2:30AM. I never feel rested. I can't shut my brain down."
- "Every morning, I feel like I've got to be the peppy guy. Then lunch hits, and I have a 30-minute break if I'm lucky. I spend it doom-scrolling on my phone just to shut down my brain. Then I rev myself back up for the afternoon ride. By the end of my day, I just think, *I can't do this anymore.* I didn't want to show the worn-out me at work, so my wife and kids get that version of me. Then, I go to bed and do it all again the next day."
- "I can't keep my cool. Every day I promise myself I'm going to, and most days, at least once, I lose it. If I don't, I'm fighting to *not* lose it. It's exhausting."

These are actual quotes I've heard from clients and leaders—words that highlight the struggles many face in the workplace today. They reveal a sobering truth: your leaders and teams are finding it difficult to experience true wellbeing. This brings us to your final inquiry: when is your time? When is the "right time" to implement this work? When is your time to prioritize and Deliver on wellbeing? As we enter the final chapter of this journey, this may be the most critical question of all. After all, if you *never Deliver*, no amount of skills or knowledge will make a difference. Without action, you will never create change.

Unfortunately, health (mental and physical) is one of those things often put on the backburner. We say, "I'll focus on that when [insert any issue or event happening in your life] is over," until we are faced with a crisis. Then, sometimes, it's already too late.

This country's health is in crisis.

Your employees' health is in crisis.

It's not too late, but it *is* time.

The world is getting more and more complicated with social media, polarizing politics, mass shootings and gun violence on the rise, and the mental health crisis in all generations (especially our kids) becoming more rampant. All of this impacts your workers and your business outcomes in significant ways, and the crisis will continue to worsen if we don't each do something to help. Time is a precious commodity, and the window to prioritize wellbeing is *now*. The stress and professional burnout that pervade today's workplaces are not abstract statistics; they are the lived realities of the people who:

- Craft your products, serve your customers, innovate transformative ideas, and make financial decisions and investments.
- Return home each night to their families and communities, shaping home environments that reflect the weight—or the relief—of their workday.
- Look to leadership for guidance and support in these unprecedented times. (If you fail to provide it, they'll find a leader or organization that will.)

We are at a place where we can bring health, wellbeing, and fitness together to solve what is otherwise clearly *not* getting solved. It's not realistic to say the pressures are going to subside on their own. That is false hope. We must understand this and build our culture to offset the reality of burnout.

Think about the legacy you want to leave—as an individual, as a leader, and as an organization. Do you want to be remembered solely for achieving financial targets? Or as someone who could do so while also transforming lives and making a lasting impact on the health of your organization, community, and country?

Viewing leadership through a wellness lens creates a ripple effect that transforms the entire organization. By committing to and delivering wellbeing leadership today, you can take a stand against the forces that undermine the health of your colleagues, communities, and beyond.

Imagine if enough organizations and leaders prioritized wellbeing—we could transform the health of this country.

A vacation is not a fix for burnout. Taking a new job is not a fix for burnout. Being a better leader or employee and fostering a working culture where employee wellbeing matters is the fix. However, this road is not the easy one. I wish it were. You'll definitely see some benefits early, and the long-term benefits will be life-changing, ensuring the long-term success of your organization. This journey is an investment into the future of your company and your people.

Investing in wellbeing as a long-term strategy is much like investing in the company's Research and Development (R&D). At first glance, it may seem like a significant spend with little immediate return. However, R&D is crucial for long-term innovation, competitiveness, and ultimately ensuring the company's growth and success. The same applies to investing in employee health:

- Both require an upfront commitment of time, money, and resources.
- Both drive long-term organizational success through that investment.
- Both provide a strategic competitive advantage.
- Both ensure long-term sustainability.

In other words, it's worth it to lead your organization "well," financially and socially. (If you don't remember the financial benefits of having a workforce that is well, please return to Chapter 2.)

So, where to start? It can seem daunting.

If you're reading this as a leader in an organization, start here. If you're reading this as an individual working on your own mental health, you can skip to the section titled "For Individuals."

FOR ORGANIZATIONAL LEADERS

Whether you're leading a team of two or of 200,000, you can deliver a culture of wellbeing to your team—but you must start by honestly answering the following question:

"Does my health and my employees' health *really* matter to me? To my organization?"

Answer this truthfully. If the answer is yes, that means you have to be willing to put resources (time, money, and thought) toward it. If it doesn't matter or doesn't matter right now, that means you're not willing to put resources toward it. It also means you shouldn't tell your employees it *does* matter to you. Otherwise, you'll lose credibility with them. Remember in Chapter 5, when I mentioned that Gallup found that 63% of HR professionals said their company cared about employee wellbeing, but only 24% of workers (in the same survey) had the same belief? You don't want to be one of those organizations where there is a disconnect. If you want it to matter, *make it matter.*

> *"I'd argue it's less about 'Can you get there?' and more like, 'You have to get there.' If we don't, millennials and Gen Zers are going to give the finger to working. 'Why would I stress myself out for you?'"*
> —BETH SMITS
> *Former SVP, Operations & Services, 24 Hour Fitness*

I'd like you to pause now and journal your answers to the following questions to fully understand your "why" for this work. This will be important when it comes time to communicate with your people. Discuss these thoughts with your executive team, leadership team, or HR partner.

- What is the connection between my team's wellbeing and their performance? What examples do I have? What does the research say? (Review Chapter 2 for some stats.)
- In what ways does employee wellbeing contribute to the organization achieving its goals?
- How committed am I to integrating wellbeing into my team/organizational culture? How would I rate this from 1–10? What is my reasoning for this rating?

If you've decided that wellbeing *does* matter, the next step is to determine how you will incorporate this into your culture. Culture is the bedrock of an organization. It shapes how employees interact, how decisions are made, and, ultimately, how the company performs. Remember the kickball team analogy from the Introduction? You already intrinsically *know* that employees who are mentally strong contribute to the team in a different way than those who are not.

A culture of wellbeing needs three things to be effective:

1. Wellbeing benefits.
2. Wellbeing policies.
3. Wellbeing leadership.

It's like a braid of rope—two strands provide support but can easily unravel. The third strand is the key to stability, it provides the strength and structure for the other two strands to work. Similarly, the first two elements, policies and benefits, support employee wellbeing and play a crucial role in creating a culture where employees can thrive.

Organizations may offer:

- Group health insurance.
- Health programs and incentives tied to smoking cessation or BMI reduction.
- Meditation programs or burnout sessions.

- Employee Assistance Programs.
- Flexible work arrangements.
- Various types of PTO and leave policies.
- DEI policies and programs.
- Gym memberships.
- Mental health days.
- Zero-tolerance harassment policies.
- Childcare support.
- Financial planning classes.

These are all helpful. However, we need to redefine the employee wellbeing experience to take their *whole life* into account. While wellbeing benefits and policies are fundamental, they cannot cultivate a holistic culture of wellbeing alone. They are only part of the equation. Effective Leadership Development and wellbeing skill development must also play a pivotal role.

1. Generous benefits and policies without leadership skills that support wellbeing lead to disengagement and lack of trust or belief in the organization.
2. Strong policies and supportive leadership are undermined when employees don't have access to adequate wellbeing benefits.
3. Generous benefits and supportive leadership without strong policies can result in inconsistencies and gaps in employee support, disintegrating the overall wellbeing culture.

You want your employees to know that the company and their leaders care about their wellbeing. You want them to know that they're protected and safe. A successful wellbeing culture relies on this multifaceted approach. Just as a braid can take three fragile strands and make them stronger when woven together, a holistic culture of wellbeing is strongest when benefits, policies, and leadership are integrated and intertwined.

This book has focused on building the skill set of wellbeing leadership, but all three components are essential. I often hear leaders say, "We're doing so much, but we just can't seem to crack the code." Leadership from a wellbeing lens is what's missing. This is a skill you can teach your leaders and all employees; a skill you can develop in your organization.

Leadership from a wellness lens looks like this:

- Development of wellbeing skills for leaders and employees.
- Modeling healthy behaviors.
- Using communication strategies that help employees feel safe to share their ideas, struggles, and concerns.
- Having open discussions about mental health and available resources.
- Intentionally using scientifically proven skills that foster mental wellbeing.
- Being aware of each employee's workload and what effective management of that looks like.
- Creating development plans that include wellbeing actions and goals tailored to each employee.
- Ensuring effective work-life integration that supports an employee's whole life experience.

As a people leader, learning the skills of The 5 Inquiries and applying them to daily operations will create an environment where wellbeing becomes second nature. You will then also be able to teach these skills to your employees, leading to improved productivity, profitability, creativity, engagement, and overall organizational success (not to mention just making the world a better place). To integrate this work holistically and cohesively into your organization, there are some steps to follow:

1. Assess your current culture.
2. Engage leadership.
3. Define organizational wellbeing language.

4. Train leaders in wellbeing leadership skills.
5. Integrate into all aspects of the employee lifecycle.
6. Communicate clearly to the organization.

Step 1: Assess Your Current Culture

Start with a comprehensive review of your culture's current values, competencies, and capabilities to understand where these currently support employee wellbeing and where there are gaps. Engaging with employees through surveys, focus groups, and interviews can provide valuable insights into how wellbeing can be better integrated. Following this, a cross-functional team, including HR, leadership, and wellbeing specialists, can draft proposed changes.

> *"People want to contribute. It's innate. When you can contribute while living the way you want to live, you have a much longer runway."*
> —STEVE WALLIN
> VP, Fortune 100 Company

Identify current cultural barriers that work *against* wellbeing:
- Which leaders don't support this philosophy? (There will be some that likely don't, and it's important to identify them.)
- Do your leaders model healthy behaviors?
- Does your culture value consensus to an unhelpful degree?
- Is "bad behavior" actually rewarded, either directly or indirectly?
- Do you implement reorgs and reporting changes too often?
- Is there a stigma around conversations about mental health?

- Does your team have the knowledge and skills necessary for wellbeing?
- Do your leaders know how to prioritize work effectively and set boundaries on less critical initiatives? Do they feel empowered to challenge or redirect initiatives that may not align with key priorities?
- Do your policies (stated and unstated) support flexibility and wellbeing?

Understanding and addressing the barriers standing in the way of a wellbeing culture in your company is essential before moving forward. This will not be a cut-and-paste, one-size-fits-all scenario. It will depend on the specific barriers that exist in your organization and with specific leaders. You must be able to identify each barrier (and its cause) to create an effective action plan. This step helps the team clearly see where they can work to overcome the most important and urgent barriers.

Step 2: Engage Leadership

Establish a company-wide expectation for employees to develop their wellbeing skills, making it a core requirement. Just as some organizations intentionally create a culture of performance or a culture of feedback, prioritize a culture where caring for and actively improving wellbeing is the norm, an expectation. Craft organizational language that resonates and reinforces this commitment.

Ensure your leaders, at all levels, are committed to leading from a place of wellbeing. Help them to see the financial, time, and social benefits of having a team that is mentally strong and resilient. Work with your HR partners on change management practices to help those who are struggling to understand the benefits and necessity of wellbeing.

Remember that just as with any other aspect of good leadership, you must surround yourself with other leaders who are willing to have the conversation and who are different from you. Women will have a different wellbeing lens to share than men, as will people of color and those from different generations. Make wellbeing a continuous dialogue.

Step 3: Define Organizational Wellbeing Language

Once you understand the current landscape, begin to define what a "culture of wellbeing" looks like in your organization. Work with the leadership team or a wellbeing project team to review your company's values, competencies, or core capabilities, to determine where to weave in wellbeing language and expectations. Incorporating wellbeing language into these constructs is necessary if you are to create a culture of wellbeing.

There are a few different approaches to this, depending on what makes the most sense for your organization.

Option A: Creating Specific Wellbeing Values and Competencies

This can involve drafting new value statements that explicitly highlight the importance of employee wellbeing. For example, a company might adopt values such as, "We prioritize mental and physical health," or, "We support work-life balance for sustained success."

Leadership competencies can also be updated to reflect these values. Competencies such as, "Promotes a culture of wellbeing," "Supports team members in managing stress," and, "Leads by example in practicing self-care," can be added to the leadership framework. These competencies should be tied to performance evaluations and leadership development programs, just like any other skill or competency, to ensure they are taken seriously and incorporated into everyday operations.

Option B: Integrate Wellbeing into Current Values and Competencies

For companies with well-established values and competencies, integrating wellbeing language into existing frameworks can be an effective strategy. This approach involves reviewing current values and competencies and identifying opportunities to weave in wellbeing-related concepts. For instance, a value like, "We strive for excellence," can be expanded to, "We strive for excellence while maintaining our wellbeing." Similarly, leadership competencies such as, "Drives results," can be rephrased to, "Drives results sustainably, in consideration of the wellbeing of the team."

It's also possible to incorporate descriptor language or sub-bullets under each value that include a focus on wellbeing. This method ensures that wellbeing becomes an integral part of the company's existing ethos without the need for significant overhauls. It also signals to employees that wellbeing is not a separate initiative but a core aspect of how the company operates and succeeds.

Option C: Embedding Wellbeing into Key Capabilities

Another approach is to embed wellbeing into the key capabilities that define how work currently gets done within the organization. This involves incorporating wellbeing metrics and practices into capability frameworks that guide various roles and functions. For example, project management capabilities might include, "Ensures project timelines are realistic to prevent burnout," or, "Incorporates regular wellbeing check-ins during project phases."

You can also extend this to the tools and resources provided to employees. This approach would include providing training programs that ensure all employees are equipped with the wellbeing skills to manage stress and burnout and checking that all managers are equipped with the skill set they'll need to lead in a way that supports their teams' wellbeing.

Incorporating wellbeing language into the company's core frameworks is a powerful step toward creating a supported, productive, and resilient workforce.

Option D: Create and Implement a Specific Wellbeing Strategy

Developing a comprehensive wellbeing strategy ensures that wellbeing becomes a deliberate and measurable component of your organization's success. It highlights its importance to employees. It requires leaders to give it the attention it deserves. A clear strategy includes the wellbeing vision or philosophy of the organization, goals and outcomes related to employee health, resources and initiatives to support these goals, and actionable steps to integrate wellbeing across all levels of the organization.

The strategy should be led and championed by the highest level of leadership, demonstrating its importance, and ensuring alignment with broader business objectives. A well-defined strategy signals to employees that wellbeing is not an afterthought but a priority essential to the company's mission and culture. It does not need to be complicated. If you're looking for a place you start, you will find the link to a sample of a general wellbeing strategy in the appendices.

Step 4: Train Leaders on Wellbeing Leadership Skills

Training leaders on the wellbeing skills outlined in The 5 Inquiries is a foundational step to delivering a culture of wellbeing. It equips leaders with the tools and mindset needed to care for their own wellbeing and to lead their teams in a way that promotes health and happiness. This holistic approach not only enhances individual and team performance, but also drives organizational success by creating a sustainable, positive work environment where everyone can thrive and contribute at a high level.

Leaders also need to know how to effectively communicate about wellbeing with their employees. More leaders than ever before are trying to engage in the conversation, but they don't lean into it fully, for several reasons. Here are a few I have heard from leaders:

- "I don't want to invade their privacy. They'll tell me if something is wrong."
- "I'm worried I'll get sued or called into HR if I say the wrong thing or violate HIPPA accidentally."
- "What if the employee needs a leave of absence? I'm already doing more with less. We won't be able to get the work done. So, I ignore it."
- "I prefer the 'don't ask, don't tell' approach."

How do we normalize health conversations? How do we normalize mental health—period? It feels way easier to deal with physical health issues. We don't hesitate to ask someone about a broken arm. It's harder to talk about mental health. Still, what's going on in your employees' lives can impact their ability to be effective in their role, and what's going on at work can very negatively impact their home life. Normalizing these conversations begins with creating an environment of trust and support, and leaders play a crucial role in setting the tone here. Normalize leaders saying to their employees:

- "How are you doing?"
- "Things seem a bit off. How can I support you?"
- "What are your physical manifestations of stress? Migraines? Insomnia? What are some resources we could bring into work to help those?"

Embedding wellbeing into the values, competencies, and capabilities in your organization helps to facilitate such discussions. Additionally, leading by example can have a powerful impact. When leaders openly discuss their own wellbeing journey or how they manage stress, it can encourage others to speak up. Using these skills during developmental conversations or regular 1:1s is imperative.

Step 5: Integrate into the Employee Lifecyle

EMPLOYEE LIFECYCLE

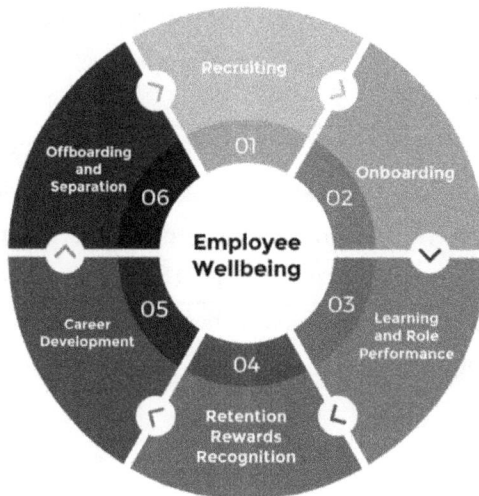

Recruiting:

Market your organization to potential candidates as one with a culture of wellbeing. Emphasize the fact that wellbeing is considered as a skill in the organization, and that employees are provided development for this skill. This is a *huge* differentiator. Almost all organizations are offering (and advertising) their wellbeing policies and benefits, but not many offer and advertise leadership through a wellbeing lens, nor do they consider wellbeing to be a skill that can be developed. This will be an excellent differentiator as candidates, especially Millennials and Gen Z, are weighing their options.

Onboarding:

Set the stage immediately with employees. Define what a culture of wellbeing means and how they will see it show up in their role and development. Communicate that wellbeing is part and parcel of everything you're doing and is not a one-off program. One leader I work with explains to all employees early on, "The only way you can be present is if your mind is healthy, and the only way we can make sure your mind is healthy is if we lay the foundations for you to be mentally and physically healthy. If you're not present, you're going to feel like whatever you're doing isn't fulfilling."

Onboarding is a perfect place to start with the first inquiry ("What Do I Believe?"). During the orientation process, a senior leader or HR leader can lead a session on helping new employees identify their inner critic and understand how it may show up at work. The employee can then take this information into their first 1:1 with their direct leader, to discuss how they'll work together.

Learning / Role Performance:
Encourage and expect continuous learning and development of the company's wellbeing skill set. Ensure 1:1s and performance reviews include discussions on workload management, overall wellbeing, and use of wellbeing skills at work.

In addition, there are a number of best practices for wellbeing 1:1s. As examples, have you ever had someone (usually a boss or your HR partner) tell you to "meet them where they are" when talking about your employees?

I bet I have said this to 100 leaders over the course of my career, and I rarely talked about *how* to do that. (I'm so sorry!) The only way to know where your employees are so you can meet them there is to *ask them*.

Your employees will respond to this in different ways. Some will want you to know them deeply. Others will not. Either way, as a leader, creating a space where they can be who they are with you is essential to their wellbeing. Before jumping into project plans and work accountability, begin 1:1s with a check-in on the employees' wellbeing. Ask open-ended questions about their stress levels, how their work is impacting their home life (and vice versa), their relationships with their coworkers, and anything outside of work that they want to discuss.

Be present. Practice your skill of mindful listening. Ask how their current projects and responsibilities are impacting their wellbeing and explore opportunities to adjust, if necessary. Review wellbeing goal(s) on their IDPs and discuss how they are helping with their stress levels. Brainstorm ideas to integrate these skills into their daily routine, to achieve their wellbeing goals. Provide support or resources as appropriate.

One of the biggest complaints I hear from employees is, "My leader skips or repeatedly reschedules my 1:1." Your employees *want* time with you. Make the commitment to keep these meetings as often as possible, and as basic as it sounds, remember these employees are human. In the words of Beth Smits, former COO at 24 Hour Fitness, "I care about humans. If humans aren't in a good place, they're not going to be effective. Start seeing them as humans. Ask, 'What do you need to be a full complete human? How can I help you be a full human with really cool stuff at work? What can I do to put you in a position to be successful so that if work is the stressor, we understand why, we can see an end to it, and we can support you as best as possible during it?'"

Best Practices for Wellbeing: Addressing Workload

One of the greatest barriers to organizational wellbeing is the challenge of balancing workloads and prioritizing tasks. Many of us have experienced the frustration of being tasked with unnecessary or low-impact work, whether it's overly detailed reports that no one reads, unnecessary process documentation, or the infamous cover sheets on your TPS reports (if you haven't seen *Office Space*, I recommend you look into it immediately!). The inability to distinguish between what truly matters and what can wait is a widespread issue that takes a toll on employee and organizational wellbeing.

The best leaders are the ones who can prioritize the team's work, understand capacity, and be in a position to notice what's going on with the team, including any signs of burnout. Not every employee is going to speak up before something becomes a problem, so have the courage to stop and say to yourself, "This isn't okay. My team is burned out. What have I done to contribute to this?" Workload and lack of prioritization are often the answer. A team only has so much capacity, and leaders need to actively manage that capacity to prevent burnout.

How do leaders manage mental capacity and work capacity with their teams and still get results? By consistently vetting what is at the bottom of the list and having the courage to say no to some of those things (*their* leaders need to make saying no okay, too). All too often, if a leader is hung up on getting promoted or feels as though they'll be seen as incapable, they're less likely to speak up for themselves and their teams. Doing the ROI on all the work so that your team is working on the highest priority tasks that make a real difference is imperative to addressing burnout. As one leader told me, "It's kind of like cleaning your closet or doing your Marie Kondo. It's about asking the question, 'What are the highest priorities right now?' constantly. There is *always* low-hanging fruit that could go away and no one would notice."

What do you do when you've eliminated everything unnecessary, yet the workload remains overwhelming for your team? Start by addressing it openly. Look at your calendar (when will it start to lessen?). Address it with the team. Thank them for hanging in there. Remind them there's a light at the end of the tunnel. Be open to listening when they're feeling overwhelmed. Give them a space to talk about it if that's what they need. Ensure they're using skills to manage their nervous system. Show them you see them, hear them, and appreciate them. Then, when this phase or project is complete, give them a space to breathe and recover, before jumping right into the next project.

Retention, Rewards, and Recognition:
Recognize and reward employees, not just for their performance, but also for their commitment to maintaining a healthy work–life balance. Include wellbeing concerns in regular 1:1s and offer incentives such as wellness days, wellness retreats, or mental health days for engagement in wellbeing practices. Provide some guidance on how an employee could use a mental health day, that would actually *encourage* mental health! See the appendices for some ideas.

Career Development:
Incorporate wellbeing goals into individual development plans (IDPs). This is a strategic approach that will align personal growth with organizational goals and objectives.

Choosing one of the wellbeing skills from The 5 Inquiries to focus on can support both personal and professional development. It also shows you care about the employee, which gives you a competitive advantage in the war for talent.

Collaborate with your team on setting measurable and achievable wellbeing goals, like consistent mindfulness practices, creating new habits, or honing the skill of self-awareness. Check in with your employees on the desired impact this skill will produce and the behavior changes associated with it. Regular review and accountability in 1:1s will help employees feel supported and cared for.

Make this an expectation in your organization. If your organization has a culture of performance, an employee should be expected to have goals around performance. If you have a culture of feedback, an employee should be expected to learn to give feedback and be held accountable in doing so. If you have a culture of wellness, an employee should be expected to work on their wellbeing.

Offboarding and Separation:

Approach offboarding with empathy, compassion, and support, whether voluntary or involuntary. Offer counseling services, conduct exit interviews that address wellbeing concerns, and provide resources to help departing employees transition smoothly. This ensures they leave with a positive impression of your organization's commitment to employee wellbeing and helps them maneuver, as a human, through what may be a very difficult time.

Step 6: Communicate Clearly to the Organization

Communication is key to successful implementation. It's therefore imperative that you clearly articulate changes to all employees, emphasizing the company's commitment to their wellbeing.

All employees need to understand the importance of wellbeing and how it fits into the company values, their personal and professional growth, and the expectations of them as an employee. The cadence of this communication will depend on how your organization generally communicates. Work with your Communication team or HR partners to determine the best cadence as the organization begins to implement these steps. Regularly assess and adjust these initiatives based on feedback and evolving needs, to ensure they remain relevant and effective.

FOR INDIVIDUALS

If you're reading this book and you're not a formal leader in your organization, the steps you need to take to deliver a culture of wellbeing (whether in your home or workplace) are similar:

1. Ask, "Does this matter to me?"
2. Determine your "why."
3. Develop the skills: Read this book and follow the steps. (Treat it like a workshop!)
4. Bring it to Life—Intentionally!

Step 1: Ask, "Does This Matter to Me?"

Begin by checking in with yourself: "Does this work resonate? Is my wellbeing something I'm willing to prioritize?" Take a moment to reflect on what wellbeing truly means to you. This initial question is crucial because lasting change requires genuine commitment—a commitment of time and action. Think about the ways you'll benefit personally, professionally, and relationally by embracing this journey. If it matters to you, you're already on the right path. If you're uncertain, keep an open mind and review some of the early chapters to understand the tangible impact your wellbeing has on your brain, your health, and the lives of those around you.

No one likes to think that they've lost control, it's an incredibly helpless feeling that often brings about embarrassment, shame, and sadness. We don't want to burden others with our problems so we keep it to ourselves and promise ourselves that we'll "do better tomorrow." But feeling burned out, like your life isn't what you want it to be, and that you're not in control of your emotions and actions is a global problem.

You are not alone.

It's not a failing in your personality, it's a result of the world we live in today. The fact that you've read this book is a great start.

Step 2: Determine Your "Why"

If your wellbeing *does* matter to you, then understanding your "why" gives power to your journey. Take a moment to ask yourself why you want to invest in your wellbeing. Maybe you want more energy so you can be present with family, or perhaps you want to reduce stress and enjoy your career more. Whatever your reason, make it personal, meaningful, and memorable. Write it down, reflect on it, and keep it visible as a reminder when challenges arise. Your "why" will ground you and keep you focused on the bigger picture when the work feels tough or unfamiliar.

Answering the questions in the Reflect to Retain sections of Chapters 1 and 4 will help you understand and define your "why."

Step 3: Read This Book and Follow the Steps

Approach this book like a personal guide. It's more than just a read; it's a practical workshop on self-discovery and personal growth. Give yourself the time and space to do the exercises, reflect on the questions, and integrate what you learn. Set a weekly time commitment and stick to it, allowing each step to build upon the last. You're not just learning about wellbeing; you're actively transforming your life one inquiry at a time. And remember, progress is steady, not instant. Be patient and consistent with yourself.

Step 4: Bring it to Life with Intention

This step is imperative, obviously, but going it alone can be tough—sustaining meaningful change is much easier when you have support. To make wellbeing a consistent and impactful part of your life, consider creative ways to engage with the material and integrate it into your daily routines. This is a place where you can call on, and nurture, your inner circle! You could start by forming an accountability group with colleagues or friends who are also interested in personal growth, providing mutual support and encouragement. Consider inviting friends to form a book club around the process so you can share insights and support each other's growth. If you're working with a therapist, this book can also be a powerful tool to deepen your sessions together, offering a structured path for exploring topics you may wish to address. And if you want additional support, check out my coaching programs, designed to complement and enhance the practices in this book.

As this work will be important in your professional world as well, consider bringing these concepts and the work you're doing to your leader during 1:1 meetings, or hiring a coach—both of whom can assist you in exploring how this work aligns with your professional development. Alternatively, share the journey with a spouse or close friend—reading and reflecting together can deepen connections and help sustain positive habits. The key is finding a method that feels natural and keeps you committed to your growth.

Summary

As you reach the end of this book and followed the steps, you've taken on the powerful work of prioritizing your wellbeing, not only for yourself, but also for those around you—your family, friends, colleagues, and community. Each step of this journey has been a testament to your commitment to leading your self and your team well and living fully and authentically.

By showing up for yourself, you're planting seeds of wellbeing that extend far beyond what you may see today. As you answer The 5 Inquiries, practice the skills, and integrate all into your life, you'll start to notice the impact on the little things: feeling calmer; responding rather than reacting; finding more energy to be present; building stronger, more meaningful connections. These small changes ripple outward, positively affecting everyone around you and creating a community (professionally and personally) rooted in authenticity, trust, and resilience.

Remember, this is ongoing work. Each step you've explored here—whether honoring your emotions, finding your strengths, or clarifying your values—is designed to grow with you over time.

Life will bring new challenges and opportunities, and as it does, revisit these inquiries, make time for reflection, and let this journey evolve. Whether you're walking this path alone or with your work team, with your therapist, or within a coaching community, you're making a real difference. Continue to nurture this commitment, both for your own transformation and for the positive impact it will bring to the lives you touch.

Thank you for being here, for prioritizing wellbeing, and for being open to change. Your journey matters, and your dedication to it is a powerful force for good in the world. Keep showing up, keep practicing, and let this work continue to support you in creating a life, an organization, and a world where wellbeing is valued and celebrated.

Reflect to Retain

What are three things I learned about myself from this chapter?

1.

2.

3.

What are three concepts I want to remember from this chapter?

1.

2.

3.

What's my "why" for my own wellbeing? What about for my team? My family?

What are the three next steps for my continued growth? What about for that of my team?

1.

2.

3.

afterword

A S I PREPARED THE FINAL EDITS of this book, a shocking event unfolded: the brazen murder of UnitedHealthcare CEO Brian Thompson. It hit close to home, not only because I live in Minneapolis and have friends who work there, but because the victim was from a small town in Iowa, near where my dad lives.

What followed was equally jarring. Public reactions were marked not by empathy, but with frustration, dark humor, and even disturbing admiration for the shooter. Memes with captions like, "My Empathy is Out of Network" revealed a painful truth: people are suffering. And many feel unheard and uncared for by the system that's supposed to care about their health.

The words inscribed on the bullets—"Deny, Defend, Depose"—echoed common critiques of our healthcare system. But this tragedy speaks to more than policy failure, it's about what happens when human wellbeing is deprioritized for too long.

The United States is facing a mental health epidemic. Rates of anxiety, depression, burnout, and despair are at historic highs. Yet, for many organizations, mental health remains an afterthought—a benefit tacked on to check a box. This is a critical misstep. Leaders need to understand that ignoring the mental health of their employees is not just a moral failure but a strategic one as well.

The data are clear: investing in mental health improves engagement, productivity, and retention. But beyond these financial metrics, it creates a culture where people feel valued, safe, and seen. Leaders and organizations have the power to lead this work and change the trajectory of the health of our nation.

The murder of a high-profile CEO is not simply an act of violence, it's a warning of what happens when people are pushed to the edge by a broken system and overwhelming stress. The tools in this book can guide the change. Now we need the will. Small, consistent investments in wellbeing can transform lives, workplaces, and our communities. That change begins with each of us.

There is a vitality, a life force, an energy, a quickening that is translated through you into action, and because there is only one of you in all of time, this expression is unique. And if you block it, it will never exist through any other medium and it will be lost. The world will not have it. It is not your business to determine how good it is nor how valuable nor how it compares with other expressions. It is your business to keep it yours clearly and directly.

—MARTHA GRAHAM

acknowledgments

I never intended to write a book, but as I look back, it seems as though every step of my path has led me to the work that has culminated into these pages. Writing it was the most difficult, lonely, trying, and challenging endeavor I've undertaken, and yet it has also been the most rewarding. To everyone who played a part in helping me bring myself and this book into the world, thank you from the depths of my heart.

To my early teachers—especially Mrs. Hauser, Mrs. Batty, Mrs. Van Gilder, Ms. Anderson and Mr. Vander Plaats—you set the foundation for my love of learning. You made it fun. Teachers like you change lives. To Ellen Mullen, my advisor at Iowa State University, thank you for always supporting my passion for leadership development, training, and coaching. And to Marilyn Deardorff, who taught with my mom and whose deep friendship my mother cherished, thank you. To all the teachers out there, you have my deepest gratitude for the work you do.

Bosses are also teachers, with the power to change the world through their leadership. Stacey Cale, my first HR boss, thank you for showing me the ropes in a challenging manufacturing environment—your lessons have stayed with me. To the Comito family—Joe, Brendan, Kieran, and Christian—a thank you for taking a chance on an inexperienced girl and shaping me into the HR professional I am today. Your unwavering support during the loss of my mother was a gift I'll never forget. And to Marce Spies-Johnson, thank you for pushing me to be a better coach and HR partner, especially when I wasn't the easiest person to lead.

Therapy and coaching have been lifelines for me during the times I couldn't figure things out on my own. To Brooks Morse, you possibly quite literally saved my life—your work with me during those difficult years remains with me. To Kayla Wagener, thank you for helping me find my footing after losing my mom. And to Christa Surerus, your support was a steady anchor when I felt lost at sea. To my two brilliant coaches, Bruce Kawahara and Ann Betz, thank you for your wisdom and guidance, during our coaching engagements and through the creation of this book.

To my friends and colleagues, thank you for enduring *countless* hours of book talk, for sharing your thoughts and invaluable professional feedback on the model and book content, and for supporting me when I couldn't see an end in sight. A very special thank you to Rick Anderson, Jennifer Bernard, Lori Cihlar, Cassidy Edstrom, Wes Feeney, Lisa Hoon, Sheila Krocak, Darcy Pietraszewski, Rebecca Rivera, Kristin Rourke, and Steve Wallin for listening, challenging, and encouraging me. Your expertise, wisdom, and ideas made this content so much better. To those who read drafts, offered edits, answered questions, and/or served as thought partners—Tracy Emmil, Mary Feyereisn, Stephanie Fitzpatrick, Antonette Gianneschi, Tony Giudicessi, Erik Jensen, Heather Powers, Beth Smits, Marce Spies-Johnson, Joyce Stokes, Christine Webster Moore, and April Whitson—you made this book stronger. To Dee Fletcher and Adam Hansen—who did all of the above *and* took the time to read and meticulously edit chapters—thank you for your time and attention to detail. Lisa Hoon, thank you for always picking up the phone in my moments of self-doubt. Fiona Barnett, thank you for being my biggest cheerleader and for your book cover ideas. A special thank you to my mentor and friend Mason Lucas, your wisdom and guidance are an ever-present facet of my daily work and life.

To my family, you have been my bedrock. To my dad—thank you for always being in my corner and cheering me on through every twist, turn, and unexpected pivot in my life. Your belief in me (even when my plans sounded..."adventurous") has meant the world. I love you. To my siblings Dan, Liza, and Ryan—thank you for being there, even when you weren't totally sure what I was doing or why! Your support (and tolerance for my many "phases") means more than you know. To my nieces and nephews—Grace, Marta, Elli, Olivia, Roen, Charlie, Harlow, Rye, Bailey, and Carter—it is truly an honor and privilege to be your aunt. Watching you grow up is one of the greatest joys of my life. You have taught me so much without even realizing it. To my mom's sisters and my Bartholomew cousins, thank you for being a part of me that I treasure, even if I don't say it often enough. To my ancestors—Dee Lenz (my amazing and wise momma), Grandpa Earl and Grandma Irene, Grandma and Grandpa B, Grandma and Grandpa Lenz, Aunt Leta, Uncle Fred—I still feel your presence, roots, and guidance. Grandma A., your wisdom continues to inspire me.

To my individual and organizational coaching clients—thank you for your openness, curiosity, willingness to try new things, and the trust you've placed in me to be a part of your story. You inspire me daily and deepen my own learning and growth. It's been an honor to walk alongside you in your journey.

Finally, this book wouldn't exist without the professional help of several incredible people. To my editor, Faye Deeran, and Hayley Paige at Onyx Publishing, thank you for making this book so much better than the manuscript you first received. To Shawn and Kelly Hodgson, thank you for your professional guidance, friendship, and unending belief in me and what I have to offer this world. Thank you for being my mirror when I most need it. Thank you to Ammad Zulfiqar and Claire Kiewatt for your design work for the graphics herein—and your patience with me in the process! To Brian and Gab, thank you for creating a space where this journey began. And to Michael Lanham, thank you for being there during those first difficult stages when this idea was just beginning to take shape. Your continued friendship, conversation, support, and love are greatly appreciated.

To everyone who has been a part of my journey, thank you for being my teachers, supporters, and guides. This book is as much yours as it is mine.

references

Chapter 2

1. Gunja, M. Z., Gumas, E. D., & Williams II, R. D. (2023). U.S. health care from a global perspective, 2022: Accelerating spending, worsening outcomes. *The Commonwealth Fund.* Retrieved November 26, 2024, from www.commonwealthfund.org/publications/issue-briefs/2023/jan/us-health-care-global-perspective-2022

2. Centers for Medicare & Medicaid Services. (2024). National Health Expenditure Data: Historical. Retrieved February 1, 2025 from https://www.cms.gov/data-research/statistics-trends-and-reports/national-health-expenditure-data/historical.

3. Gunja, M. Z., Gumas, E. D., & Williams II, R. D. (2023). U.S. health care from a global perspective, 2022: Accelerating spending, worsening outcomes. *The Commonwealth Fund.* Retrieved November 26, 2024, from www.commonwealthfund.org/publications/issue-briefs/2023/jan/us-health-care-global-perspective-2022

4. National Institute of Mental Health. (2024). Mental Health Information: Statistics: Mental Health. Accessed February 1, 2025 from https://www.nimh.nih.gov/health/statistics/mental-illness?utm_source=chatgpt.com.

5. The Standard. (2021). *Nearly Half of American Workers Now Suffer from Mental Health Issues During COVID-19.* Accessed February 1, 2025 from https://www.standard.com/get-to-know-standard/newsroom/press-releases/nearly-half-american-workers-now-suffer-mental-health.

6. World Health Organization (WHO). (2022). *COVID-19 Pandemic Triggers 25% Increase in Prevalence of Anxiety and Depression Worldwide.* Accessed February 1, 2025 from https://www.who.int/news/item/02-03-2022-covid-19-pandemic-triggers-25-increase-in-prevalence-of-anxiety-and-depression-worldwide.

7. National Center for Health Statistics. (2021). *Drug Overdose Deaths in the U.S. Top 100,000 Annually.* Accessed February 1, 2025 from

https://www.cdc.gov/nchs/pressroom/nchs_press_releases/2021/202
11117.htm.

8. Kestel, D. (2002), cited by World Health Organization. *COVID-19
Pandemic Triggers 25% Increase in Prevalence of Anxiety and Depression
Worldwide.* Accessed February 1, 2025 from https://www.who.int/
news/item/02-03-2022-covid-19-pandemic-triggers-25-increase-in-
prevalence-of-anxiety-and-depression-worldwide.

9. Park, C. S., Choi, E.-K., Han, K.-D., Ahn, H.-J., Kwon, S., Lee, S.-R.,
Oh, S., Lip, G. Y. H., (2023), in European Journal of Preventative
Cardiology. *Increased Cardiovascular Events in Young Patients with
Mental Disorders: A Nationwide Cohort Study.* Accessed February 1,
2025 from https://academic.oup.com/eurjpc/article/30/15/1582/
7146568.

10. BusinessWire. (2021). *Nearly Half of American Workers Now Suffer from
Mental Health Issues During COVID-19.* Retrieved February 1, 2025
from https://www.businesswire.com/news/home/20210202005236/
en/Nearly-Half-of-American-Workers-Now-Suffer-from-Mental-
Health-Issues-During-COVID-19.

11. World Health Organization (WHO). (2019). *Burn-out an "occupational
phenomenon": International Classification of Diseases.* Accessed
February 1, 2025 from https://www.who.int/news/item/28-05-2019-
burn-out-an-occupational-phenomenon-international-classification-
of-diseases.

12. Deloitte. (2018). *Workplace Burnout Survey: Burnout without Borders.*
Deloitte. Retrieved February 1, 2025, from
https://www2.deloitte.com/us/en/pages/about-
deloitte/articles/burnout-survey.html.

13. U.S. Department of Labor. (2024). Trendlines Employment and
Training Administration. *Changes in the U.S. Labor Supply.* Accessed
February 1, 2025 from https://www.dol.gov/sites/dolgov/files/ETA/
opder/DASP/Trendlines/posts/2024_08/Trendlines_August_2024.ht
ml.

14. Gallup. (2018). *4 Things Gen Z and Millennials Expect from Their
Workplace.* Accessed November 28, 2024 from
https://www.gallup.com/workplace/336275/things-gen-millennials-
expect-workplace.aspx.

15. Maese, E., Dupreé, W. & Lloyd, C. (2022), cited in Gallup. *Level the Playing Field for Development With Fair Recognition.* Accessed February 1, 2025 from https://www.gallup.com/workplace/400064/level-playing-field-development-fair-recognition.aspx.

16. Center for American Progress. (2022). *Health Insurance Costs Are Squeezing Workers and Employers.* Accessed February 1, 2025 from https://www.americanprogress.org/article/health-insurance-costs-are-squeezing-workers-and-employers/.

17. Mayer, K. (2024), in Society for Human Resource Management (SHRM). *Employers Project 8%-9% Rise in Health Care Costs for 2025.* Accessed February 1, 2025 from https://www.shrm.org/topics-tools/news/benefits-compensation/employers-project-8--9--rise-in-health-care-costs-for-2025.

18. Mayer, K. (2024), in Society for Human Resource Management (SHRM). *Employers Project 8%-9% Rise in Health Care Costs for 2025.* Accessed February 1, 2025 from https://www.shrm.org/topics-tools/news/benefits-compensation/employers-project-8--9--rise-in-health-care-costs-for-2025.

19. Wallert, J., Held, C., Madison, G., Olsson, E. M. G. (2017), in Science Direct. *Temporal Changes in Myocardial Infarction Incidence Rates are Associated with Periods of Perceived Psychosocial Stress: A SWEDEHEART National Registry Study.* Accessed February 1, 2025 from https://www.sciencedirect.com/science/article/pii/S0002870317301709.

20. Freichel, R. & O'Shea, B. A. (2023), in Nature. *Suicidality and Mood: The Impact of Trends, Seasons, Day of the Week, and Time of Day on Explicit and Implicit Cognitions among an Online Community Sample.* Accessed February 1, 2025 from https://www.nature.com/articles/s41398-023-02434-1.

21. National Center for Chronic Disease Prevention and Health Promotion (NCCDPHP). (2024). *About the Division for Heart Disease and Stroke Prevention.* Accessed February 1, 2025 from https://www.cdc.gov/nccdphp/divisions-offices/about-the-division-for-heart-disease-and-stroke-prevention.html.

22. Slack. (2023). *The State of Work in 2023.* Accessed February 1, 2025 from https://slack.com/intl/en-gb/blog/news/state-of-work-2023.

23. World Health Organization (WHO). (2024). *Mental Health at Work*. Accessed February 1, 2025 from https://www.who.int/news-room/fact-sheets/detail/mental-health-at-work.

24. Wigert, B. & Agrawal, S. (2018), in Gallup. *Employee Burnout, Part 1: The 5 Main Causes*. Accessed February 1, 2025 from https://www.gallup.com/workplace/237059/employee-burnout-part-main-causes.aspx.

25. Occupational Health & Safety (OSHA). (2021). *A Shared Responsibility: Preventing Violence in the Workplace*. Accessed February 1, 2025 from https://ohsonline.com/articles/2021/05/04/a-shared-responsibility-preventing-violence-in-the-workplace.aspx.

26. U.S. Bureau of Labor Statistics. (2021). *Homicides and Other Workplace Assaults by Gender in 2019*. Accessed February 1, 2025 from https://www.bls.gov/opub/ted/2021/homicides-and-other-workplace-assaults-by-gender-in-2019.htm.

27. U.S. Bureau of Labor Statistics. (2022). *Workplace violence: homicides and nonfatal intentional injuries by another person in 2020*. Accessed February 1, 2025 from https://www.bls.gov/opub/ted/2022/workplace-violence-homicides-and-nonfatal-intentional-injuries-by-another-person-in-2020.htm.

28. Occupational Health & Safety (OSHA). (2021). *A Shared Responsibility: Preventing Violence in the Workplace*. Accessed February 1, 2025 from https://ohsonline.com/articles/2021/05/04/a-shared-responsibility-preventing-violence-in-the-workplace.aspx.

Chapter 3

1. Centers for Disease Control and Prevention. (2024). Adult obesity facts. *cdc.gov*. Retrieved December 5, 2024, from https://www.cdc.gov/obesity/php/data-research/adult-obesity-facts.html

2. Oxford English Dictionary. (2024). *Food (n.), sense II.6*. doi:https://doi.org/10.1093/OED/5853062517

3. Merriam-Webster. (n.d.). *Food*. Retrieved November 26, 2024, from www.merriam-webster.com/dictionary/food

4. Hopkins, A. (2024). What is GRAS? *Environmental Working Group*. Retrieved November 26, 2024, from https://www.ewg.org/news-insights/news/2024/03/what-gras

5. Kindy, K. (2014). Food additives on the rise as FDA scrutiny wanes. *The Washington Post*. Retrieved December 5, 2024, from https://www.washingtonpost.com/national/food-additives-on-the-rise-as-fda-scrutiny-wanes/2014/08/17/828e9bf8-1cb2-11e4-ab7b-696c295dd

6. Gabriel, J. (2023). *Landmark Legislation Banning Dangerous Food Additives Signed by Governor Newsom*. Accessed February 1, 2025 from https://a46.asmdc.org/press-releases/20231007-landmark-legislation-banning-dangerous-food-additives-signed-governor.

7. The Wall Street Journal. (2025). FDA Bans Artificial Dye Red 3 From Food. Accessed April 21, 2025, from https://www.wsj.com/health/healthcare/fda-bans-artificial-dye-red-3-from-food-26c9c0e1?utm

8. Riehm, K. E., Feder, K. A., Tormohlen, K. N., *et al.* (2019), in JAMA. *Associations Between Time Spent Using Social Media and Internalizing and Externalizing Problems Among US Youth*. Accessed February 1, 2025 from https://jamanetwork.com/journals/jamapsychiatry/fullarticle/2749480.

9. Balt, E., Mérelle, S., Robinson, J., Popma, A., Creemers, D., van den Brand, I., van Bergen, D., Rasing, S., Mulder, W. & Gilissen, R. (2023), in BioMed Central. *Social Media Use of Adolescents who Died by Suicide: Lessons from a Psychological Autopsy Study*. Accessed February 1, 2025 from https://capmh.biomedcentral.com/articles/10.1186/s13034-023-00597-9.

10. Qui, T. (2021), in Stanford University. *A Psychiatrist's Perspective on Social Media Algorithms and Mental Health*. Accessed February 1, 2025 from https://hai.stanford.edu/news/psychiatrists-perspective-social-media-algorithms-and-mental-health.

11. Stempel, J., Bartz, D., & Raymond, N. (2023, October 25). Meta's Instagram linked to depression, anxiety, insomnia in kids—US states' lawsuit. Reuters.

12. New York City Government. (2024). Mayor Adams announces lawsuit against social media companies fueling nationwide youth mental health crisis. *nyc.gov*. Retrieved November 26, 2024, from

https://www.nyc.gov/office-of-the-mayor/news/125-24/mayor-adams-lawsuit-against-social-media-companies-fueling-nationwide-youth-mental-health#/0

13. KFF. (2022). *2022 Employer Health Benefits Survey*. Accessed February 1, 2025 from https://www.kff.org/report-section/ehbs-2022-section-13-employer-practices-telehealth-provider-networks-and-coverage-for-mental-health-services/.

14. Statista. (2025). *Domestic and international revenue of the U.S. pharmaceutical industry from 1975 to 2023*. Accessed April 16, 2025 from https://www.statista.com/statistics/245473/market-share-of-the-leading-10-global-pharmaceutical-markets/

15. Moynihan, R., Heath, I., & Henry, D. (2002). Selling sickness: The pharmaceutical industry and disease mongering. *BMJ, 324*(7342), 886–891. doi:https://doi.org/10.1136/bmj.324.7342.886

16. Faria, J. (2023). *Pharma and Healthcare Industry Advertising in the U.S. — Statistics & Facts*, published in Statista. Accessed February 1, 2025 from https://www.statista.com/topics/8415/pharma-and-healthcare-industry-advertising-in-the-us.

17. Strong, D. (2021). *Dopesick* miniseries. Hulu.

18. Macy, B. (2018). *Dopesick: Dealers, doctors, and the drug company that addicted America.* Little, Brown and Company.

19. Buntz, B. (2023). Timeline: Navigating Johnson & Johnson's talc lawsuits and their stock performance impact. *Pharmaceutical Processing World*. Retrieved November 28, 2024, from https://www.pharmaceuticalprocessingworld.com/timeline-navigating-johnson-johnsons-talc-lawsuits-and-their-stock-performance-impact

20. Rosenthal, E. (2017). *An American sickness: How healthcare became big business and how you can take it back.* Penguin Press.

21. Rosenthal, E. (2024). Ouch. That 'free' annual checkup might cost you. Here's why. *California Healthline*. Retrieved November 28, 2024, from https://californiahealthline.org/news/article/preventive-care-free-annual-checkup-aca-surprise-billing

22. Levey, N. N. (2022). 100 million people in America are saddled with health care debt. *KFF Health News*. Retrieved November 28, 2024,

from https://kffhealthnews.org/news/article/diagnosis-debt-investigation-100-million-americans-hidden-medical-debt

23. Sayki, I. (2023), in OpenSecrets. *Despite record federal lobbying spending, the pharmaceutical and health product industry lost their biggest legislative bet in 2022.* Accessed February 1, 2025 from https://www.opensecrets.org/news/2023/02/despite-record-federal-lobbying-spending-the-pharmaceutical-and-health-product-industry-lost-their-biggest-legislative-bet-in-2022/.

24. Regan, D. T. (1971). Effects of a Favor and Liking on Compliance. Journal of Experimental Social Psychology, 7(6), 627–639.

25. Center on Budget and Policy Priorities (CBPP). (2020). *The Far-Reaching Benefits of the Affordable Care Act's Medicaid Expansion.* Accessed February 1, 2025 from https://www.cbpp.org/research/health/chart-book-the-far-reaching-benefits-of-the-affordable-care-acts-medicaid-expansion.

26. TPG Family of Companies. (2025). *Pills and Surgery vs Lifestyle Changes.* Accessed April 22, 2025 from https://thetpgfamily.com/pills-and-surgery-vs-lifestyle-changes/.

Chapter 4

1. Kitterman, T. (2024) in Great Place to Work. *5 Ways Workplace Culture Drives Business Profitability.* Accessed February 1, 2025 from https://www.greatplacetowork.com/resources/blog/5-ways-workplace-culture-drives-business-profitability.

2. National Safety Council (NSC). (n.d.) *Prioritizing Employee Mental Health.* Accessed February 1, 2025 from https://www.nsc.org/workplacementalhealth.

3. Deloitte. (2024). *2024 Gen Z and millennial survey: Living and working with purpose in a transforming world.* Deloitte. Retrieved November 28, 2024, from https://www.deloitte.com/global/en/issues/work/content/genzmillennialsurvey.html

4. Headspace (2024). *Workforce State of Mind: Sixth Annual Workplace Mental Health Trends Report.* Available at: https://5327495.fs1.hubspotusercontent-na1.net/hubfs/5327495/Headspace%202024%20Workforce%20State%20of%20Mind%20Report.pdf

5. Rosenthal, E. (2017). *An American sickness: How healthcare became big business and how you can take it back.* Penguin Press.

Chapter 5

1. KFF. (2022). *2022 Employer Health Benefits Survey*. Accessed February 1, 2025 from https://www.kff.org/report-section/ehbs-2022-section-13-employer-practices-telehealth-provider-networks-and-coverage-for-mental-health-services/.

2. Wigert, B. (2022), cited in Gallup. *Top 6 Things Employees Want in Their Next Job*. Accessed February 1, 2025 from https://www.gallup.com/workplace/389807/top-things-employees-next-job.aspx.

Chapter 6

1. Castenada, Carlos. (1972). *Journey to Ixtlan: The Lessons of Don Juan*. New York: Simon & Schuster, p. 81.

2. Maguire, E. A., et al. (2000). "Navigation-related Structural Change in the Hippocampi of Taxi Drivers." Proceedings of the National Academy of Sciences, 97(8), pp. 4398–4403.

3. Woollett, K., & Maguire, E. A. (2011). "Acquiring 'the Knowledge' of London's layout drives structural brain changes." Current Biology, 21(24), 2109–2114.

Chapter 7

1. University of Rochester. (no date). *Journaling for Emotional Wellness*. Accessed February 1, 2025 from https://www.urmc.rochester.edu/encyclopedia/ content?ContentID=4552&ContentTypeID=1.

2. Pennebaker, J. W. & Smyth, J. M. (2016). Expressive Writing: Words That Heal. Independently Published.

3. Baikie, K. A. & Wilhelm, K. (2005). Emotional and Physical Health Benefits of Expressive Writing. *Advances in Psychiatric Treatment*. pp. 338–346. Available at https://practicalneurology.com/articles/2015-sept/the-science-behind-the-powerful-benefits-of-having-a-purpose.

Chapter 8

1. Kross, E. (2021). *Chatter: The Voice in Our Head, Why It Matters, and How to Harness It*. New York: Crown Publishing Group.

2. Singer, M. A. (2007). *The Untethered Soul*. p. 13; p. 21; p. 31.

Chapter 9

1. Ma, X., Yue, Z.-Q., Gong, Z.-Q., Zhang, H., Duan, N.-Y., Shi, Y.-T., Wei, G.-X. & Li, Y.-F. (2017), an original research article in Frontiers. Accessed February 1, 2025 from https://www.frontiersin.org/journals/psychology/articles/10.3389/fpsyg.2017.00874/full.
2. Yackle, K., Schwarz, L. A., Kam, K., Sorokin, J. M., Huguenard, J. R., Feldman, J. L., Luo, L., & Krasnow, M. A. (2017). Breathing Control Center Neurons that Promote Arousal in Mice. Science, 355(6332), pp. 1411–1415.
3. Huberman, A. (Host). (2021). *Huberman Lab Podcast*. Huberman Lab Media. Retrieved November 28, 2024, from https://www.hubermanlab.com/podcast
4. Tennant, A. (Director). (2002). *Sweet Home Alabama* [Motion Picture]. Touchstone Pictures.
5. Singer, M. A. (2007). *The Untethered Soul*. p. 13; p. 21; p. 31. Need to find correct pages. I'm not in MN now and will do that when I get home.
6. David, L., & Seinfeld, J. (Creators.) (1989–1998). *Seinfeld* [TV Series]. Season 6, Episode 15. NBC.

Chapter 10

1. Felitti, V. J., Anda, R. F., Nordenberg, D., Williamson, D. F., Spitz, A. M., Edwards, V., Koss, M. P., & Marks, J. S. (1998). Relationship of Childhood Abuse and Household Dysfunction to Many of the Leading Causes of Death in Adults: The Adverse Childhood Experiences (ACE) Study. American Journal of Preventive Medicine, 14(4), pp. 245–258. Accessed February 1, 2025 from https://linkinghub.elsevier.com/retrieve/pii/S0749379798000178.
2. Ficarra, G., & Requa, J. (Directors). (2011). *Crazy, stupid, love* [Motion Picture]. Carousel Productions; Di Novi Pictures.

Chapter 11

1. Frankl, V. E. (1946). *Man's search for meaning*. Beacon Press. p. 13; pp. 133–134; pp. 135–138.
2. Kabat-Zinn, J. (1979). *Full Catastrophe Living*.

3. Hoshaw, C. (2022) in Healthline. *What is Mindfulness? A Simple Practice for Greater Well-being.* Accessed February 1, 2025 from https://www.healthline.com/health/mind-body/what-is-mindfulness.

4. Isbel, B., Weber, J. & Lagopoulos, J. *et al.* (2020), in Scientific Reports. Neural Changes in Early Visual Processing After 6 Months of Mindfulness Training in Older Adults. Accessed February 1, 2025 from https://doi.org/10.1038/s41598-020-78343-w.

5. Isbel, B., Weber, J. & Lagopoulos, J. *et al.* (2020), in Scientific Reports. Neural Changes in Early Visual Processing After 6 Months of Mindfulness Training in Older Adults. Accessed February 1, 2025 from https://doi.org/10.1038/s41598-020-78343-w.

6. Datta, K., Malllick, H. N., Tripathi, M., Ahuja, N. & Deepak, K. K. (2022). Electrophysiological Evidence of Local Sleep During Yoga Nidra Practice. Front. Neurol. 13:910794. doi: 10.3389/fneur.2022.910794.

7. Gunjiganvi, M., Rai, S., Awale, R. B., & Mishra, P. (2023). Efficacy of Yoga Nidra on Depression, Anxiety, and Insomnia in Frontline COVID-19 Healthcare Workers: A Pilot Randomized Controlled Trial. International Journal of Yoga Therapy, 33(2023). https://doi.org/10.17761/2023-D-22-00011.

Chapter 12

1. Schwartz, S. H., & Sortheix, F. M. (2018). Values and subjective well-being. In D. S. Dunn (Ed.), *Positive psychology: Established and emerging issues*, 245–263. Routledge.

2. Csikszentmihalyi, M. (1990). *Flow: The psychology of optimal experience.* Harper & Row.

3. Schultz, W. (2015). Neuronal reward and decision signals: From theories to data. Physiological Reviews, 95(3), 853–951. doi:https://doi.org/10.1152/physrev.00023.2014.

4. Ritvo, E. (2014), in Psychology Today. *The Neuroscience of Giving: Proof that Helping Others Helps You.* Accessed February 1, 2025 from https://www.psychologytoday.com/us/blog/vitality/201404/the-neuroscience-giving.

5. Boyle, P., Buchman, A., Barnes, L. & Bennett, D. (2010). "Effect of a Purpose in Life on Risk of Incident Alzheimer Disease and Mild

Cognitive Impairment in Community-Dwelling Older Persons." Arch Gen Psychiatry. 2010:304–310.

6. Abellaneda-Pérez, K., Cattaneo G., & Cabello-Toscano, M. *et al.* (2023). Purpose in Life Promotes Resilience to Age-Related Brain Burden in Middle-Aged Adults. Alz Res Therapy 15, 49. Available at https://doi.org/10.1186/s13195-023-01198-6.

7. Fotuhi, M., & Mehr, S. (2015, September). *The science behind the powerful benefits of having a purpose.* Practical Neurology

8. Frankl, V. E. (1946). *Man's search for meaning.* Beacon Press. p. 13; pp. 133–134; pp. 135–138.

9. Deloitte. (2019). The Deloitte Global Millennial Survey 2019. Accessed February 1, 2025 from https://www2.deloitte.com/content/dam/Deloitte/global/Documents/About-Deloitte/deloitte-2019-millennial-survey.pdf.

10. Deloitte. (2023). Making waves: How Gen Zs and Millennials are Prioritizing—and Driving Change in the Workplace. Accessed February 1, 2025 at https://www2.deloitte.com/us/en/insights/topics/talent/recruiting-gen-z-and-millennials.html.

11. Stein, D., Hobson, N., Jachimowicz, J. M., & Whillans, A. (2021) in Harvard Business Review. "How Companies Can Improve Employee Engagement Right Now." Accessed February 1, 2025 from https://hbr.org/2021/10/how-companies-can-improve-employee-engagement-right-now.

12. Nink, M. & Robison, J. (2016) in Gallup. The Damage Inflicted by Poor Managers. Accessed February 1, 2025 from https://news.gallup.com/businessjournal/200108/damage-inflicted-poor-managers.aspx.

Chapter 13

1. Burton, L. R. (2020). The Neuroscience and Positive Impact of Gratitude in the Workplace. American Association for Physician Leadership. Retrieved from https://www.physicianleaders.org/news/the-neuroscience-and-positive-impact-of-gratitude-in-the-workplace.

2. Michaels, L. (1975). *Saturday Night Live* [TV Series]. NBC.

3. Hampton, D. (2019) in The Best Brain Possible. *The Neuroscience of How Affirmations Help Your Mental Health.* Accessed February 1, 2025 at

https://thebestbrainpossible.com/affirmations-brain-depression-anxiety/.

Chapter 14

1. Maslow, A. (1943). A Theory of Human Motivation. Psychological Review, 50(4), pp. 370–396.
2. Darabont, F. (Director). (1994). *The Shawshank Redemption* [Motion Picture]. Castle Rock Entertainment.
3. Taylor & Francis (2012). "Oxytocin, Social Sharing and Recovery from Trauma." ScienceDaily. Accessed on February 1, 2025 at www.sciencedaily.com/releases/2012/12/121218111558.htm.
4. Wong, S. F., Cardoso, C., Orlando, M. A., Brown, C. A. & Ellenbogen, M. A. (2021). Depressive Symptoms and Social Context Modulate Oxytocin's Effect on Negative Memory Recall, Social Cognitive and Affective Neuroscience, Volume 16, Issue 12, December 2021, pp. 1234–1243. Available at https://doi.org/10.1093/scan/nsab072.
5. American Medical Association. (2022). AMA Adopts New Public Health Policies to Improve Health of Nation. Accessed February 1, 2025 from https://www.ama-assn.org/press-center/press-releases/ama-adopts-new-public-health-policies-improve-health-nation-5.
6. World Health Organization. (2022). WHO Launches Commission to Foster Social Connection. Accessed February 1, 2025 at https://www.who.int/news/item/15-11-2023-who-launches-commission-to-foster-social-connection.
7. Finley, A. J. & Schaefer, S. M. (2022). Affective Neuroscience of Loneliness: Potential Mechanisms underlying the Association between Perceived Social Isolation, Health, and Well-Being. J Psychiatr Brain Sci. 2022;7(6):e220011. doi: 10.20900/jpbs.20220011.
8. National Academies of Sciences, Engineering, and Medicine. (2020). *Social Isolation and Loneliness in Older Adults*. Accessed February 1, 2025 from https://doi.org/10.17226/25663.
9. Bowers, A., Wu, J., Lustig, S. & Nemecek, D. (2022). "Loneliness Influences Avoidable Absenteeism and Turnover Intention Reported by Adult Workers in the United States", Journal of Organizational Effectiveness: People and Performance, Vol. 9 No. 2, pp. 312–335. https://doi.org/10.1108/JOEPP-03-2021-0076.

10. U.S. Bureau of Labor Statistics. (2019). *Employer Costs for Employee Compensation.* Accessed February 1, 2025 from https://data.bls.gov/timeseries/CMU2010000000000D.

11. BetterUp (2019), in Harvard Business Review. The Role of Belonging at Work and the Outsized Consequences of its Absence. Accessed February 1, 2025 at https://hbr.org/2019/12/the-value-of-belonging-at-work.

12. Yao, L., Xu, M., & Pellegrini, E. K. (2021). The boss's long arm. *Frontiers in Psychology, 12*(Article 780030). doi:https://doi.org/10.3389/fpsyg.2021.780030

Chapter 15

1. Chester, D. S. & Nathan DeWall, C. (2016) in Oxford Academic Social Cognitive and Affective Neuroscience. *The Pleasure of Revenge: Retaliatory Aggression Arises from a Neural Imbalance toward Reward.* Accessed February 1, 2025 from https://doi.org/10.1093/scan/nsv082.

2. Harvard Health Publishing. (2021). *The Power of Forgiveness: The REACH method teaches how to overcome lingering bad feelings toward someone who did you wrong.* Accessed February 1, 2025 from https://www.health.harvard.edu/mind-and-mood/the-power-of-forgiveness.

3. Ricciardi E, Rota G, Sani L, Gentili C, Gaglianese A, Guazzelli M, Pietrini P. (2013). How the Brain Heals Emotional Wounds: The Functional Neuroanatomy of Forgiveness. Front Hum Neurosci. 2013 Dec 9;7:839. doi: 10.3389/fnhum.2013.00839. PMID: 24367315; PMCID: PMC3856773. Accessed April 28, 2025 from https://pmc.ncbi.nlm.nih.gov/articles/PMC3856773/?utm_

4. John Hopkins Medicine (no date). *Forgiveness: Your Health Depends on It.* Accessed February 1, 2025 from https://www.hopkinsmedicine.org/health/wellness-and-prevention/forgiveness-your-health-depends-on-it.

5. David, L., & Seinfeld, J. (Creators.) (1989–1998). *Seinfeld* [TV Series]. Season 9, Episode 2. NBC.

6. Cloud, H. & Townsend, J. (1992). *Boundaries: When to Say Yes, How to Say No to Take Control of Your Life.* Zondervan.

7. Tawwab, N. G. (2021). Set Boundaries, Find Peace: A Guide to Reclaiming Yourself. TarcherPerigee.

8. Pansini, M., Buonomo, I. & Benevene, P. (2024). Fostering Sustainable Workplace Through Leaders' Compassionate Behaviors: Understanding the Role of Employee Well-Being and Work Engagement. Sustainability. 2024; 16(23):10697. https://doi.org/10.3390/su162310697)

9. Klimecki, O. M., Leiberg, S., Lamm, C., & Singer, T. (2013). Functional neural plasticity and associated changes in positive affect after compassion training. *Cerebral Cortex, 23*(7), 1552–1561. doi: https://doi.org/10.1093/cercor/bhs142

10. Kirby, J. N. (2017). Compassion interventions: The programmes, the evidence, and implications for research and practice. *Psychology and Psychotherapy: Theory, Research and Practice, 90*(3), 432–455. doi:https://doi.org/10.1111/papt.12104

11. Klimecki, O. M., Leiberg, S., Lamm, C., & Singer, T. (2013). Functional neural plasticity and associated changes in positive affect after compassion training. *Cerebral Cortex, 23*(7), 1552–1561. doi: https://doi.org/10.1093/cercor/bhs142

12. Stanford Medicine. (2025). Compassion Cultivation Training. Details accessed on February 1, 2025 from https://med.stanford.edu/psychiatry/education/cme/cct.html.

13. Neff, K. D., Rude, S. S., & Kirkpatrick, K. (2007). An examination of self-compassion in relation to positive psychological functioning and personality traits. *Journal of Research in Personality, 41*, 908–916. doi:https://doi.org/10.1016/j.jrp.2006.08.002

14. McClelland, D. C. (1961). The Achieving Society. Princeton, NJ: D. Van Nostrand Company.

Chapter 16

1. Zhang, H. Li, X. & Li, Y. (2023). The Impact of Authentic Leadership on Employee Innovation Behavior and Work Engagement in Specialized, Fined, Peculiar and Innovative SMEs. Open Journal of Business and Management, 11, pp. 238-259. doi: 10.4236/ojbm.2023.111014.

2. Van den Bosch, R. & Taris, T. (2018) in Frontiers. *Authenticity at Work: Its Relations With Worker Motivation and Well-being.* Accessed February

1, 2025 from https://www.frontiersin.org/journals/communication/articles/10.3389/fcomm.2018.00021/

3. Zak, P. (2017) in Harvard Business Review. *The Neuroscience of Trust.* Accessed February 1, 2025 from https://hbr.org/2017/01/the-neuroscience-of-trust.

4. RHR International. (2020). *Promoting Intimacy at Scale.* Accessed February 1, 2025 from https://rhrinternational.com/blog/solutions-assessment/promoting-intimacy-at-scale/.

5. Brown, B. (2012). *Daring greatly: How the courage to be vulnerable transforms the way we live, love, parent, and lead.* Avery.

6. Eisenberger, N. I., Lieberman, M. D., & Williams, K. D. (2003). Does rejection hurt? An FMRI study of social exclusion. *Science, 302*(5643), 290–292. doi:www.science.org/doi/10.1126/science.1089134

7. West, T. V., Thorson, K., Grant, H., & Rock, D. (2018). *Asked for vs. unasked for feedback: An experimental study.*

8. Edmondson, A. C. (2018). *The fearless organization: Creating psychological safety in the workplace for learning, innovation, and growth.* Wiley.

9. Hugander, P., & Edmondson, A. C. (2024). Skills training links psychological safety to revenue growth. *MIT Sloan Management Review.* Retrieved December 5, 2024, from https://sloanreview.mit.edu/article/skills-training-links-psychological-safety-to-revenue-growth

Chapter 17

1. Resolve. (No date). *Creating Structure and Stability Through Routines: Part 1 Routines and The Brain.* Accessed February 1, 2025 from https://www.kcresolve.com/blog/creating-structure-and-stability-through-routines-part-1-routines-and-the-brain.

2. Suckow, E. J., Henderson-Arredondo, K., Hildebrand, L., Jankowski, S. R., Killgore, W. D. S. (2023). 70 Daily Routine and Psychological Resilience. Journal of the International Neuropsychological Society.

3. Elrod, H. (2012). *The miracle morning: The not-so-obvious secret guaranteed to transform your life: Before 8AM.* Hal Elrod.

4. Clear, J. (2018). *Atomic habits: An easy & proven way to build good habits & break bad ones.* Avery, p. 38.

appendix a

deep dive—resource list

Here you'll find a list of books that I have found incredibly helpful in my own journey to Lead My Self Well. This is a great place to start if a topic has struck a chord with you and you'd like to dive deeper to further your own learning, growth, and development.

Parts I and II: The Problem and The Solution

Topics: Neuroscience, Journaling, the state of the Health of America
- Calm Clarity—Due Quach
- The Art of Changing the Brain—James Zull
- Writing to Heal: A Guided Journal for Recovering from Trauma and Emotional Upheaval—James W. Pennebaker
- Dopesick: Dealers, Doctors, and the Drug Company that Addicted America—Beth Macy
- An American Sickness: How Healthcare Became Big Business and How You Can Take it Back—Elisabeth Rosenthal
- Dying for a Paycheck—Jeffrey Pfeffer

Part III: Discover—What Do I Believe?

Topics: The Inner Critic, Self-Talk, and Breath
- The Untethered Soul—Michael A. Singer
- Think Again—Adam Grant
- Taming Your Gremlin—Rick Carson
- Breath: The New Science of a Lost Art—James Nestor
- The Power of Now—Eckhart Tolle

Part IV: Diagnose—Where Have I Been?

Topics: The Inner Child, Trauma, and Mindfulness
- The Power of Attachment: How to Create Deep and Lasting Intimate Relationships—Diane Poole Heller

- The Body Keeps the Score: Brain, Mind and Body in the Healing of Trauma—Bessel van der Kolk
- Becoming the One: Heal Your Past, Transform Your Relationship Patterns, and Come Home to Yourself—Sheleana Aiyana
- A Mindfulness-Based Stress Reduction Workbook: Bob Stahl and Elisha Goldstein

Part V: Define—Why Am I Here?

Topics: Purpose, Meaning, and Affirmations
- The Purpose Factor—Brian Bosché and Gabrielle Bosché
- Man's Search for Meaning—Viktor Frankl
- What to Say When You Talk to Yourself: Powerful New Techniques to Program Your Potential for Success—Shad Helmstetter

Part VI: Devote—Who Do I Influence?

Topics: Forgiveness, Boundaries, Community, and Compassion
- Forgiving Unforgivable: The 4 Essential Secrets to Overcome Trauma, Stand Empowered, and Step into Purpose—Natalie Baird-King
- The Community-First Advantage: How Modern Leaders Leverage Community to Lead, Connect and Drive Growth—Chris Catania
- Boundaries: When to Say Yes, How to Say No to Take Control of Your Life—Henry Cloud and John Townsend
- Love Works: Seven Timeless Principles for Effective Leaders—Joel Manby
- Connectable: How Leaders Can Move Teams from Isolated to All In—Ryan Jenkins and Steven Van Cohen
- Compassionomics: The Revolutionary Scientific Evidence That Caring Makes a Difference—Stephen Trzeciak and Anthony Mazzarelli

Part VII: Dedicate—How Do I Show Up?

Topics: Vulnerability, Trust, Habits, and Routines

- Daring Greatly: How the Courage to be Vulnerable Transforms the Way We Live, Love, Parent, and Lead—Brené Brown
- The Miracle Morning: The Not-So-Obvious Secret Guaranteed to Transform Your Life—Hal Elrod
- The Speed of Trust: The One Thing That Changes Everything—Stephen M. R. Covey
- Atomic Habits: An Easy and Proven Way to Build Good Habits & Break Bad Ones—James Clear

Part VIII—Deliver—When is My Time

- The STAY Challenge: A Leaders' Guide to Managing Unwanted Turnover and Regrettable Retention—April Whitson

appendix b

finding a qualified therapist

Signs It's Time to Seek a Licensed Therapist

There are times when our mental health challenges extend beyond what we can manage through self-reflection, personal development tools, or support from friends and family. Recognizing when it's time to seek the help of a qualified and licensed therapist can be a crucial step toward healing and growth. Therapy is not just for moments of crisis—it's a resource for anyone seeking a deeper understanding of themselves, healthier coping strategies, and improved emotional wellbeing.

A key indicator is the presence of unhealthy coping mechanisms, such as overusing substances like alcohol or drugs, engaging in disordered eating, or relying on excessive work or distractions to numb emotional pain. These behaviors might provide temporary relief but often worsen the underlying issues over time. A therapist can help uncover the root causes and guide you toward more sustainable, healthy strategies.

Trauma—whether from past experiences or recent events—can also be a reason to seek professional help. If you are experiencing flashbacks, nightmares, or intense emotional reactions tied to a specific memory, a therapist trained in trauma-informed care can help you process these experiences in a safe and supportive environment. Similarly, unresolved grief, whether from losing a loved one, a major life change, or a loss of identity, may require therapeutic intervention to navigate effectively.

Finally, if you've tried self-help methods but feel stuck or like you're going in circles, therapy may be an approach that can help you move forward. Licensed therapists are trained to identify patterns that may be invisible to you and to offer insights and tools tailored to your unique situation. Seeking therapy is not a sign of failure; it's an act of courage and self-respect. It's a commitment to your own growth, resilience, and overall wellbeing.

How to Find a Therapist

Finding the right therapist for you can feel like an overwhelming task, especially when you feel like you need help RIGHT NOW! I know, I've been there. I've had a couple of not-so-great experiences with therapists and one completely terrible experience (that's a story for another day!). What's important is that you find a person with whom you feel comfortable. Being willing to openly share with the therapist you choose will go an incredibly long way in helping them to help you. Here are a few tips to help you find an excellent match:

1. **Know Your Needs:** Are you seeking help for anxiety, trauma, addiction, family issues? Knowing your specific needs will help find a qualified and licensed therapist in that area of expertise.

2. **Use Trusted Resources:** Your company EAP is a great place to start if you have mental health benefits through your organization. They generally offer confidential services that are complimentary for the first several visits.

   When looking externally, there are directories that can assist in finding a licensed therapist in your state. Psychology Today has an excellent search option for this use. You can also ask for recommendations from friends, family, or your doctor.

If you're finding it difficult to find a provider locally or that works with your busy schedule, there are online resources like BetterHelp and Talkspace that offer convenient access to licensed therapists via video, phone, or chat.

3. **Check with Your Insurance Provider:** If you carry mental health benefits, get a list of in-network therapists and ask about out-of-pocket expenses before your first session.

4. **Schedule a Consult**: Many therapists offer a free or low-cost initial consultation to assess for fit. Use this session to ask questions about their approach, experience, and fees. If paying out of pocket, you can ask if they offer sliding-scale options. Ask what a typical session looks like and pay attention to your comfort level during this interaction— it's a great indicator of whether they'll be a great fit for you.

5. **Stay Open but Trust Your Gut:** This relationship is key to success in therapy. If you feel heard, understood, respected, and safe, that's a great sign. If not, keep looking until you find someone who makes you feel that way. Be patient. Finding the right therapist can take some time, but it's worth the effort.

If you're not feeling it, be comfortable explaining that to the therapist. A good therapist won't get their feelings hurt—they'll welcome the feedback and help refer you to someone who might be a better fit. Don't give up. I would have never found my favorite therapist if I'd let the terrible experience with the first one keep me from searching for help.

appendix c

values list

Achievement
Accountability
Accuracy
Adventure
Altruism
Ambition
Assertiveness
Authenticity
Balance
Beauty
Belonging
Boldness
Calmness
Challenge
Collaboration
Commitment
Community
Compassion
Competition
Connectedness
Consistency
Contribution
Cooperation
Courage
Creativity
Curiosity
Determination
Diligence
Discipline
Diversity
Efficiency
Empathy

Empowerment
Enthusiasm
Equality
Excellence
Fairness
Family
Focus
Freedom
Fun
Generosity
Grace
Growth
Happiness
Harmony
Health
Helping Others
Honesty
Honor
Humility
Humor
Inclusivity
Independence
Individuality
Integrity
Joy
Leadership
Learning
Legacy
Love
Loyalty
Nurturing
Orderliness

Partnership
Peace
Practicality
Professionalism
Power
Recognition
Reliability
Resourcefulness
Results-Oriented
Risk-Taking
Self-Expression
Selflessness
Service
Simplicity
Spirituality
Stability
Strategic
Strength
Success
Supportiveness
Taking Action
Team-Oriented
Thoughtfulness
Tolerance
Tradition
Trust
Understanding
Uniqueness
Vitality

appendix d

tools and resources

Free Tools

Real transformation happens when knowledge turns to action. To help you move to action, I've included access to a Wellbeing Strategy Toolkit – a collection of practical tools you can download and use as you move through each step of the journey. Just scan the QR code or go to www.caralenz.com to dive in!

Weekly Wellbeing Tracker

Free download. A simple but powerful tool designed to help you monitor and keep accountable to key wellbeing habits, including the Daily Practice Ideas. Use it to set and check in on the intentions, affirmations, and wellbeing strategies you create for yourself.

Organizational Wellbeing Strategy—Sample

Free download. This organizational wellbeing strategic plan framework is a starting point for any organization attempting to embed wellbeing in the overall strategy. This plan can also be adapted for an individual to set their own personal strategic plan around their health.

Quick Balance Strategy

Free download. When stress or overwhelm takes over, use this tool to bring you to balance—fast. This simple technique is designed to help you reset and refocus when you need to do it in the moment. This is a printable pinup you can place at your desk or anywhere you want a reminder to find your center quickly.

Mental Health Day Guide

Free download. Taking a mental health day for self-care is necessary at times. But it's easy to let the day slip by in habits that may feel comforting in the moment but don't actually contribute to mental health. This guide provides practical strategies that bring joy, reduce stress, and help return to daily life feeling more balanced and capable.

Talking About Wellbeing: A Guide for Employees and Leaders

Free download. This guide is a practical framework for initiating meaningful conversations about wellbeing in the workplace—whether you're an employee seeking support or a leader wanting to foster a more resilient, high-performing team. It includes scripts, prompts, and strategies to navigate these often-sensitive conversations.

appendix e

how to work with me

Lead Well Platform: Individuals, Leaders, and Organizations

At the heart of everything I do is a passion for helping people cultivate wellbeing—for themselves and their teams. For information on tools and resources to help organizations and individuals take action on wellbeing, please visit my website at www.caralenz.com.

Lead Well Workshops

Designed to be interactive and practical, these workshops equip individuals, leaders, and teams with tools and strategies to integrate wellbeing into their daily operations. Topics range from managing burnout and fostering resilience to building cultures of trust and accountability. Workshops are customized to meet your organization's specific needs.

Individual and Group Coaching Programs

For those ready to go deeper, coaching offers a personalized approach to growth. Individual coaching provides one-on-one support to help you navigate challenges, set goals, and develop sustainable wellbeing practices. Group coaching programs guide participants through The 5 Inquiries using a collaborative space for peer learning and building community.

351 | Appendix E

Certifications

Elevate your expertise with certifications in my signature Lead Well methodology. This program is perfect for HR professionals, coaches, and organizational leaders who want to champion wellbeing and drive cultural transformation within their organizations.

Speaking and Webinars

Bring the message of wellbeing to life through engaging and inspiring talks. Whether it's an in-person keynote or a virtual webinar, I deliver actionable insights and real-world strategies that resonate with leaders at all levels. Topics include the ROI of Wellbeing, Balancing Health and Life, and Unlocking the Power of Wellness as a Skill.

If you're ready to make wellbeing a cornerstone of your leadership and your life, I encourage you to connect. Together, we can create a strategy that works for you and your organization, and build a world where everyone thrives! I welcome you here.

www.ingramcontent.com/pod-product-compliance
Lightning Source LLC
Chambersburg PA
CBHW031423270326
41930CB00007B/554